BRITISH DIPLOMACY AND FINANCE IN CHINA

BRITISH DIPLOMACY AND FINANCE IN CHINA, 1895–1914

E. W. EDWARDS

CLARENDON PRESS · OXFORD
1987

HF
1534.5
.C5
E39
1987

Oxford University Press, Walton Street, Oxford OX2 6DP

Oxford New York Toronto
Delhi Bombay Calcutta Madras Karachi
Petaling Jaya Singapore Hong Kong Tokyo
Nairobi Dar es Salaam Cape Town
Melbourne Auckland

and associated companies in
Beirut Berlin Ibadan Nicosia

Oxford is a trade mark of Oxford University Press

Published in the United States
by Oxford University Press, New York

British Library Cataloguing in Publication Data

Edwards, E. W.
British diplomacy and finance in China,
1895—1914.
1. Great Britain—Foreign relations—
China   2. China—Foreign relations—
Great Britain   3. Great Britain—Foreign
relations—1837—1901   4. Great Britain—
Foreign relations—1901—1936   5. China—
Foreign relations—1644—1912
1. Title
327.41051   DA47.9.C5
ISBN 0-19-822916-X

Library of Congress Cataloging in Publication Data

Edwards, E. W.
British diplomacy and finance in China, 1895—1914.
Bibliography: p.
Includes index.
1. Great Britain—Foreign economic relations—China.
2. China—Foreign economic relations—Great Britain.
3. Great Britain—Foreign relations—China.   4. China—
Foreign relations—Great Britain.   5. Investments,
British—China—History.   I. Title.
HF1534.5.C5E39 1987   337.41051   86-28567
ISBN 0-19-822916-X

Typeset by Joshua Associates Limited, Oxford
Printed and bound in Great Britain by
Biddles Limited Guildford and King's Lynn

IN MEMORY OF MY WIFE
AND FOR LOUISE AND SARAH

Acknowledgements

I am grateful to the British Academy for the award of a fellowship that enabled me to visit Japan and for a grant from its research fund; to the Leverhulme Trust for an award at an earlier stage of my research; to University College, Cardiff for a period of study leave and to its Department of History and its Library for facilities accorded me since my retirement.

For permission to quote from copyright material I owe thanks to the Marquess of Salisbury, Miss R. Addis, the Gloucestershire County Archivist, the Mitchell Library, Sydney, the Thomas Fisher Rare Books Library of the University of Toronto and the British Library.

Crown copyright material in the Public Record Office is published by permission of the Controller of Her Majesty's Stationery Office.

I have also to thank the Mitchell Library and the Thomas Fisher Rare Books Library for making available on loan microfilms of material from the diary of G. E. Morrison and the papers of J. O. P. Bland respectively, and the editors and publishers of the *English Historical Review* and the *Journal of Oriental Studies* for allowing me to include portions of articles which I contributed to these journals.

I am obliged to Columbia University Press for permission to make use of the map of British financed Chinese Railways in 1911 in *Chinese Railways and British Interests 1898–1911* by E-tu Zen Sun (King's Crown Press, Columbia University 1954) on which the map in this study is based.

To Dr Yuichi Inouye I offer thanks for many kindnesses during my stay in Tokyo; to Mrs Katagiri I am grateful for translations of documents from Japanese.

I owe much to my friends Professor Ian Nish and Dr Peter Lowe and the late Ifor B. Powell. My thanks go also to Professor D. C. M. Platt, Mr P. D. Coates, and Mr John Orbell, who kindly answered enquiries, to the librarians and archivists who allowed me to see documents in their care, and to the staff of Oxford University Press for their helpful guidance.

I am particularly grateful to Mrs Beryl Richards for the care and patience with which she typed the manuscript.

Preface

This study is concerned with the attitude of the British government to aspects of British financial and industrial enterprise in China during a period of economic activity involving major powers and marked by phases of international competition and co-operation. Two areas of British policy are examined: relations between the government and financiers, and relations between the government and other powers seeking to advance economic interests in China. The work is based primarily upon the records of the Foreign Office. It also draws upon the private papers of some of the principal figures involved. Though permission to consult the archives of the Hongkong and Shanghai Banking Corporation and the British and Chinese Corporation was not accorded, the papers of Sir Charles Addis and J. O. P. Bland, and especially the correspondence with the bank and corporation contained in the Foreign Office records, provided much information on the policies of the bank and its associates.

Contents

Abbreviations

ACDC	American China Development Company
BCC	British and Chinese Corporation
BD	*British Documents on the Origins of the War, 1898–1914*
CAB	Cabinet Papers
DDF	*Documents diplomatiques français, 1871–1914*
DMI	Department of Military Intelligence
EHR	*English Historical Review*
FO	Foreign Office Records in the Public Record Office, London
FRUS	*Foreign Relations of the United States*
GP	*Die grosse Politik der europäischen Kabinette, 1871–1914*
HJ	*Historical Journal*
NGB	*Nihon gaikō bunsho* (Japanese diplomatic documents)
PRO	Public Record Office
T	Treasury Papers

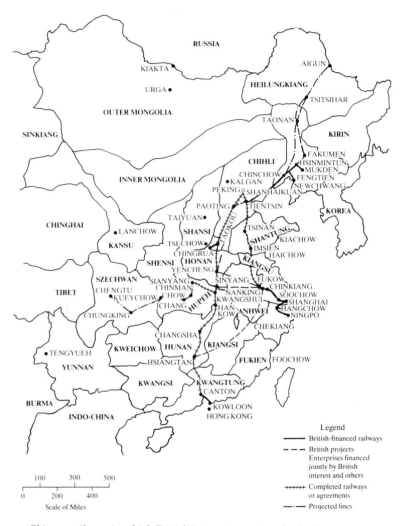

Chinese railways in which British interests were involved, 1895–1914

Introduction

THE last quarter of the nineteenth century saw a major shift in the focus of international relations. Rivalry among the Great Powers, which for years previously had been concentrated on European issues, was extended to Africa and eastern Asia. From about 1890 territorial and economic interests outside Europe, which had hitherto been of secondary significance, became the dominating concern of foreign-policy makers in the European capitals.

For Britain this new phase brought serious difficulties, for there were now competitors where previously the British had enjoyed virtually a free hand. Moreover the situation was made more difficult by the course of international relations. In the 1890s Britain's relations with other powers did not offer the conditions for bold decision. By 1894 the *rapprochement* between France and Russia had been consolidated into an alliance. The grouping of two naval powers whose imperial ambitions had long caused problems for Britain threatened serious embarrassment for British policy if the allies followed a joint policy—particularly in the Mediterranean but also in Africa and Asia. Unease was compounded by the erratic course on which Germany, hitherto regarded by British governments as a stabilizing force in Great Power relations, embarked in the 1890s. The uncertain nature of German policy in the post-Bismarck years disquieted British ministers and was an additional factor enjoining caution upon a Britain having to recognize a decline in freedom of manœuvre.[1]

In Africa, rivalry resulted in annexation and counter-annexation until almost the whole of the continent was partitioned. In Asia, too, there was annexation, notaby in Burma and Indo-China; but where long-established state structures were still functioning, the situation was more complicated. In the new age of competition, British policy was generally defensive, having as its aim to preserve economic and strategic positions acquired when challenge had been limited.

[1] On the background of international relations, see W. L. Langer, *The Diplomacy of Imperialism* (2nd edn., New York, 1951), A. J. P. Taylor, *The Struggle for Mastery in Europe, 1848–1918* (Oxford, 1954), C. J. Lowe, *The Reluctant Imperialists* (2 vols., London, 1967) and J. A. S. Grenville, *Lord Salisbury and Foreign Policy* (London, 1964).

This was certainly so in China. The British had been drawn there in search of trade, and at the end of the nineteenth century trade was still their prime concern. British policy had been directed to the removal of barriers set up by the Chinese authorities. Successive Anglo-Chinese treaties, from the Treaty of Nanking (1842) onward, had opened the way to some degree for foreign trade. Apart from small territorial acquisitions none of the British treaties had sought exclusive rights, nor indeed had those negotiated by other powers. British governments in China had held firmly to the conventions of *laissez-faire* doctrine. The function of government was limited to securing the conditions for free and fair competition thereafter remaining strictly detached from the operations of British business in competition either with foreign or British rivals. An important factor in the maintenance of equitable trading in China, the Imperial Maritime Customs Service, had come into existence in the 1850s largely under British auspices because of the chaotic conditions at the ports resulting from the Taiping rebellion. The service, a department of the Chinese government, had become responsible for the collection of duties at ports designated by treaty for foreign trade. It was international in its personnel, consisting in 1895 of some 700 foreign inspectors, more than half of them British, and 3,500 Chinese. Under Robert Hart, inspector-general from 1863, high standards of integrity were established, and foreign traders could rely upon the impartial enforcement of treaty tariff provisions upon all comers.[2]

Under these conditions British trading and financial interests had advanced to dominate China's foreign trade. Jardine, Matheson and Butterfield and Swire were the most important merchant and coastal shipping firms. The Hongkong and Shanghai Banking Corporation (hereafter the Hongkong Bank), with its interests concentrated in Far Eastern business had, after early tribulations following its foundation in 1864, moved ahead of its rivals to become the leading foreign bank. It was the first bank in the region to emerge as the result of local initiative. Its founders were major merchant houses in Hong Kong, and its shareholders were initially almost entirely drawn from the foreign trading community in China and Japan. Of the great merchant houses only Jardine, Matheson remained aloof from the bank—until 1877 when its chairman William Keswick became a director, marking

---

[2] For a succinct account of the service, see J. K. Fairbank *et. al.* (eds), *The I.G. in Peking* (2 vols., Cambridge, Mass., and London, 1975), pp. 3–30.

the start of an enduring association between the two institutions. By this time the Hongkong Bank had appointed Thomas Jackson as its chief manager. Under his able guidance it made significant progress, though in 1896 it was still judged to be 'rather a "provincial institution" and . . . not on the first line'.[3]

The China market never expanded during the nineteenth century as optimists had expected. Its place in the overall pattern of British overseas trade was to become more significant after 1900, however, and in the years up to 1914 the China market, together with India and Japan, was to provide surpluses that helped to offset adverse trading balances with Canada, the United States and the Argentine. Up till then it was of limited importance. As an investment area for British capital it hardly counted. The British trading community attributed this to the restrictions still imposed by the Chinese authorities on foreign entry into inland trade. If these were removed, great expansion, they argued, would follow. Official opinion was sceptical of these claims. British consuls and the Board of Trade were well aware of the reality—that China had little need of foreign imports because she would herself produce virtually all she needed. Officials and traders agreed that only if China embarked upon modernization could there be major opportunities for British industry.[4] Still, the prospect of a vast potential market, particularly for textiles, was firmly established in the minds of politicians. Though they withstood the demands from merchants for a vigorous policy to break down China's resistance to foreign trade, they recognized an actual stake, and still more a prospect, which ensured that no British government could ignore developments in China that might threaten the position which had been built up.

Until the Sino-Japanese War in 1894–5, coming when the spirit of imperialism had gripped the Great Powers, exposed the extent of China's weakness, there was no major threat, though the eighties had brought signs of an attitude on the part of some governments that foreshadowed departure from the conventions which had hitherto prevailed in foreign trade. A sense of common interest and a willingness to share trade relaxations extracted from the Chinese authorities had marked the relations of the powers in China. Trading had been

[3] A. S. J. Baster, *The International Banks* (London, 1935), pp. 165–75; M. Collis, *Wayfoong* (London, 1965), pp. 23–9, 58; Fairbank *et al.*, 2, no. 1011; F. H. H. King, 'The Bank of China is Dead', *Journal of Oriental Studies* 7 (Jan. 1969), pp. 39–62.

[4] N. A. Pelcovits, *Old China Hands and the Foreign Office* (New York, 1948), pp. 1–7; S. B. Saul, *Studies in British Overseas Trade, 1870–1914* (Liverpool, 1960), chap. 3.

competitive among the foreign enterprises, but governments had kept aloof. Now government participation began to emerge. The approach of a new phase was signalled by provisions in the Franco-Chinese treaty of Tientsin, 1885, which ended the Tongking war. France secured preferential duties on border trade between Tongking and China and an undertaking that China would turn to French industry when she decided to build railways, though this did not constitute an exclusive privilege. Germany, too, was intent upon expanding her trade in China, and German diplomats involved themselves, giving support to their nationals in securing contracts from the Chinese authorities. The foundation of the Deutsch-Asiatische Bank in 1889 marked a further step. The bank was designed to provide the financial base for a major commercial offensive in China. It was from the first a semi-state bank created by the German government, which had brought together reluctant financial interests by promising very favourable guarantees of support. When it opened in Shanghai it had behind it banks 'representing almost all German financial capital with overseas interests'. The State Bank of Prussia was included in the syndicate and this, together with the provision that the appointment of the bank's president was subject to the approval of the German emperor, underlined its function as an agent of national policy intended to challenge for commercial supremacy in China.[5]

But it was Japan's victory in 1895 that created the conditions for the new tendencies to emerge in full power. It opened a period of fierce international competition for economic primacy in which the prizes were viewed by successful and unsuccessful as means to political as well as economic advance, for no power was in a position to use crude military force against rivals. The Europeans were too remote. Japan was exhausted. Until the trans-Siberian railway was complete, Russia lacked the necessary communications. The British, if they had judged the stake as sufficient to demand forceful defensive measures, no longer had freedom of deployment for their naval strength, for the Franco-Russian alliance made it hazardous for forces to be withdrawn from Europe. China thus became an economic battleground in which governments joined bankers to fight for loan and railway contracts, a process in which China had to relinquish new areas of control within her sovereign territory. In essentials, this situation, promising national

---

[5] Baster, p. 182; J. E. Schrecker, *Imperialism and Chinese Nationalism. Germany in Shantung* (Cambridge, Mass., 1971), pp. 10–11.

and private advantage to the victor governments and their financiers, was not confined to China. The British had to meet it elsewhere, in Persia and the Ottoman Empire particularly, though there the issues were at least as much strategic as economic. New weapons were now being employed in the struggle for mastery in weak but still viable states. Economic diplomacy was added to political. In this field Britain had resources in financial power and industrial enterprise to match any competitor. What was lacking was organization in the manner of continental rivals, for in France and Russia as in Germany the state was able to influence financiers and industrialists in ways that were outside the power and indeed alien to the outlook of British governments. By the end of 1895 the Russo-Chinese Bank had been founded with Russian direction and French funds; and in 1898, by order of the French government, the Banque de l'Indo-Chine appeared in China to co-ordinate French financial operations there.[6]

In face of the employment of political finance by rivals resulting in serious inroads into the China market, British governments came to modify the rigid conventions that had kept government and private enterprise for the most part at arm's length. In China, in accordance with established practice, official detachment in the matter of loans by British financial institutions to the Chinese authorities had been strictly observed. It was a general principle that the government should give no guarantees for payment of interest on loans outside the Empire except in the rare instances where political considerations made such an undertaking necessary.[7] The Hongkong Bank had successfully established itself as the principal source for China's overseas borrowing, but the loans, small in amount, that it had negotiated from 1874 to 1895 were private operations. On two occasions the bank had asked for diplomatic assistance to secure assurances from the Chinese authorities. In 1877 it failed to get support over conditions for a loan which was the first to be secured on the customs revenue; the Foreign Office approved the legation's view that it was not for diplomatic agents to involve themselves in negotiations for any loan. In 1884, when the British minister in Peking had assisted the bank to

---

[6] O. Crisp, 'The Russo-Chinese Bank: An Episode in Franco-Russian Relations', *Slavonic and East European Review* 52 (1974), pp. 197–212; R. D., Quested, *The Russo-Chinese Bank: A Multinational Financial Base of Tsarism in China* (Birmingham, 1977), p. 6. In 1910 the bank became the Russo-Asiatic Bank.

[7] D. C. M. Platt, *Finance, Trade and Politics in British Foreign Policy, 1815–1914* (Oxford, 1968), p. 13.

get imperial sanction for a loan to the Canton provincial authorities, he was criticized by the parliamentary under-secretary for foreign affairs. This incident, however, revealed that official circles recognized that traditional principles mght need reconsideration to meet competitors actively supported by their governments. Salisbury, foreign secretary in 1885–6, and Rosebery, who succeeded him when the Liberals took office in February 1886, both authorized British representatives to support British firms in such circumstances. Rosebery also instructed Bryce, his parliamentary under-secretary, to examine how far the Foreign Office could go in supporting commerce without impairing the standards and repute of the diplomatic and consular service or establishing connection with private firms. Bryce's report recommended closer contact, and the mid-eighties brought action in support of British enterprise faced in China with threats of competition from rivals backed by their diplomats. But this was temporary, and the tenor of the Bryce report showed that the doctrine of detachment still prevailed.[8] Developments in China during the years covered by this study were to contribute significantly to its erosion.

The first phase, from 1895 to 1904, was a decade of international rivalry in which British concerns met opposition in financial and industrial enterprise, notably Chinese government loans and railway contracts, from European rivals organized and supported by governments interested in varying degrees as much in political as in commercial advantage. These years saw growing participation by the British government in economic policy as a defensive strategy evolved bringing the Foreign Office into close association with the Hongkong Bank and the enterprise it founded in 1898 with Jardine, Matheson for railway business: the British and Chinese Corporation.

From 1904 the tendencies of the preceding decade were reversed as the powers moved from competition to co-operation. In Britain the Liberal government that came in at the end of 1905, with Sir Edward Grey succeeding Lord Lansdowne as foreign secretary, accepted and continued this movement of policy. The Anglo-French railway agreement of 1905–6 embraced the governments as well as financial interests. A triple entente of bankers came in 1909 in consequence of

. [8] Pelcovits, pp. 135–8; Platt, pp. 271–4; David McLean, 'Commerce, Finance and British Diplomatic Support in China, 1885–86', *Economic History Review* 2nd. series, 26 (Aug. 1973), pp. 464–76. For a general survey of official attitudes towards economic activity abroad, see Platt.

the stalemate in the Hukuang loan that led to the admission of the German group. By mid-1909 the United States had forced itself into the Hukuang negotiations, and from this emerged in 1910 the four-power banking consortium for railway and financial operations in China in which the banking groups were closely associated with and supported by their respective governments. In these developments the British role was central. It involved a new relationship, modifying still further the traditional detachment between the government and the British 'group' which consisted in effect of one institution—the Hongkong Bank. This latter fact was to create problems for the British government.

The Chinese revolution in 1911 created a new situation, bringing Russia and Japan into the consortium and creating strains within it. The withdrawal of the United States from the consortium was dramatic but not seriously damaging. More significant for Britain was the rivalry among the remaining members, the thrusts by Japanese and French interests into what were held to be British preserves, the tensions within British financial circles illustrated by the Crisp loan and involving the Foreign Office in controversy, and the attempt by the Foreign Office to evolve a new national strategy to maintain Britain's economic position in China as the phase of international co-operation gave way in 1913–14 to a resumption of competition.

I

Chinese Government Loans 1895–1900

THE Treaty of Shimonoseki (April 1895) made plain the gains that Japan expected from victory, but they were not all to be secured. Three of the major powers—Russia, France, and Germany—jointly brought pressure to which Japan was forced to yield. She had to relinquish the prize of the Liaotung Peninsula and to recognize that for some years to come she could not exercise any effective influence on developments in China. The way was left open for the three European powers to attempt to realize long-held ambitions of financial, commercial, and territorial expansion in China. The heavy indemnity imposed by Japan, which meant that China's foreign borrowing had to increase greatly, offered a means of influence. If the three powers succeeded, the independence and integrity of China would be threatened. If economic expansion were pursued under the conditions of free and fair competition that had hitherto governed foreign commercial relations in China, there would be no complaint from British interests, for British merchants were confident of their ability to meet fair competition. If, however, the tendencies already visible in the eighties of political intervention in commercial relations through pressure for preferential treatment and exclusive rights were to prevail, then British interests, actual and prospective, would be under threat. Furthermore, undue pressure upon the fragile structure of the Chinese state might result in collapse and disintegration. This would bring a serious problem for the British government: the matter of the administration of the centre of British activity, the densely populated Yangtze Valley. To abandon it to anarchy or to other hands would damage interests; to take it into control would mean assuming the impossible burden of another India. As viewed from London, the Chinese situation in 1895 was unclear. If the harmony that on the whole had marked the relations of the Western powers there were to prevail, there was little to fear. If, however, competitors for economic supremacy were to employ political influence, the British position could be under severe strain.

British policy in the spring of 1895 was in the hands of the Liberal government headed by Lord Rosebery, who had become prime minister in March 1894 following the resignation of Gladstone. Lord Kimberley was foreign secretary, the office Rosebery had himself held before he succeeded Gladstone. The response of the Rosebery Cabinet to the unexpected completeness of Japan's victory was hesitant and vacillating. Though invited to do so by Russia it did not participate in the intervention against Japan, nor on the other hand did it take action to oppose it. Partly this was because some provisions of the Treaty of Shimonoseki were welcomed, but most of all because any danger of involvement in conflict in the Far East (which might come if Japan decided upon resistance to the powers) had to be avoided at a time when the limitations of British power in the face of the Franco-Russian alliance were becoming plain. Rosebery and Kimberley expected that British finance would be represented in the loan that China would have to seek from foreign banks in order to meet the large indemnity. If the whole amount were to be raised in one loan, as initially seemed likely, then the London market would have to be called upon to supply part of the funds.[1] It was obvious that whatever arrangements were made for the loan must be highly political: prestige, profit, and, more important, power would accrue to the lending banks and their governments. The situation was quite new in relation to China, for hitherto her foreign borrowing had been small and of no political significance.

The Hongkong Bank, very conscious of its own interest in securing the loan contract, understood from the first that this was a matter on a different scale from the numerous loans it had negotiated for China in the past. Not only was the amount involved much greater, but the bank knew that this time there was the certainty of competition from European rivals backed by their governments. The Chinese authorities, as they had done on previous occasions when seeking loans, turned to Sir Robert Hart, the inspector-general of the Imperial Maritime Customs. Over the years Hart had come to recognize the competence of the Hongkong Bank in Chinese business. He did not 'consider the H. Bank people *first-class* bankers . . . but the H. Bank has a large Chinese connection and it is easier to work through it than go to others who again would have to use its assistance', he had

---

[1] I. H. Nish, *The Anglo-Japanese Alliance* (London, 1966), pp. 28–33; L. K. Young, *British Policy in China, 1895–1902* (Oxford, 1970), pp. 27–8.

observed in January 1895. The success of the bank in floating a war loan for China in 1894 after the Bank of England had refused to lend, followed by a second loan in 1895, had added to its standing and now it was to the Hongkong Bank that Hart advised the Chinese to turn.[2]

The bank was ready to take the business, large assignment (some £40 million) though it was, and was confident that with backing from German bankers it could raise the money. It recognized that in this matter it would need official support. Early in May 1895, Ewen Cameron, its London manager, made contact with the Foreign Office. Pointing out that there was news of foreign competition, he raised fears that if the loan went to European rivals they might use it as a means to take control of the customs and other areas that would enable them to injure British commerce. Through he was coolly received the Rosebery ministry clearly recognized from the first that the loan was a political question, and that the government must involve itself and call in financiers to represent British interests.

This was not an innovation: that there were limits to *laissez faire* when major political interests were involved was well established. The purchase of the Suez canal shares was one instance, and official support for the foundation of the Imperial Bank of Persia in 1889 was another. Initially it appears that Rosebery accepted the prospect of a British loan to be handled by the Hongkong Bank; when however it became evident that France and Germany would oppose, he proposed an international loan to be organized by Rothschilds. This would ensure the preservation of the existing British predominance in the Chinese maritime customs administration. It was also in the tradition of British policy in China, which had always looked to co-ordinated international action and had never sought special advantages. The decisive factor, however, was the urgent need to avoid friction with other powers.[3]

It is unnecessary to follow in detail the manœuvres that thwarted the plan for a joint loan in which all interested powers would have shared and brought the business into the hands of Franco-Russian finance. Witte, the Russian finance minister and chief architect of Far Eastern policy, had originally not been anxious to participate. When,

---

[2] Fairbank *et al.*, *The I.G.*, 2, no. 962; S. F. Wright, *Hart and the Chinese Customs* (Belfast, 1950), pp. 652, 657–8; Collis, pp. 69–70.

[3] FO 17/1252, memorandum by Sanderson, 7 May 1895; FO 17/1253, Rosebery to Sanderson, 17 May 1895; D. McLean, 'The Foreign Office and the First Chinese Indemnity Loan, 1895', *HJ* 14, no. 2 (1973), pp. 303–21.

however, he was invited by French bankers to form a group of Russian banks to share in the loan, he responded rapidly. The Franco-Russian group organized and secured the loan for themselves alone.[4] The Germans, who as partners in the triple intervention against Japan had looked for a share in the business, found themselves excluded. Witte had gained a considerable success thanks to ample French finance and Chinese resentment against Britain's failure to come forward with aid against Japan. As it became clear that there was to be no place for Germany in the loan, and equally clear that the international loan for which the British government hoped had failed, the Deutsch-Asiatische Bank and the Hongkong Bank joined forces with the support of their governments in a rival but abortive bid for the business. Their pressure, however, together with the wish of the Chinese not to put themselves entirely into the hands of one Western group, had ensured that the Franco-Russian loan accounted only for a portion of the indemnity payment. The Treaty of Shimonoseki provided for payment of the indemnity in instalments. The Franco-Russian loan was for a sum sufficient to meet the first payment. For the second portion China undertook to look to British and German sources.

For the British government and the Hongkong Bank the bid for the loan, though unsuccessful, marked an important stage. It brought the bank into close contact with the government, and particularly with senior officials in the Foreign Office.[5] It initiated what was to become, as the China situation developed, a close and persisting connection between the government and private finance that marked a significant departure from the tradition of official detachment from private enterprise. The bank had made its case in the Foreign Office as an institution ready to fight to maintain its position and the interests of British commerce with which it was closely linked. No other British bank operating in China seems to have shown interest in the indemnity loan business. If there was an obvious element of self-protection in the Hongkong Bank's case, it also quickly became plain that Cameron's warnings that the Franco-Russian combination would exploit its victory were well founded. Finance had become a political weapon in China, as the Foreign Office recognized; exclusion of British interests from the loan had been a set-back politically as well as for

---

[4] Wright, pp. 658–60; Crisp, p. 197.

[5] *DDF* 1st series, 12, no. 64, Montebello to Hanotaux, 12 June 1895; A. Gérard, *Ma mission en Chine* (Paris, 1918), pp. 126–8; Wright, pp. 660–1; Mclean, p. 32.

the Hongkong Bank's prospects. Participation in the loans yet to be raised to meet the remaining instalments of the indemnity offered some opportunity for regaining lost ground.

For the contract for the second portion of the indemnity loan and for longer-term action in what was now plainly to be a highly competitive market in which major industrial projects (particularly railways) were likely to be sanctioned by a Chinese government awakened to the necessity of modernization, the bank prepared itself by cementing its association with the Deutsch-Asiatische Bank. On 27 July 1895, a few weeks after the Franco-Russian group had gained the first indemnity loan contract, the two banks signed in Berlin an agreement covering all loans and advances that might be concluded with the Chinese government or any of the provinces within the Chinese Empire.

The agreement provided that all business of this nature offered to either bank, and any loans or advances made to government departments and companies and having imperial or provincial government guarantees, were to be dealt with jointly. Joint action in respect of financial operations with railways or other companies not having such guarantees would require special agreements for each separate case. The agreement was made on the basis of parity, each bank taking an equal share in the operation and jointly signing all contracts. The representative of the Hongkong Bank, however, subject to other arrangements, was to conduct negotiations with the Chinese authorities on terms agreed by the two banks. If the Hongkong Bank, in the event of a large loan, decided to take in another issuing house in London, it undertook in the first instance to offer the business to N. M. Rothschild and Sons. Finally, the two parties declared their willingness to enter agreement to foster their mutual interests in Asia outside of the Chinese loan and advance business, and to enter into negotiation for that purpose shortly.

The Foreign Office appears to have had no part in bringing about this banking alliance. When Lord Salisbury (who had come into office at the end of June 1895 as prime minister and foreign secretary in the Conservative government succeeding the Liberal administration that Rosebery had headed) was made aware of its existence and of proposed joint action by the parties on railways in northern China, he saw no objections in principle, but the association on the British side between government and bank was loose. The agreement, Cameron reported, was submitted to and approved by the German government, which kept close control over the German group. The Foreign Office did not ask to see the agreement, let alone give it official approval, and indeed did not see its text until 1905.[6] In part, no doubt, this was because it was regarded as a business venture from which the government should remain detached. It was also, however, an association that Salisbury would regard cautiously on political grounds. In the prevailing international situation, he did not wish to tie himself too closely to Germany. His principal object was to improve relations with Russia, and that would not be assisted by the government's involvement in a partnership whose aims in northern China could bring opposition from Russia.

Contact between the Foreign Office and the Hongkong Bank developed more closely as negotiations for the second indemnity loan got under way. Gérard, the French minister in Peking, made strenuous efforts to secure the contract for France, but Hart—well aware of the dangers that award of this loan to the Franco-Russian group would bring, particularly to the administration of the customs—used his considerable influence on behalf of the Anglo-German group. His agent in London, J. D. Campbell, approached a member of the Cabinet to stress the importance of blocking the French. In Peking the British legation was active in support of the Anglo-German offer.[7] Cameron's emphasis in discussions over the first indemnity loan on the danger to British predominance in the administration of the customs if foreign powers were allowed to take the lead in financing the Chinese government had clearly made an impression in the Foreign Office. When it had seemed that the German government was seeking to obtain primacy for the German bank in the second indemnity loan, Francis Bertie, the assistant under-secretary in charge of the Far Eastern department, resisted. Having come to resent the assertiveness Germany had shown in other matters, he now urged that Germany be told that Britain wanted joint representation to the Chinese government for a single loan by the Hongkong and Deutsch-Asiatische banks. Salisbury approved, the Germans concurred, and the contract was secured by the two banks in March 1896—though the Chinese, assisted by Gérard's raising fears of a French counter-bid

---

[6] FO 17/1254, Sanderson to Cameron, private, 31 July 1895; Cameron to Sanderson, 1 Aug. 1895; FO 17/1686, memorandum by Langley, 4 Feb. 1905; FO 17/1687, Addis to FO, 6 Apr. 1905.
[7] Fairbank *et al.*, *The I.G.*, 2, no., 1013; Wright, pp. 660–1; FO 17/1276, Beauclerk to FO, 27 Feb. and 11 Mar. 1896.

and by an offer from an American group, brought the Anglo-German syndicate to agree to terms considerably more favourable to China than had been their original intention.[8]

When the preliminary agreement for the loan was signed on 7 March, Cameron immediately sought government assistance to ensure the success of the issue in the London market. He feared that its terms could influence the market adversely unless it was accorded some special status, and of course he was anxious to advance the standing of the Hongkong Bank. He asked that the loan be inscribed at the Bank of England. He stressed the extent to which his bank, by granting terms scarcely warranted by the standing of Chinese credit, had averted a serious threat to British interests; and the stipulation the bank had secured in the loan contract to the effect that administration of the Chinese maritime customs would continue as at present for the next thirty years. In this the bank was helping itself, for its own position was bound up with the predominant position of British commerce in China, which might suffer from any departure from the system and standards established by Hart. Still, there was undoubted substance in Cameron's argument, which was supported by Hart and the British legation in Peking. Further, as Sir Thomas Sanderson, the permanent under-secretary at the Foreign Office pointed out, if inscription were not accorded by the Bank of England, the Germans, who had given the loan a special status in their market, would get first place in the matters connected with it. There was, in fact, a community of interest between the Hongkong Bank and the Foreign Office (where the case for inscription was easily accepted), for political standing in Peking could be influenced by the response of British investors.

The approval of the Treasury was, however, necessary for an approach to the Bank of England, and there the response of the chancellor of the exchequer, Sir Michael Hicks Beach, was very different. Hicks Beach, a staunch upholder of official detachment from private financial operations, had a poor opinion of financiers. It seemed to him that the government was being asked to request inscription

to enable the Hongkong and Shanghai Bank and their friends to make more profit out of an arrangement they had already concluded.

[8] FO 17/1256, memorandum by Bertie, 9 Nov. 1895; Gérard, loc. cit. On Bertie and other FO personalities, see Z. S. Steiner, *The Foreign Office and Foreign Policy, 1898–1914* (Cambridge, 1969).

The Bank of England are very reluctant to have anything to do with the matter—the only precedent being in the case of Egypt—and I do not think we should be justified in asking them to assist us on such a ground as this.

I have a complete mistrust of these Foreign Loan Syndicates. I don't believe their agent would have been allowed to conclude the matter if they are not satisfied they could make a good thing of it without the assistance of the Bank of England. But they naturally would like to make it better. Of course, if on political grounds you press the matter that would be another thing.

Hicks Beach saw himself as the guardian of financial morality, but times were changing and finance was becoming a major political weapon in rivalry in weak, ill-organized states. In Persia and the Ottoman Empire as in China the need to meet political finance by similar means was to be increasingly recognized in the Foreign Office. Political necessity was bringing a widening official involvement in financial and economic policy. Salisbury shared much of Hicks Beach's view as to the proper relations between finance and government, but he gave primacy now to political considerations. On 26 March, the Bank of England agreed to inscribe the whole issue of the loan.[9]

To secure the contract for the second indemnity loan was a political gain, though foreign competition had not been determined despite the fears raised by Gérard. For the Foreign Office it had been of assistance to find in the Hongkong Bank a British institution ready to take the loan. The matter had strengthened its links with the bank, which had again shown itself eager for Chinese government loan business, mindful of wider British interests, and in good standing with Hart and the Peking legation. Moreover there was no serious competition for the loan from other British banks. The Chartered Bank had serviced a loan in 1895, but other than that seems to have handled no Chinese government loans and appears to have shown no interest in the second indemnity loan. An approach was made to the Foreign Office late in the day by the Ottoman Bank, which had received official assistance in April 1895 for a proposed small loan to China, but this was rejected because support was by that time pledged to the

---

[9] FO 17/1287, Cameron to Sanderson, 10 Mar. 1896; memorandum by Sanderson, 17 Mar. 1896; Bank of England to Treasury, 26 Mar. 1896; Salisbury Papers, box 17, Hicks Beach to Salisbury, 11 Mar. 1896.

Hongkong Bank and its associates.[10] This did not indicate a departure from the accepted principle of official impartiality and detachment from competition in economic matters, for the indemnity loan was primarily a political question. What it did show was that the Foreign Office was fully alive to the need for political support of British finance in a transaction with wide implications. The time had not come when the government was prepared to back, even to encourage, a vigorous push by British enterprise in China. There was no demand that it should do so. There was as yet no realization by British public opinion or even by the British community in China of the new situation, in which fair competition in the China market was to be threatened by the operations of governments seeking and securing exclusive advantages for their finance and industry. There had been concern in the eighties over the terms of the Franco-Chinese Treaty of Tientsin, and subsequent French policy directed to divert the trade of Yunnan into Tongking at the expense of Hong Kong had caused some stir in the colony. But neither French exclusivism, exemplified in the positions secured by Gérard in 1895–7, nor the Russian advance in Manchuria roused serious anxieties. The prospect of intensified competition was recognized, but confidence in the ability of British commerce to meet it was the prevailing attitude.[11]

The jolt came in the winter of 1897–8, with Russia's move into the Liaotung Peninsula following the German seizure of Kiaochow. The China question was caught up in the wave of popular imperialism. Between 1895 and 1898 there was no change in the long-standing public apathy in Britain towards China. There was not one debate on China in the parliamentary sessions of 1896 and 1897, and only a handful of questions were put. Apart from some pressure by chambers of commerce, mainly in the textile towns, for a railway from Burma into Yunnan to tap what was thought to be a rich market, there was no public interest. The China Association, established in 1889 to organize British business involved in the China trade into a pressure group, worked in the background. Its aims continued to be those that had been reiterated for many years before its foundation; to bring the British government to secure the removal by China of restrictions upon foreign trade in general. There were, however, indications that

---

[10] FO 17/1287, Ottoman Bank to FO, 17 and 26 Feb. 1896; Sanderson to Bertie, 27 Feb. 1896; Wright, p. 656.

[11] Pelcovits, pp. 166–7, 190–1.

some of the leading figures recognized the emergence of a new situation requiring significant modification of the principle that had hitherto governed British commercial policy, the preservation of an open door.

William Keswick of Jardine, Matheson, who was now established in London after long years in China and influential in the London committee of the association (which was dominated by the major trading firms) quickly saw the shape of things to come after Japan's victory. He judged that the solution to the inevitable push of Russian exclusivism lay in agreement upon spheres of influence, in which British recognition of Russian economic predominance in the north was set against Russian recognition of similar British predominance in the Yangtze Valley. The London committee accepted his views and on 16 November 1895 he led its deputation, which incuded Ewen Cameron, to Salisbury, emphasizing the need to protect British interests, above all in the Yangtze Valley, and the importance of reaching an understanding with Russia. The case for a recognition of spheres, while not explicitly stated, was obviously implicit in his remarks. Salisbury was non-committal as to spheres, but his assurance of intention to defend British interests and his recognition of the importance of the China market satisfied the deputation; they were plainly not seriously alarmed and were therefore content with a policy of precaution as they were to remain for two years further.[12]

This was all that Salisbury intended. He did not regard British interests in China as of decisive importance. There were positions to be defended, but others could be yielded without serious loss. He did not need Keswick to tell him of the desirability of an understanding with Russia. He was only too well aware of the limitations of British power, which restricted his actions in areas of greater moment than China. The Franco-Russian alliance, however, did not unduly disturb him. 'I do not believe that the junction of Russia and France in a maritime war is at all a probable contingency . . .', he wrote to Hicks Beach in January 1896. Indeed, at the height of the Venezuela crisis, he was more concerned about relations with the United States. 'A war with America—not this year but in the not distant future—has become something more than a possibility . . . It is much more of a reality than the future Russo-French coalition.' Even so, the existence of the alliance had seriously restricted British freedom of action in the

---

[12] Pelcovits, pp. 178–91, 205–6;FO 17/1256, record of interview, 16 Nov. 1895.

Mediterranean and added another burden to what had been the major preoccupation of British foreign policy throughout the nineteenth century, the Russian threat to India. For Salisbury, therefore, Russia's advance in China was not without its compensations. Manchuria was a long way from the Khyber Pass. In the China question he saw an issue that distracted Russia from more sensitive areas, and the continuation of expenditure there of Russian interest, energy, and resources was not without advantages.

The attitude of the China Association deputation, in its concentration on the Yangtze Valley, may well have influenced his thinking on the possibility of an arrangement with Russia. He looked to compromise with Russia but he did not intend to abandon the principle of the open door. He understood that Witte was engaged upon a slow advance in Manchuria a policy of peaceful penetration that did not bring any immediately serious threat to British interests in northern China, let alone the Yangtze Valley. There and in the south it was French activity that seemed to carry implications, particularly of the threat to the open door, wherever the French with their determinedly protectionist policy might succeed in establishing themselves. He was not alarmed by the bogey of a joint Franco-Russian thrust in the Far East, for he did not believe they shared the necessary harmony of interest in the area on which alone a really dangerous pressure could be mounted.[13]

In this assessment Salisbury was correct. Hanotaux, the French minister for foreign affairs, and Gérard, the minister in Peking, came to resent the secondary position assigned to France in the Russo-Chinese Bank established with French capital in December 1895, and the somewhat cavalier way in which France was treated by Russia and kept in ignorance of policies in which she was financially involved. The essential weakness of the French position, the lack of an impregnable base from which to operate, perhaps accounts for the almost frenetic zeal with which Gérard grasped at every opportunity for securing concessions and advancing French interests. The fact was that Indo-China was not a defensible position. With the British holding Burma and Malaya and with a military reserve in India as well as command of the seas, France was very vulnerable in the Far East. Her major asset was availability of investment capital, not military

---

[13] Hicks Beach Papers, PCC/69, Salisbury to Hicks Beach, 2 Jan. 1896. On Salisbury's view of Russian aims in China, see Grenville, chap. 6.

strength. Her whole position depended upon the support of an associate, and if that were not forthcoming collapse was always likely as the price of over-extending her power. Moreover, even if Russia could be counted upon for consistently solid support, the French were aware of weakness in the position of their ally. Until the trans-Siberian railway was completed, Russia would be unable to undertake a conflict with a superior sea power who could cut her communications. Patience and prudence were necessary until secure communications were established, and in view of the slow progress of the railway that would not be for several years.[14]

Salisbury's inclination also was for patience and prudence and in this he was able to proceed unhampered until 1898, by an aroused public opinion. His position rested on the assumption that reasonable settlements safeguarding British interests were possible. His strategy was twofold: to press China for concessions that would assist the opening of trading opportunities British enterprise could expoit; and to settle conflicts of interest with Russia and France peacefully and in such a way as to fend off challenges to British interests in the present or future. He was ready to admit the interest of other powers—as indeed he did publicly, repeating on 9 November 1895 Disraeli's phrase 'In Asia there is room for us all'—and ready to adjust differences by diplomacy. Agreement with France on as many as possible of the colonial questions in Asia and Africa that had disturbed relations was a primary aim of his policy. In it he saw the most practicable means of averting the danger of concerted action by a wide-ranging extension of the 'East Asian Dreibund' of 1895. In Paris Hanotaux, anxious to obtain greater freedom of action for France within the Russian alliance, understood that this was possible only if she could add to her friendships. Subordination to Russia would be eased by improvement in relations with Britain; hence the Anglo-French agreement of January 1896, which covered a variety of issues in Africa as well as in Asia. It provided for the neutralization of Siam and for mutuality rights in respect of 'all commercial and other privileges and advantages' that had been conferred on the two powers in Yunnan and Szechwan by virtue of the conventions of 1 March 1894 and 20 June 1895 or which might in the future be granted to them there.

The mutuality agreement was a shrewd stroke by Salisbury. There

---

[14] *DDF* 1st series, 13, nos. 55, 170, Gérard to Hanotaux, 3 Jan. and 28 Mar. 1897; FO 17/1361, report by Major Bower, 18 July 1898.

was no intention on the part of the British government to sanction the use of public funds to develop railway communications from Burma into southern China; the formidable engineering difficulties and the enormous cost were pointed out to chambers of commerce attracted to the project by the efforts of publicists. It had no support in the Foreign Office or in the China Association, whose members saw no reason to assist the trade of Burma at the expense of Hong Kong. In their view the natural route was that of the rivers, the Yangtze to Shanghai and the West River to Canton and Hong Kong where the commercial outlets were dominated by British firms. The aim of British policy should be to remove barriers to this natural flow created by Chinese restrictions, and to resist attempts by France to deflect commerce from its natural outlets. French fears that the British would build a Burma railway (which in fact they had no intention of doing) offered an opportunity Salisbury was quick to take: the agreement on reciprocity ensured the way would be open to British enterprise to profit from French efforts to penetrate Yunnan and Szechwan. True, in neither area were British commercial interests particularly active. Though the China Association in November 1895 had mentioned access to Szechwan and publicists had stressed its prospects as a market, Salisbury's action had not been a response to determined pressure from private interests. On the contrary, the initiative was much more that of the Foreign Office intent on ensuring that opportunities were opened for enterprise to exploit if it wished.[15]

The Anglo-French agreement was one arm of a dual policy designed to limit the encroachment of rivals on British interests and to extend opportunities for British enterprise. The other arm was direct pressure by Britain on the Chinese government. The contract for the second indemnity loan had provided some security for the important customs administration. Before its conclusion came the appointment of the strong man to the Peking legation that the China Association had called for. The movement away from the policy of detachment towards active safeguarding of positions of political and economic significance was given direction with Sir Claude MacDonald's arrival. In February 1897 he secured an Anglo-Chinese agreement that, in addition to rectification of the Burmese–Chinese frontier, recognized

---

[15] J. D. Hargreaves, 'Entente manquée: Anglo-French Relations 1895–1896', *Cambridge Historical Journal* 11 (1953), pp. 65–92; Chandran Jeshurun, *The Contest for Siam, 1889—1902* (Kuala Lumpur, 1977), chap. 4; W. B. Walsh, 'The Yunnan Myth', *Far Eastern Quarterly* 2 (1943), pp. 272–85.

Britain's right to extend Burmese railways into Yunnan when the time came. This was little more than a further political weapon to quieten those at home who from time to time called for a Burma railway, but it also indicated a movement towards response in kind to the new imperialism. More important was the undertaking by China to open the West River from Wuchowfu in Kwangsi to Canton for navigation. This, also among the actions asked for by the China Association, marked a serious setback to French hopes of attracting the trade of south-western China to Hanoi in place of Hong Kong.

Between 1895 and 1897 Salisbury had done pretty well at no cost, and he had satisfied the China trading interests. Not all were completely happy, but general equanimity was undisturbed. Agitation for the Burma railway continued among chambers of commerce, but the leading houses in the mercantile community were content with the government's dual policy up to the middle of 1897. Then the clear indications of exclusivism in French and Russian intentions began to cause concern. The contract for the third portion of the indemnity loan, an amount of £16 million, occupied the Hongkong Bank through 1897. It was recognized in the Foreign Office that it was important to keep it out of French and Russian hands, but as the Chinese seemed disposed to deal with the Anglo-German group as in 1896 there was no great concern.

The German occupation of Kiaochow changed the situation and the question of the indemnity loan became increasingly disturbing. Negotiations between the Chinese government and the Hongkong Bank had begun in February 1897, but dragged on because the bank and its German partner wanted more control over the security offered—the *likin* and the salt revenues—than the Chinese were ready to allow, maintaining that unless this was accorded they would find difficulty in floating the loan on the London and Berlin markets. The bank kept the Foreign Office informed but asked only for unofficial help. Clearly it had now established a close relationship with the Far Eastern Department. Hicks Beach was told that 'The Hong Kong and Shanghai Bank communicate information to the Foreign Office . . . and the Foreign Office let the Bank know unofficially what is reported from Peking and elsewhere as to any offers made by foreign syndicates to the Chinese government.'[16]

What brought the matter to the forefront was a report from

---

[16] Hicks Beach Papers, PC 72/2/3, unsigned FO memorandum, 9 July 1897.

MacDonald on 22 December 1897 that the Chinese had arranged a Russian loan for the £16 million, in return for which Russia was to have a monopoly of railways in northern China and the inspector-generalship of the customs. This seems to have been a negotiating move by the Chinese seeking to play off prospective lenders, for they asked MacDonald to ascertain whether the Anglo-German group would renew its previous offer for the loan. The Hongkong Bank was not prepared to accept the Chinese terms, but indicated that they could raise the money required if the British government would give a partial guarantee of 1 or 1½ per cent interest. Cameron also made other proposals: that in case of default the government should administer the revenue pledged; and that the loan should be issued by the Bank of England, either alone or in conjunction with the Hongkong Bank. On Bertie's suggestion, Cameron put his views before Salisbury. Thus the question of government participation in a loan to China was again raised. Clearly the political advantages and dangers involved in the loan were both significant; equally clearly the chancellor of the exchequer disliked association with the Hongkong Bank. If the government were to accept any responsibility for the loan—and it was the Russian offer that influenced him to approve that proposal—he hesitated between a direct loan, which he preferred, and a guarantee. But in his view, if this course were followed, Parliament would require more than a retention of the present commercial position and would want some clear step towards predominance such as the purchase of the Suez Canal shares had brought, but done 'with the utmost secrecy and *not* through Cameron or his bank'.[17]

The possibility that the government, while undertaking to guarantee the loan, would not use the Hongkong Bank seems to have become known to Cameron. At all events, on 7 January, he put his case to Bertie for his bank by itself or in conjunction with the Bank of England to be entrusted with the floating of the loan. He justified his claims by the high credit the bank enjoyed in England as well as in the East, the magnitude of the interests it represented in China, and what it had done to promote British trade there in the last thirty-four years. The bank had been closely associated with the Chinese government, which he was confident would wish the management of the loan to be entrusted to it. If it were not, he claimed,

---

[17] Salisbury Papers, A/90, Hicks Beach to Salisbury, 26 and 27 Dec. 1897; FO 17/1356, memorandum by Norton, 1 Jan. 1898.

we will suffer great loss of prestige and our influence in the East will be
seriously impaired. We are now fighting a hard battle with Russian, French,
and German semi-state banks in China and I am proud to say we are more
than holding our own. If, however, we are ignored by our Government in an
important transaction like this, which legitimately comes within our field, our
position will be very much damaged.

At the same time, in what must have appeared as a concerted pressure,
MacDonald telegraphed from Peking:

I think it very important that the position of the Hongkong and Shanghai Bank
should be recognized in connection with the issue or agency of the loan as
representing British finance in China. The Russian Bank here receives strong
official support from Russian Government and competes strongly with our
Bank for Chinese government business. If left outside in this matter the
position of the Hongkong and Shanghai Bank would be seriously impaired in
the eyes of the Chinese government.

Hart added his support too, but Cameron's plea was curtly dismissed by the chancellor, who minuted the letter: 'I trust that this will
be left unanswered. I think it time that communications from
Mr. Cameron should be discouraged.' Salisbury concurred.[18]

It is thus evident that in the senior ranks of the Cabinet there was no
disposition to assist the Hongkong Bank in what must have seemed a
crude attempt to advance its interest and standing further by appearing as the agent of the government. But the government was ready to
use financial weapons. Hicks Beach proposed a direct loan to China
and an approach to Russia for agreement on their respective interests.
A loan of £12 million was approved as a political operation to prevent
Russian gains, particularly in the customs service. The security
demanded was the customs, salt, and *likin* revenues, which in the
event of default were to be placed under British control. Further
concessions, it was indicated, would be required.

The Chinese authorities, confronted now by Russian and British
offers and only too well aware of the consequences likely to follow
acceptance of the one in preference to the other, reverted to their
initial position. They rejected the British government's offer and
again appeared ready for what could be presented as a bankers' loan.

At all events, by the beginning of February the Hongkong Bank
seems to have felt that the situation was moving in that direction. On

---

[18] FO 17/1356, Cameron to Bertie, 7 and 8 Jan. 1898, FO 17/1340, MacDonald to
Salisbury, 8 Jan. 1898.

10 February, Cameron reported that the Chinese government was ready to contract a loan on the security of the *likin* and customs revenues. Hart had asked the bank to make a first offer. Cameron presented this as an opportunity to regain lost ground, to be taken without delay. Would the government give the bank sufficient support for it to act? Hicks Beach once again refused to sanction the guarantee the bank was obviously seeking. He viewed the situation now as likely to be a question between rival financiers of different nations, and he did not think it proper to support a private bank in the very indefinite manner suggested.

When the Chinese, fearful of Russia, rejected the British offer of a direct loan, Salisbury, regarding this as an affront for China had formally requested the loan, demanded compensation, including a pledge of the non-alienation of the Yangtze Valley and confirmation that the inspector-general of the customs should continue to be a British subject so long as British trade was predominant. Following Chinese acquiescence he doubted whether any British loan would be necessary since he had secured sufficient safeguards. Bertie, however, emphasized other factors. He told Salisbury that if the money were found by foreign banks, either under a Russian, German, or French indirect or modified guarantee (such as the appointment of inspectors in case of default) the governments concerned would have strong claims to flood the customs with their nominees. What the Hongkong Bank wanted, since a direct guarantee was impossible, was that the Bank of England should join with them to issue the loan; or they would stand aside if the Bank of England would undertake it alone. Bertie said that Cameron understood the Bank of England would not participate unless pressed by the government, and his submission stressed the Russian threat. He maintained that without some kind of government assurance no Chinese loan could be floated at present in view of the effect of recent events on Chinese credit. If there were no British loan, the Chinese would turn to Russia and in a few months Russia would guarantee the loan. If the government would not help, Cameron saw an international loan bringing in Russia and France as the only hope of preventing a Russian success.[19]

[19] *BD* 1, no. 1, memorandum by Tilley, 14 Jan. 1905; FO 17/1356, Cameron to FO, 10 Feb. 1898, with minute by Hicks Beach; Bertie to Salisbury, 10 Feb. 1898; Cameron to Bertie, 11 Feb. 1898, with minute by Hicks Beach. The Deutsch-Asiatische Bank had been inclined at an earlier stage in the negotiations to bring in French and Russian banks to the loan with international control of the security; memorandum by Norton, 1 Jan. 1898.

Bertie's support of the Hongkong Bank's case is an indication of the position it had established in the Foreign Office. Senior officials (Bertie himself, and Sanderson), saw it as a useful instrument of policy. Salisbury, however, was cool, and Hicks Beach hostile. The possibility of the international loan that dismayed Cameron was not unwelcome to the chancellor, who supported the efforts Salisbury was making to find a *modus vivendi* with Russia. For the Hongkong Bank it was something to be avoided. The bank wanted the business for itself and its German partners and went ahead on its own account, concluding a preliminary agreement with the Chinese on 19 February 1898 for a loan of £16 million of which the Germans were to provide half. If the Hongkong Bank's portion were to be successfully floated in London, however, some official assistance was necessary. Cameron, his position strengthened by the loan agreement, resumed his search, bringing Lord Rothschild's influence to bear on Salisbury to persuade the Bank of England to issue as well as to inscribe the loan, for this would ensure its success. Hicks Beach now became more amenable. He thought inscription would suffice, arguing that issue by the Bank of England would be regarded as equivalent or almost equivalent to a loan supported by the government and would lead to friction with Russia. If, however, it was thought advisable for political reasons to ask the Bank of England to issue, he would act on a request from the Foreign Office. In the event, possibly because of the chancellor's warning, assistance was limited to a request for inscription, which was accorded by the Bank of England though with some reluctance. This limitation affected the success of the issue, which was made at the height of the Port Arthur crisis. Bertie commented:

For the £8m. portion of the Chinese loan issued at Berlin £38m. have been applied for. Of the £8m. offered in London only £2m. have been subscribed by the public. The difference is to be accounted for by the confidence felt in Germany of government support in case of default and the contrary feeling here.[20]

Though following the compensation obtained from China Salisbury had set less store by the loan, its conclusion was a further

---

[20] Salisbury Papers, Special Correspondence E, box 154, Schomberg McDonnel to Salisbury, 23 Feb. 1898, with enclosures; FO 17/1357, memoranda by Bertie, 22 and 24 Feb. and 24 Mar. 1898; FO to Treasury, 16 Mar. 1898. Hamilton Papers, BL Add. MSS 48614, Hicks Beach to Hamilton, 23 Feb. 1898.

buttressing of the British position at a time when public opinion was pressing for action to counter Russia's advance. If Franco-Russian banks had secured the loan contract, it would have added to criticism of the government for weakness over China. The Hongkong Bank had served usefully at a time when China would not take a direct British government loan for fear of provoking Russia.

The loan was certainly important for the bank. Despite the poor response to the issue, the operation had added to its prestige. More and more it came to appear as the financial agent of the British government in China. The determination and persistence of Cameron in face of rebuffs, the support the bank had mobilized from Rothschild, Hart, MacDonald, and within the Foreign Office (particularly from Bertie), together with the political situation in China, which had prevented acceptance of a direct loan from the British government, had enabled it to make a further advance. The key to its success was enterprise. It was efficient, had good connections with the Chinese, and was eager for loan business. Ever since 1895 when the changed climate had brought foreign governments to interest themselves in China's finances, it had adjusted to circumstances. It was ready in its own interests to act as the British counter to the continental state banks.

As for the British government, it was being brought to recognize that in China, as in Persia, it needed a British financial institution to take business of political significance. Traditionalists in the Treasury were more reluctant than officials in the Foreign Office to accept the necessity of association with private finance, but if the Hongkong Bank had not existed in the new China scene it would have been necessary to invent it. The Chartered Bank, now the only serious rival to the Hongkong Bank among British financial institutions in China, had lagged behind. When early in 1898 it did seek a share in the loan, its approach to the Foreign Office met with the response that, while its offer would be mentioned, 'our communications on Chinese financial questions during the last few years had mainly been with the Hongkong and Shanghai Bank'. Three years later the Chartered Bank, now 'very jealous and not unnaturally so' of the Hongkong Bank, made another approach, this time for a share in any of the banking business connected with the Boxer indemnity and asking for a seat on the committee of bankers at Shanghai that was to supervise the transfer of funds. The British seat, however, went to E. G. Hillier, the able and experienced Peking agent of the Hongkong Bank, and with it the business attached.[21] Hillier's appointment symbolized the further strengthening of ties between the bank and the Foreign Office that had developed between 1898 and 1901. This was especially the result of the bank's involvement in the new phase that had begun in 1898—the struggle to dominate China's railway communications—but the Boxer Rising had reaffirmed the value of a financial institution eager to make itself available.

In August 1900 the viceroy at Hankow applied for the assistance of the British government in raising a loan of £75,000 to pay his troops. If they were not paid, the viceroy's influence would suffer. The Yangtze Valley had remained quiet during the Boxer disturbances and the viceroys had been friendly, and it was obviously in the British interest that this should continue. The Hongkong Bank was ready to find the money but asked for a government guarantee to cover the loan, not only to safeguard the bank but also to ensure that the transaction had its maximum effect. Competitors, Russian and Belgian, it was hinted by Cameron, were in the field. Salisbury, initially dubious as to the advantage to be gained by the loan, as was Hicks Beach, soon came round to stress to the Treasury the importance of upholding the viceroy, and suggested that the matter be best arranged through the Hongkong Bank. Hicks Beach, however, had shed none of its prejudices. He suspected that the viceroy's request had been prompted by the bank's agents at Shanghai. He agreed to guarantee only part of the interest that the bank intended to ask and instructed, 'If Cameron hesitates tell him we will employ some other bank and ... advance money either ourselves or through Bank of England ... Cameron cannot afford to lose prestige of government employment now and in future'.

The loan went through on Treasury terms but the fact of the guarantee, if only partial, marked a further step away from traditional principles. The chancellor had not welcomed official participation and when a request for a further loan to the viceroy in order to forestall offers from foreign banks was made in November 1900, he reacted with an unrestrained denunciation of the Hongkong Bank, which he saw as seeking to manipulate the government to advance its own interests.

[21] FO 17/1356, Chartered Bank to Treasury, 25 Jan. 1898; memorandum by Sanderson, 27 Jan. 1898; FO 17/1507, Chartered Bank to FO, 1 Aug. 1901; FO 17/1511, Chartered Bank to FO, 27 and 28 Nov. 1901. Hamilton (Treasury) to Campbell, 3 Dec. 1901. For a good analysis of the Persian issues, see D. McLean, *Britain and her Buffer State* (London, 1979).

All these proposals come really from one quarter—the Hongkong and Shanghai Bank, and its creatures and supporters in China. It is very easy to understand why they should wish us to place them in a better position in China than even the Russo-Chinese Bank, by giving them direct guarantees for business which, everywhere in the past, English banks have done where it was worth doing without such assistance. For years they have consistently worried the Foreign Office with this end in view. Even if I trusted them it is not a policy I could adopt. But I do not. I know that their agent suggested this application to the Viceroy when arranging the security for the loan already granted—and, in my opinion, they failed to consider our interests as they ought to have done in settling the security for that loan . . . I will not place the purse of the country at the disposal of these people as I believe it practically would be if these applications are agreed to . . . They say the security of the new loan is adequate and that German, Belgian and French financiers or syndicates (not governments) are ready to lend. Why in that case cannot the H & S Bank find this comparatively small amount themselves? If our bankers are less wealthy or less enterprising than their foreign competitors in China so much the worse for them and our merchants there. But this has not hitherto been considered sufficient ground for government guarantee.[22]

The chancellor's views did not prevail. The Cabinet decided in favour of the new loan as politically desirable. The viceroys were clearly regarded by the Foreign Office as important allies. Hicks Beach had thought it unwise and impracticable for Britain to try to keep foreign trade out of the Yangtze Valley by subsidizing the viceroys; the Foreign Office took a different view and was now quite ready to use the financial weapon. Lansdowne, who represented the 'do something' group in the Cabinet, had become foreign secretary in October 1900. He was ready to adapt to a new situation with new methods. In April 1901 he was sounding the chancellor on further financial aid to the viceroys.[23] This, too, without question, would be

[22] FO 17/1443, Cameron to FO, 6 Aug. 1900; FO 17/1444, FO to Treasury, 10 Aug. 1900; Cameron to Bertie, 10 Aug. 1900; Hicks Beach to Brodrick, 10 Aug. 1900; Hicks Beach Papers, PC 72/2/2, Salisbury to Hicks Beach, 12 Aug. 1900; Salisbury Papers, box 17, Hicks Beach to Salisbury, 11 Nov. 1900; Young, pp. 180–1.

[23] Hicks Beach Papers, PCC/84, Lansdowne to Hicks Beach, 7 Apr. 1901. But in 1904 Cameron failed to secure a pledge from the government to ensure that the bank would be repaid if it made a loan to the viceroy of Canton. He argued that the loan would strengthen British influence in a province where the French were pressing. On advice from Austen Chamberlain, now chancellor of the exchequer, Lansdowne would not agree to do more than promise that the British consul-general would use his best endeavours to ensure repayment (FO 17/1653, Cameron to Campbell, 29 Jan. and 1 Feb. 1904; Chamberlain to Lansdowne, 30 Jan. 1904; Campbell to Cameron, 1 Feb. 1904).

through the Hongkong Bank, for the Foreign Office had now come to view it as a major auxiliary in the protection of British interests in China. The knighthood conferred on Cameron in 1900 was an obvious recognition of the services he had rendered. The bank stood out as the financial arm of British policy, the complement of the semi-state banks of France, Russia, and Germany. In some respects the comparison was just, but the Hongkong Bank differed in significant aspects. It was a private institution and it was individual. It did not, as did the continental banks in China, represent a consortium of domestic banks, nor did it have close links with industry as they did. Moreover it was not entirely British, for from its foundation there had been non-British directors among the Hong Kong merchants who sat on its board. From the appointment of Thomas Jackson as its chief manager in 1875, its management had been British as was the great bulk of its shareholding; but the presence of German directors was to cause problems for the bank in the years to come.

2

British Enterprise and Chinese Railways, 1898–1904

THE government's support of the Hongkong Bank in the indemnity loans and in subsequent loans to the Yangtze viceroys was in an area of obvious political significance. These episodes had indicated a growing recognition in the Foreign Office of the importance of finance as a weapon in the armoury of diplomacy, and a readiness to work in conjunction with a private financial institution. The attitude of the Treasury, however, and the reluctance of the Bank of England to inscribe the issue of the third indemnity loan, had shown the distaste felt by the financial hierarchy for government participation, even to this limited extent, in a private banking operation. But the course of events in China in 1897–8 had already created a situation that was bringing the Foreign Office into involvement in more obviously commercial transactions, thus breaching more sharply the established convention of *laissez faire*, the shibboleth of British economic policy. There had indeed in 1885 been indications in relation to the affairs of China that the government would modify its policy of detachment if foreign competitors of British enterprise received support from their governments, and it had long been recognized that certain enterprises, particularly railways, could be of political significance. The Bryce Report of 1886, however, was markedly cautious in its view of the proper extent to which British representatives abroad should involve themselves in the market place.

The German occupation of Kiaochow and still more the appearance of the Russians at Port Arthur brought a dramatic change in what had earlier seemed for Britain to be disturbing but not alarming developments. The government's concern over the third indemnity loan and the stir in public opinion were indicative of the movement of the China question into the centre of British politics. Hitherto the pressure of rivals had not brought calls for drastic counter-action. British interests in Manchuria if not negligible were limited, and neither the Foreign Office nor the China Association seemed to attach great importance to the area. There had been some concern about French designs in southern China, but this was diminished by Salisbury's successful acquisition of countering positions. Opinion in the British community was that the natural force of geography would thwart French plans for diverting trade routes to Indo-China. Even their railway schemes did not cause serious alarm. This general unconcern, reflected in the feeling of the British community in China that even after 1895 the advances made by other powers were really for the good of all traders in China, disappeared rapidly in 1897–8 as Germany pressed for, and secured in the Sino-German Treaty of 6 March 1898, preferential rights for her enterprise in Shantung.

The Chinese Government binds itself in all cases where foreign assistance, in persons, capital or material may be needed for any purpose whatever within the Province of Shantung, to offer the said work or supplying of materials in the first instance to German manufacturers and merchants engaged in undertakings of the kind in question.[1]

At the same time, Russia moved into the Liaotung Peninsula, France sought to strengthen her position in the South and Japan likewise in Fukien, all aiming if not at territorial acquisition then at the creation of spheres from which the trade and enterprise of other powers would be more or less completely excluded. The government rapidly took measures to protect British trade. Pledges were obtained that safeguarded the Yangtze Valley and ensured that the direction of the customs service would remain in British hands. These measures conformed to the principle that defence of economic interests in a general sense was a legitimate and necessary function of foreign policy. But more was necessary. Before Japan's victory the Chinese government was coming to accept the need for technological modernization. The Imperial Railway Administration was established in 1891 to construct a railway from Peking to Mukden, with a branch to Newchwang on which work had begun before the outbreak of war. After defeat the urgency of rapid modernization as a condition of

---

[1] J. V. A. MacMurray (ed.), *Treaties and Agreements with and concerning China* (2 vols., New York, 1921), 1, p. 116. The award of a provisional contract for the Peking–Hankow railway to a Belgian group in May 1897 had caused concern in the British legation but not to the Anglo-German financial group, which did not believe that the contract would be carried out; see G. Kurgan-van Hentenryk, *Leopold II et les groupes financiers belges en Chine* (Brussels, 1971), pp. 117–18.

survival was recognized, and schemes had been drawn up for major developments in mining and particularly in railways. Now, with further evidence in Kiaochow and Port Arthur of China's helplessness in face of pressure, and with awareness of the significance of mines and railways as means not only of acquiring or buttressing political influence but also as sources of profit (through loans, construction, or operating rights), demands from foreign enterprises mounted in Peking for concessions to build the planned railways and others thought desirable.

The Chinese authorities recognized that China did not have sufficient resources to construct the railway system she needed, and that foreign money and foreign technology would be necessary. These were in fact being pressed upon her, but often with barely concealed motives attached. British political aims were defensive: to protect commercial interests and prospects from invasion by rivals who, by differential railway tariffs among other means, might restrict free competition. The Chinese were concerned that railway concessions accorded to foreign governments were intended to establish political controls. Agreements made with British enterprises were commercial contracts made with private firms; the railways to be constructed formed the security for the loan but were the property of the Chinese railway administration. In the event of default the lenders were empowered to take control until arrears were redeemed.

The Chinese, well aware of the dangers from the award of concessions, endeavoured as far as they could to prevent any one power gaining railway predominance in a particular area.[2] This aim was not realized in Manchuria or Shantung, but elsewhere it had partial success, sometimes to the chagrin, at other times to the satisfaction of the British government and British enterprises vigorously involved in the battle for concessions.

The Foreign Office quickly recognized that in the new situation, mining and especially railway concessions in foreign hands could threaten British trade in its main centres. In free and fair competition the British, it was held, would dominate the field; but competition was not free and fair. Heavy diplomatic pressure was being applied by European rivals organized for economic war with their financial and

---

[2] E-tu Zen Sun, *Chinese Railways and British Interests, 1898–1911* (New York, 1954), pp. 42–8. P. H. Kent, *Railway Enterprise in China* (London, 1907), pp. 94–5. Most British contracts gave the lenders a dominant place in operating the line for the duration of the loan.

industrial forces grouped more or less closely under the leadership of semi-state banks, each responsive to the wishes of its government. Britain had to extend defensive strategy into the railway field. The concessions obtained by Russia for the Chinese Eastern Railway and by the French for a line from Indo-China into Yunnan had not caused alarm for one reason or another. Now with large schemes afoot, particularly for a major trunk line connecting Peking with Canton (thus traversing the Yangtze Valley) and parliamentary and public opinion calling for action over railways as well as in other fields in China, it was politically impossible for the government, even if it desired, to keep out of the battle. It had to join in, and it would have to use weapons to match those of its adversaries. It would have to come down into the arena of competing enterprise.

Here it was plain there was no shortage of British contenders. As the long-dreamed-of China market seemed at last to show real prospects, a flood of concession hunters appeared. But what was needed, if there were to be a significant British presence in mines and railways, was financial strength. Few among this variegated throng were worthy of serious consideration. One that merited attention was the Pekin Syndicate, founded in 1897 and involved mainly in mining ventures. It had Italian connections, but it was a British concern backed by solid City interests. Lord Rothschild was a principal shareholder. With the support of MacDonald, the Pekin Syndicate succeeded in obtaining important mineral concessions in Shansi, including what was claimed to be the largest anthracite coalfield in the world.[3] With its mining interests went a concern with railway construction for the transport of its minerals, which was to give it a place of some significance as the railway situation developed. Here, however, the one serious enterprise that appeared was the British and Chinese Corporation, in which the Hongkong Bank was a major shareholder.

Participation in railway financing had been envisaged in the Hongkong Bank's agreement with the Deutsch-Asiatische Bank in 1895, but the British bank does not seem to have been very eager to push business in this sector where in any case opportunities were few. When they did appear in 1898, the Hongkong Bank's relations with its German partner in railway questions became strained. By March

---

[3] FO 17/1357, Earl of Mayo to Salisbury, 21 Feb. 1898; FO 17/1363, Pekin Syndicate to FO, 27 Sept. 1898.

1898, the Germans were blocking a Chinese project for a line from Tientsin to Chinkiang to be financed by British and American capital by insisting that the option for the section through Shantung be given to German interests. Yet at the same time as they claimed an exclusive position in Shantung, they were seeking participation in railway business in the Yangtze Valley.

How far this determined the Hongkong Bank to separate from the German group and form a powerful British syndicate is uncertain. Undoubtedly it was a factor, as was the limitation its function as bank put upon its freedom of action in railway business. Also important, however, and perhaps decisive, was the indication the bank received in the middle of March 1898, possibly from MacDonald, that the British government was now disposed to promote British railways in China.[4] Although Cameron was advised by Bertie to hold on to the Germans as long as they were in any way reasonable, the bank decided to end the partnership in respect of railway business and to work separately. The first target of the 'strong, representative and influential syndicate' they intended to form, the Foreign Office was told, would be the concession for the Shanghai–Soochow–Nanking line, which Cameron said was very important to secure for Britain.

Cameron was clearly making a bid for tacit recognition as the British standard bearer in the railway battle. There was another group of substance in the City aiming at the Shanghai–Nanking line, which promised to be a profitable venture. This included Cosmo Bonsor (a director of the Bank of England), and the banking houses, Barings and Hambros, but Cameron was able to bring them into the Hongkong Bank's syndicate that came into being early in June 1898: the British and Chinese Corporation. The bank and Jardine, Matheson, who were the major shareholders, were to be joint managers, with Jardine's taking responsibility for supply and construction work and the bank issuing and servicing loans. The other subscribers included Rothschild's, Baring's, Hambros and other merchant banking houses, but no industrial interests apart from the railway engineers, Pauling and Co. The British and Chinese Corporation was essentially a financial concern and therefore not comparable with the European groups that concentrated financial and industrial resources into large units, but its

---

[4] FO 17/1357, memorandum by Bertie of conversation with Count Arco-Valley, 13 Mar. 1898; FO 17/1358, Cameron to Bertie, 28 Mar. and 4 Apr. 1898; FO 17/1343, MacDonald to Salisbury, 17 Mar. 1898, indicates Salisbury's interest in British participation in railway development in China.

City backing seemed to promise it considerable funds. The objects of the corporation were to apply for concessions to construct, administer, manage or control public works of all kinds, including railways, tramways and docks. Cameron presented the list of subscribers to the Foreign Office as 'really a very good and representative one', and the Far Eastern Department, aware of MacDonald's belief that if a reliable syndicate prepared to take some risk were formed he could get important railway concessions, judged it to be a strong group. Apart form the Pekin Syndicate there was no other group of comparable strength in the field.

The formation of the corporation, apparently without official pressure, seemed to dispose of a problem. The Foreign Office was looking for an instrument and found it to hand in the British and Chinese Corporation. The chambers of commerce were calling for direct financial participation by the government in Chinese railways. This was quite impossible, for Parliament would never permit it even if the Cabinet agreed. Now that the corporation, with apparently ample financial resources at its call, was ready to bid, it seemed that the Foreign Office had a group whose applications it could support, confident that the group would be able to raise the necessary funds. This assurance, which was required from all applicants for support, appeared amply provided in the list of subscribers presented by Cameron.[5]

At the time of the formation of the corporation, battle had already been joined with the German group on the issue of the Shanghai–Nanking concession, and this had brought in the governments. Cameron, in asking for official support, emphasized what was involved:

The German syndicate have laid a scheme before the Chinese authorities and we think it probable, unless we close at once, the German plan will be accepted. I need not point out what a serious blow it would be to British prestige if the railway system in the rich provinces of Kiangsu and Chekiang were to pass under the control of any other Power and it becomes a question under these circumstances whether pressure similar to what is exercised by other Powers should not be brought to bear on the Chinese government.

[5] FO 17/1358, Macrae to Campbell, 21 Apr. 1898; FO 17/1359, Cameron to Bertie, 9 June 1898; Pelcovits, pp. 234–5. The absence of industrial participation reflected the degree to which British industry, in constrast with the continental pattern, was detached from bank control; see Platt, pp. 23–4.

Assuming that Germany will carry through the projected system of railways through Shantung to Chinkiang, and they now secure the Shanghai–Nanking line, they will virtually command all railway communication from Tientsin to Shanghai and up the Yangtze valley to Nanking.

I take the liberty of pointing out these facts and trust the government will be able to induce the Chinese to grant the delay we require and in any case not to allow railways in Kiangsu and the Yangtze Valley to pass into the hands of Germany or any other Power than Great Britain.[6]

The Foreign Office responded robustly. When the German ambassador asked that MacDonald's demand for the Shanghai–Nanking line as a political concession be withdrawn, adding that if the Deutsch-Asiatische Bank failed to get the line it would have a most unfortunate effect on public opinion in Germany, Bertie retorted vigorously. The Germans, he said, had just got a concession in Shantung; now they sought one in opposition to us in the Yangtze region. 'Were Germans to have all the railways?' He made the same point later on to Lord Rothschild, who had close links with the German group. 'They wanted Shantung all to themselves and to share the rest of China with us and others taking the plums for themselves.'

What was at issue seems to some extent to have been a question of prestige. The two groups envisaged co-operation in financing, constructing, and working the Shanghai–Nanking railway, but the British entirely refused the Deutsch-Asiatische Bank's claim that the company to be established to build and work the railway should have a German name. Salisbury was determined that this should not be so. He made two proposals to Germany. The profits of the venture, he suggested, should be equally divided between the two groups, but the company to build and operate the line should be registered as an English company, under English management, and with an English name. (Cameron's emphasis on prestige had clearly made an impression on the Foreign Office.) Salisbury's second proposal was for a general Anglo-German agreement on railways, whereby all railways in Shantung for which either bank might obtain concessions should be under German management with equal division of profits, while in the Yangtze Valley British management should operate, again with division of profits. The German government rejected both proposals. It claimed a special position for Germany in Shantung by reason of the occupation of Kiaochow and its agreement with China, but main-

---

[6] FO 17/1358, Hongkong Bank to FO, 22 Apr. 1898.

tained that the Yangtze area, where nothing was occupied by Britain, was still unreservedly open to German enterprise. Thereupon MacDonald was instructed to continue to oppose the claims of the German group to the Shanghai–Nanking line.[7]

Following the award of concessions to the French, the British had demanded the Shanghai–Nanking contract as a political concession in compensation, and in May 1898 Jardine, Matheson negotiated a preliminary agreement for the line on behalf of the British group. The breach between the British and German groups, though not intended on the British side to prevent co-operation in the future, was distressing to some in the financial world, and successful efforts were made by the Rothschilds to bring them together. Alfred de Rothschild claimed to have been responsible for arranging the meeting in London, early in September 1898, from which emerged the two groups' recognition of each other's sphere of interest for railway concessions in China—the Germans taking Shantung and the Hoangho Valley, the British taking the Yangtze Valley. They also agreed to co-operate in the Tientsin–Chinkiang railway, the Germans to finance and construct the northern section to the border of Shantung and the British the southern portion. The British government seems to have had no hand in bringing the agreement about. It was notified of its conclusion and of the resolution agreed on by the groups that it was 'desirable for the British and German governments to agree about the spheres of interest of their countries regarding the railway concessions in China and to mutually support the interests of either country', and with the German government approved it, but that was all. The minutes of the meeting 'do not appear to have been confirmed or ratified either by the governments or by their groups'.[8] However important it may have seemed at the time, the agreement was of limited significance and was not to be regarded by the Germans in later years as excluding them from the Yangtze Valley.

Successful resistance to the Germans was some consolation in the depressing China scene in the summer of 1898, but there had been damaging progress by other rivals. In July, Salisbury was pessimistic.

---

[7] FO 17/1359, memoranda by Bertie, 3, 4, and 6 May 1898; Cameron to Bertie, 17 May 1898; Hongkong Bank to FO, 23 May 1898; FO 17/1362, memorandum by Norton, 12 Aug. 1898.

[8] FO 17/1359, A. de Rothschild to Bertie, 4 May 1898; FO 17/1360, memorandum by Bertie, 6 July 1898; FO 17/1363, Hongkong Bank to FO, 3 Sept. 1898; Salisbury Papers, Special Correspondence E, box 154, A. de Rothschild to Salisbury, 16 Jan. 1899; FO 371/851, Addis to FO, 23 Apr. 1910, on the significance of the agreement.

The battle of concessions does not seem to be going well for us and we must face the possibility that the mass of Chinese railways if they come into existence will be in foreign hands. One evil of this is that we shall lose all orders for material; that we cannot help. The other evil is that the managers of the railways by differential rates and privileges may strangle our trade. This we ought to be able to prevent by pressing that proper provisions for equal treatment be inserted in every concession . . .[9]

The definitive award of the Peking–Hankow contract to the Belgian group was felt in London to be a very hard blow because it was thought that the Belgians were simply a screen for Franco-Russian masters. There was certainly a strong French element, but in fact Russia's involvement was limited to diplomatic assistance to the Belgian group in its application for the contract. Though public opinion in Britain was stirred by fears that the line would open the way for Russia to enter the Yangtze Valley, the Foreign Office came to accept that the Russo-Chinese Bank was not associated with the Belgian syndicate.[10] Moreover, experts consulted by MacDonald did not think that the Peking–Hankow line would pay. In his view the Hongkong Bank would be ill advised, even if the possibility existed, to exchange for it the loan contract that the bank had negotiated in June 1898 for the extension of the Imperial Railways of North China (the Northern Railway) beyond Shanhaikuan, at the western end of the Great Wall, to Hsinmintun in Manchuria, with a branch to Newchwang. The bank had already made loans in 1894, 1896, and 1897 for the Peking–Shanhaikuan section, which was being constructed under the direction of a British engineer, C. W. Kinder.[11] The extension was to be built on the same basis, as a Chinese railway not as a concession. The project was politically sensitive because, as well as promising lucrative traffic, it would have the effect of keeping direct railway communication between Manchuria and Peking out of the hands of Russia if construction were financed from other sources.

It may well be that the decision of the Chinese authorities in April 1898 to offer the loan contract to the Hongkong Bank was influenced

[9] FO 17/1339, Salisbury to MacDonald, 13 July 1898.

[10] Kurgan-van Hentenryk, Leopold II, pp. 168–79; Quested, p. 56.

[11] FO 17/1344, MacDonald to Salisbury, 22 July 1898; an exchange had been urged by the China Association on the assumption that there was a Russian interest in the Peking–Hankow line (Pelcovits, pp. 236–7). For text of the contract, see MacMurray, i, pp. 179–81.

by rivalries within the Chinese railway administration.[12] Political considerations, the knowledge that the most obvious opponent of Russia among the powers was Britain, must also have been in the minds of the Chinese. Russia certainly saw the decision in that light. Furthermore, the approach to the British at a time when Russian ambitions in Manchuria were only too plain was in accordance with Chinese tactics in the distribution of railway contracts. The choice of the Hongkong Bank was a further indication of the special position it held among British financial institutions in China as that most closely involved in Chinese official loans. MacDonald may well have encouraged the Chinese to turn to the British bank. He had maintained vigorous opposition since his arrival in Peking to Russian attempts to harass Kinder's work on the line. At that time, issues of pride and prestige appear to have been the main motives fuelling the resistance to actions designed to dislodge the British presence in the railway. But in the spring of 1898, with Russia in Port Arthur, more substantial factors were coming into play.

MacDonald left the Foreign Office in no doubt of the importance of the opportunity he saw to secure a position for British interests in the extended line. In reporting the offer he added, 'I think it very desirable offer should be accepted promptly as it is certain if taken elsewhere it will be certain to be accepted.' A few days later he was more emphatic: 'It is most important that control of this line should not slip out of British hands. Please inform Hongkong Bank if they cannot accept offer I must request Pekin Syndicate to consider it. If we do not accept Director-General's offer Germans or Russians most certainly will.'[13]

The bank took the offer, signing early in June 1898 a preliminary agreement on behalf of the British and Chinese Corporation, which it was then forming. Whatever the commercial case for it, the operation was plainly highly political and a direct challenge to Russia. It quickly drew protests from St Petersburg, where the provision in the contract that the Shanhaikuan–Newchwang extension was to be part of the security for the loan and that in the event of default it could be taken over by the corporation was regarded as particularly disturbing. Counter-protests followed from London against the Russian attempt to interfere with British private enterprise involved in a purely

---

[12] A. Rosenbaum, 'The Manchurian Bridgehead; Anglo-Russian Rivalry and the Imperial Railways of North China, 1897–1902', *Modern Asian Studies* 10 (1976), pp. 41–64.
[13] FO 17/1340, MacDonald to Salisbury, 25 and 30 Apr. 1898.

Chinese undertaking. Salisbury took MacDonald's advice and withdrew the suggestions he had made of willingness to exchange the British interest in the Peking–Newchwang contract for a similar position in the Peking–Hankow line.[14] This seems an indication that Salisbury saw political advantage in holding on to the Northern Railway. Arthur Balfour, who took charge of the Foreign Office in Salisbury's absence on vacation, was critical of MacDonald's policy in the matter, considering it rash to challenge Russia without reckoning on a reaction. Balfour regarded the Northern Railway extension as a wasting asset of no great value to Britain. But he did see it as a bargaining counter that might be exploited to get Russia to renounce interest in concessions in the Yangtze Valley, in return for a similar renunciation by Britain in respect of Manchuria.[15] This was in Salisbury's mind too, and was eventually to be achieved in April 1899 but without sacrifice of British interest in the Northern Railway. Before then significant developments had taken place in the relations between the government and the Hongkong Bank.

Cameron had soon made it plain that the British and Chinese Corporation looked for official assistance going beyond diplomatic support. In July 1898 he enquired as to the prospect of a direct government guarantee or, failing that, a promise of a subsidy for a few years in case of need for a line from Peking to Chinkiang.[16] To raise the necessary five or six million pounds unaided was beyond any combination of finance in the City, yet the line was likely to prove a great commercial success and it was important that it should be in British hands. This request reflected the thinking of the China Association and the chambers of commerce that state finance employed by Britain's rivals in China should be met by state finance. But it cut across one of the strictest conventions of British economic diplomacy—that there should be no involvement of public funds in private commercial enterprise—and was therefore turned down.

Within a few months, however, Cameron made another request. He was now concerned about the success of the approaching flotation of the loan for the Northern Railway extension. Though they had

[14] FO 17/1360, memorandum by Campbell, 21 June 1898; Rosenbaum, p. 53; *BD* 1, no. 56, minute by Salisbury on MacDonald to Salisbury 25 July 1898.

[15] Salisbury Papers, vol. 89, memorandum by Balfour, 13 July 1898, quoted in part by Young, pp. 93–4. BL Add. MSS 49691, Balfour Papers, Balfour to Salisbury, 30 Aug. 1898. Balfour's memorandum came before the cabinet in Aug. 1898, CAB 37/46.

[16] FO 17/1361, Cameron to Bertie, 14 July 1898.

succeeded in forcing the withdrawal of the Shanhaikuan–Newchwang section as part of the security for the loan, which was now to consist solely of the line from Peking to Shanhaikuan, the hostility of the Russians to the projected extension was unabated and was expected to cause investors to hold off from the loan. To prevent this, Cameron asked for authority to insert in the prospectus an assurance from the government that it would uphold the contract. This, he pointed out, had as one of its conditions that the Chinese government would pledge in writing that the security should not be alienated. This was the political core of the transaction because it would keep the railway approach to Peking out of Russia's grasp. Balfour, evidently viewing the line as a diplomatic asset, saw no objection to Cameron's proposal. Hicks Beach, however, was less impressed by its political significance than by the danger that the proposal might result in domestic embarrassment for the government. He doubted if it would be

advisable to place HM subjects who invest their capital in railway enterprise in China in a better position, as regards their right to government support, than those who invest it in other enterprises abroad and any action on the part of Her Majesty's Government of the kind asked for must have this effect if it is worth anything at all.

If any support were given, he felt it ought to be confined to lines within the British sphere—the Yangtze district and the neighbourhood of Hong Kong. If the Northern Railway loan were to be regarded as a special case, he would not go beyond permitting a statement in the prospectus, 'in carefully chosen words to be approved of by us beforehand coupled with a disclaimer of pecuniary liability', to the effect that the government took note of the assurance to be given by the Chinese to MacDonald pledging the non-alienation of the security as a binding pledge on the part of the Chinese government.[17] Salisbury agreed with the chancellor, and Cameron accepted the limitations; but at the end of November he again asked the government to give an assurance that the contract would be upheld, for in view of developments in China he no longer thought that it would be possible to carry out the flotation of the loan on the basis of the undertaking he had received in September. 'I need not point out', he concluded, 'how important it is that the railway entering into China

[17] FO 17/1363, minutes by Sanderson, 19 Sept., Bertie, 20 Sept., and Balfour, 21 Sept. 1898; memorandum by Hicks Beach, 23 Sept. FO 17/1364, Salisbury to MacDonald, 27 Sept. 1898.

from Manchuria should be under British control, and that the important trade of Newchwang shall not be diverted to Port Arthur or Talienwan.' He was initially rebuffed but at the end of January got some part of what he wanted. Salisbury accepted Bertie's advice that the bank be authorized to include in the prospectus both a statement that the loan had been arranged with the knowledge of the British government, and a Foreign Office letter taking note of the Chinese promise that none of the lines named in the contract as security would be alienated to any foreign power, as a binding engagement on the part of the Chinese government.[18] This, following upon the indemnity loans and the numerous railway concessions secured in the Yangtze Valley, was one more advance by the bank, carrying with it now the British and Chinese Corporation, towards public acceptance that it enjoyed a special relationship with the government in operations in China.

Official support had also been given elsewhere in issues where there was a substantial applicant and where the area was of political significance. The Pekin Syndicate had been backed diplomatically in its application for concessions in Shansi, and the Yunnan Company was given support in its effort to secure a concession for road, railway, and telegraph lines from the Burmese frontier to the Yangtze. Official opinion had always been sceptical of the long-mooted proposals for a Burma–Yangtze railway. The project had, however, attracted powerful support from publicists and from chambers of commerce, particularly in the textile towns and consequently the government had to give it some acknowledgement—especially when French competition in south-west China whipped up public feeling. Hence its inclusion in one form or another among the various demands made on China since 1895.

The emergence of the Yunnan Company owed nothing to government prompting, though it was not unwelcome since its existence and activity would stifle complaints that nothing was being done to realize the Burma–Yangtze dream. Its backers were British merchants in India and Burma who had been brought together by John Halliday, a substantial commercial figure in India and head of the Araccan Company. One of the initial subscribers, Robert Miller, a director of Burma Railways, was also a director of the Pekin Syndicate, but there

---

[18] FO 17/1364, Hongkong Bank to FO, 23 Nov.; FO to Hongkong Bank, 2 Dec. 1898; FO 17/1398, memoranda by Bertie, 26 and 28 Jan. 1899.

do not appear to have been other links between the two groups. Halliday was known to Lansdowne, a former viceroy of India, whom he approached in July 1898 for support from the government for the concession the company sought from China. The concession, he told Lansdowne, would be not for the company only but for the government, and would be of immense assistance in the competition with France and Russia in western China which, unless something was done, would cut Burma off from China altogether. He was in touch with Burma Railways and had some contacts with the Military Intelligence Department.

The Foreign Office welcomed the appearance of the company, not because it believed in the feasibility of the scheme but, as Curzon put it, 'if people can be found to spend their money on such an enterprise by all means let us encourage them. It will relieve the government and gratify the chambers of commerce.' The military authorities saw practical advantage to be drawn from the survey of a route that the company proposed to make, and the director of Military Intelligence argued that the railway could bring in important advantages politically and commercially; but the India Office was as sceptical as the Foreign Office. Bertie proposed that the concession be included in the demands made on China in retaliation for the award of the Peking–Hankow railway concession to the Belgians, 'not that it is likely to be feasible as a commercial enterprise but in order to satisfy a persistent and noisy though perhaps small section of the public at home', and a small group of technical officers and an escort were lent to the company to make the survey.[19]

Developments in 1898 showed that the British government was ready within limits to support serious British enterprise in specific economic ventures in China where advantages judged worthwhile were to be obtained. It had resisted German claims to the Shanghai–Nanking Railway; it had defended the position of the British and Chinese Corporation against Russian pressure over the Northern Railway loan. It would not commit itself to financial assistance or to obligations that, in the event of default by the Chinese on loan contracts, might involve it in intervention where it would be difficult

[19] FO 17/1361, War Office to FO, 20 July 1898, encl. Halliday to Lansdowne, 16 July 1898; Yunnan Co. to Salisbury, 26 July 1898, with minutes; DMI to FO, 26 July 1898. FO 17/1362, India Office to FO, 12 Aug. 1898; memorandum by Bertie, 17 Aug. 1898; Chandran Jeshurun, pp. 282–6. The Burma–Yangtze concession was in fact made the subject of a separate demand.

to bring British power to bear. This was one reason, apart from the general repugnance to become involved in debt-collecting, why support in the form of a binding assurance was withheld from a proposed Anglo-American combination hoping to take over the American-held concession for the Hankow–Canton line.[20] Where there was political pressure at home the government could be brought to advance claims of little importance, as over the Burma–Yangtze railway. Largely because the powerful senior official in the Foreign Office, Francis Bertie, and MacDonald in Peking were ready to engage in vigorous defence of British interests and to view Cameron's requests for support sympathetically, the government was pushed into implicit commitments over the Northern Railway that went further than some of its members wished. Certainly in the eyes of interested parties the government had done well. Cameron did not hide his satisfaction with the way things had gone.

He was sarcastic in regard to Lord C. Beresford and similar critics, and with reference to the recent rush for railway and other concessions, he was more optimistic—a good deal more—than Sir C. MacDonald as to England having come out at the top. In fact, according to the H & S Bank it is a case of England first and the rest nowhere. This very rosy view may be somewhat induced by the Bank's own affairs. They seem to have been coining money in China lately. He stated confidentially that their dividend for the last half of 1898, including bonus, would mean 40 per cent to the shareholders, and 30 per cent for the whole year. The figures were 'simply phenomenal'.[21]

Co-operation between the government and the financiers in 1898, while not without friction, had been on the whole harmonious. The vigorous counter-action in the battle of concessions had brought political profit and the prospect of material gains for the groups that with official backing had secured mining and railway concessions. It soon became evident, however, that the contract for the Northern railway extension was to raise an unanticipated problem for the government—what action to take when the British and Chinese Corporation wished to sell Russia a contract that the government had helped to secure and fianance.

From the inception of the scheme to extend the railway, it was plain that British participation would bring a continuation of the Russian

---

[20] FO 17/1362, Macrae to Bertie, 25 and 30 Aug. 1898; FO 17/1363, FO to Macrae, 26 Sept. 1898. The importance of the line was recognized.

[21] FO 17/1398, memorandum by Campbell, 14 Jan. 1899.

opposition that had already been directed against Kinder in 1897 when he was constructing the line to Shanhaikuan. Russian apprehensions had been compounded by the provisions of the loan agreement. Scott, the British ambassador in St Petersburg, understood their attitude. In March 1899 he wrote to Salisbury:

It is a thousand pities that our Bank could not have taken some other security for their loan than one that ostensibly spells 'control' of the Manchurian line. There is a Russian side to the story. The line is in Manchuria and Curzon's book describes it as having a political strategical value rather than a mercantile one—and the eagerness with which we have been trying to establish a quasi-control of the line seems suspicious to the Russians who understood that we wanted principally to secure the Yangtze valley for our enterprise.[22]

It was, however, the failure of the Chinese railway administration to observe the terms of the loan contract that from February 1899 the British and Chinese Corporation complained of. By April complaints had multiplied, despite pressure by the legation on the Chinese government for action to end infringements. Interest on the loan for recent months had not been paid, nor had earnings of the line been deposited with the Hongkong Bank. The interests of the bondholders, therefore, were endangered.

In the Foreign Office a senior official in the Far Eastern department, Francis Campbell, was sympathetic to the corporation's request for assistance, arguing that not only was there clear breach of assurances made by the Chinese to the British government but further, that support for the corporation which apart in a lesser degree from the Pekin Syndicate, was the one substantial British concern engaged in railway enterprise in China, was necessary on wider grounds: 'If the British and Chinese Corporation fail in this what chance is there for any other British railway enterprise which must be in a much less favourable position?'

Salisbury did not oppose a warning to the Chinese but modified the language proposed. He feared to create a dangerous precedent. 'To use the fleet to collect the Hongkong Bank's debts will bring down upon us all the British capitalists in any part of the world who are being cheated by the local government.'[23]

---

[22] BL Add. MSS 52303, Scott to Salisbury, 23 Mar. 1899. I owe this citation to Ian Nish. *Problems of the Far East* by G. N. Curzon was published in 1894.

[23] FO 17/1399, BCC to FO, 18 Feb. 1899; FO 17/1400, Cameron to FO, 30 Mar. 1899; BCC to FO, 7 and 17 Apr. 1899; FO 17/1401, minutes by Campbell and Salisbury, 25 Apr. 1899.

Official detachment remained his position as the matter developed. By June 1899 the corporation, anxious to be rid of what they now regarded as a liability, were contemplating a deal with the Russians, whom they felt to be responsible for their difficulties. The Foreign Office was informed that an Anglo-Russian partnership had been suggested to them for the Peking–Newchwang line and for other developments in northern China. The proposal was that the corporation should hand over on completion the portion of the railway outside the Great Wall while receiving running powers over it, with the Russians receiving running powers over the intramural section.

This proposal evoked contrary views. St John Brodrick, parliamentary under-secretary at the Foreign Office, favoured it on satisfactory conditions. Balfour seems to have hesitated but then came down against advising the corporation to barter its rights to Russia. Bertie thought Britain should press China to fulfil the contract, but if the corporation wished to make an arrangement with the Russo-Chinese Bank they were to do so on their own responsibility. This advice was approved by Salisbury.[24]

It then became clear that there was divergence of views among the financiers. The London group, led by William Keswick, was for a sale to the Russians. Hongkong Bank officials in China, on the other hand, were opposed. They emphasized the growing trade of northern China and the great prospects opening there. They saw Russian motives as political and insisted that the bank must do nothing to further Russian designs. This divergence was not new. Keswick had long favoured concentration on the Yangtze Valley; the bank's senior officials in China, with wider interests, had taken a wider view and had opposed a sphere-of-interest policy.[25] Moreover it now emerged that one reason behind the proposals for sale was the desire of the firm of Panmure Gordon, brokers to the Northern Railway loan, to dispose of stock in the loan to the value of £60,000. Because of the well-publicized difficulties on the line, the stock had dropped eight points in the market, and a sale to the Russo-Chinese Bank would save the brokers from loss by raising the price. It would also, in the view of some members of

---

[24] FO 17/1450, memoranda by Bertie, 3, 16, 22 June, and Brodrick, 8 June 1899, with minute by Salisbury, 22 June 1899.

[25] FO 17/1403, Cameron to Bertie, 28 June and 6 July 1899; FO 17/1362, Cameron to FO, 16 Aug. 1898, communicating opinions of the Tientsin agent of the bank and of Thomas Jackson, its chief manager, stressing the importance of northern and southern China and urging adherence to the open-door policy.

the corporation, open the way to a working arrangement by which they could float other enterprises, some with and some without the co-operation of the Russo-Chinese Bank. The senior partner in Panmure Gordon, a Belgian named Koch whose brother was in the Russian service, had gone to St Petersburg, Bertie reported, to negotiate an arrangement. MacDonald had found Koch to be pro-Russian. 'We therefore cannot expect patriotism from Koch', Bertie commented.

Opinion in the Foreign Office hardened against sale when Koch's proposals were received. Bertie was critical of the absence of safeguard against the mortgage and control over the Peking–Shanhaikuan section passing to Russia, for this would be a great danger to China and Britain. Salisbury continued to argue for official detachment from the matter, stressing that the government must not take any responsibility for advice. Bertie had never looked favourably upon the sale proposal and St John Brodrick had declared himself strongly against an unconditional sale. He thought Koch's proposals equivalent to handing over the line to Russia. On 4 August Keswick was informed that the Foreign Office saw no reason for the government to desire any change in the existing control of the line, to which considerable support had been given by the government on public grounds.[26]

The affair marked one more stage in the evolution of British economic diplomacy in China. The government had become involved in the Northern Railway loan in 1898 because of the political significance of the line. It was aware of its commercial importance as well. Political interest—the certainty of criticism if a sale were made to Russia—together with the wish to preserve an economic jumping-off point in the general interests of British trade combined to shape the official attitude and to block a transaction that, if to the advantage of some financiers, was judged to be injurious to the British position as a whole. Salisbury, influenced by a traditional distaste for official involvement in the affairs of private enterprise and by the political aim of improved Anglo-Russian relations, was in the end alone in opposing any advice to the corporation. His wishes were represented by the Scott–Muraviev agreement of April 1899, which in addition to the British renunciation of intention to seek railway concessions north of the Great Wall in return for a similar renunciation by Russia in respect of the Yangtze basin, stipulated that in the Shanhaikuan–Newchwang

[26] FO 17/1403, memoranda by Bertie, 3 July 1899, and, FO 17/1404, 28 July 1899, with minutes by Brodrick and Salisbury; FO to BCC, 4 Aug. 1899; Young, p. 95.

railway the British loan contract did not constitute a right of property or foreign control, and that the line was to remain a Chinese line under the control of the Chinese government and could not be mortgaged or alienated to a non-Chinese company. Plainly the sale of the contract to Russia would have reinforced the agreement. Salisbury did not prevail. As for the corporation, it remained technically free to decide on its own course, though given the attitude of the Hongkong Bank representatives in China it is by no means certain that the sale would have gone ahead if the Foreign Office had remained aloof. But the official disapproval was decisive. If support of the corporation in general was, as Campbell had argued, in the national interest, so too official support was needed if it were to prosper in the future. It could not go against the Foreign Office. The limitations of its position as an unofficial instrument of policy had been demonstrated.

For the Foreign Office, the rich commercial prospects in northern China had become an additional reason for preserving British interests in the Northern Railway. During the Boxer Rising, the Russians took over the greater part of the line. The director of Military Intelligence, arguing that they would probably get it eventually, suggested that they should be allowed to keep the railway in return for agreement to a free hand for Britain at Shanghai and the Yangtze 'where our material interests are far greater'. Campbell, much impressed by the arguments of E. G. Hillier, the Hongkong Bank's agent in Peking, would have none of this, remarking that the director of Military Intelligence underrated British material interests in the north. The trade of Tientsin was growing far more rapidly than that on the Yangtze.[27]

In January 1901 came more evidence of divergent views between the London and China groups in the Hongkong Bank hierarchy. Cameron, arguing that unless the British government were prepared to resist, Russia would retain control of the Shanhaikuan–Newchwang portion of the line and that this would take away the security of the bond holders, proposed that the Foreign Office should allow the corporation to negotiate with Russia over that section of the line. What he had in mind, obviously, was a sale of the British interest. This was contested from Hong Kong by Thomas Jackson. The corporation, he urged, should stand on the loan agreement. He would look upon a

---

[27] FO 17/1438, Cameron to FO, 22 Mar. 1900, enclosing memorandum by Hillier; FO 17/1442, memorandum by Ardagh, 17 July 1900, with minute by Campbell.

handover of the line to Russia with extreme disfavour, a view applauded by Campbell who minuted 'one could hardly have a better opinion'. The China-based group within the bank took a longer view than their London colleagues, who seemed to be influenced by short-term financial considerations. Foreign Office opinion was now firmly convinced of the importance of the British economic stake in northern China. The corporation was given clear indication that the Foreign Office would not welcome a sale of the contract to Russia. Though in February 1901 Lansdowne was prepared to consider a sale on condi-tions if Russia's right to remain in occupation of Manchuria had to be recognized, that was put aside as Russia's attitude on Manchuria became more moderate and the prospect of restoring the *status quo* on the railway brightened.[28]

There were still problems. In July 1901 no funds were available to pay the coupon on the Northern Railways loan, since the Chinese authorities (not being in possession of the line, part of which was still held by Russia), could not provide the money. Following an appeal from the British and Chinese Corporation, the Foreign Office proposed to the Treasury that the government should advance the amount necessary, pointing out that default would be very detrimental to British interests in northern China. Hicks Beach objected to a proposal that would put British interests in the railway in a more favourable position than other claimants who had suffered through the Boxer troubles, but did agree to a partial indemnity for the corporation in respect of the proportion of the coupon corresponding to that part of the line in British military hands. This was not accept-able to the Foreign Office, which feared that the resultant partial default might lead to Russia getting permanent possession of the Shanhaikuan–Newchwang section.[29]

A compromise was arrived at, but the conflict between the tradi-tional *laissez-faire* policy and the political approach was once more

---

[28] FO 17/1450, Hongkong Bank to FO, 2 Jan. 1901, and Hongkong Bank, Hong Kong, to London Office, 7 Jan. 1901; CAB 37/56, memoranda by Bertie 12 Feb. and Lansdowne 15 Feb. 1901; Young, pp. 275–81.

[29] FO 17/1506, FO to Treasury, 16 July 1901; FO 17/1507, Treasury to FO 25 July; memorandum by Campbell, 25 July 1901. The danger was of the bondholders taking control of the British-held line which could result in Russia appropriating the section she was holding. Campbell proposed a means (the use of Chinese bonds due under Boxer damage claims) whereby the corporation could pay the coupon and receive an indemnity without liability to the Treasury. This was accepted (Treasury to FO, 29 July 1901).

plain to see. The Foreign Office was now firmly attached to the support of substantial British enterprise, especially in railways, as a means of preserving and advancing the British economic stake in China, even to the point of making public funds available where the need was acute and the enterprise of particular significance. Since 1898 the government had moved into a quite close relationship with the Pekin Syndicate and the British and Chinese Corporation in response to the threat posed by the state or semi-state organizations sponsored by Russia, France, and Germany. The concessions obtained by the British groups were judged as strategic positions in the battle to keep China as a whole open to British commerce.[30] Lansdowne wanted to be rid of military involvement in China, the legacy of the Boxer Rising, but he wanted to secure the British position. He was more concerned with the Far East than Salisbury had been. The alliance with Japan was very much a Foreign Office and Admiralty policy, disliked by many of the Cabinet but accepted because there seemed no alternative.[31] It registered a determination to maintain the British stake in China.

There were, however, signs of growing doubts about the methods of the two British groups. Hicks Beach had been consistently critical of the operations of the financiers. In August 1901 when the British and Chinese Corporation was seeking government assistance to pay the coupon due on the Northern Railway extension loan, a Treasury official commented that the Foreign Office was incapable of dealing with such people as the corporation. The private correspondence of Sir Ernest Satow, British minister in Peking since 1900, with Lansdowne must have created unease about the corporation and the Pekin Syndicate. He thought that the syndicate's mines in Shansi, about which G. E. Morrison, *The Times* correspondent, was later to be very critical, were no more than an *affaire de bourse*, while the corporation's requirements over the negotiations for the return of the Northern

---

[30] This was illustrated in April 1902 when, after its sequestration during the Boxer period, the Northern Railway system was restored to China, and Satow secured the insertion of a clause that defined Article III of the Northern Railway agreement of 1898 so as to prevent a line from Tientsin to Paotingfu from passing out of the Northern Railway's control, and thus blocked a projected link route that would have given the Peking–Hankow line an outlet to the coast. See FO 17/1531, Clause V of the agreement between Satow and the administrator-general of the Imperial Railways of North China, 29 Apr. 1902; MacMurray, 1, p. 334.

[31] Nish, *The Anglo-Japanese Alliance*, pp. 369–70. G. W. Monger, *The End of Isolation: British Foreign Policy 1900–7* (London, 1963), pp. 58–66.

Railway to civil administration were a burden. 'Everyone complains of Jardine, Matheson and particularly Mr Keswick for being too grasping. Then exacting from China the full interest of 5 per cent on the whole railway loan and omitting to credit them with the interest earned in London on the unexpended balance seems quite indefensible.' Two years later he thought that the delay in building the Canton–Kowloon railway was because it would damage the Hong Kong–Canton–Macao steamboat line in which Jardine, Matheson were probably shareholders. He went on to say:

Men in high positions out here in the Hongkong Bank openly express their regret that Ewen Cameron and others entered into a combination with Jardine, Matheson and Co. to form the British and Chinese Corporation because they believe it is Wm. Keswick who is the obstructionist who prevents anything being done with the railway concessions.[32]

By 1903 the attention of the Far Eastern Department in the Foreign Office was concentrated on consolidation of the British position in the Yangtze Valley. Several concessions had been obtained by the corporation in 1898–9 with official support, but all were dormant. Russians, Germans, French, and Belgians were actively constructing the lines they had gained. Yet, apart from the Northern Railway extension, no work had begun on any of the contracts held by the corporation, and none had advanced beyond the stage of preliminary engagements. The shortcomings of the corporation were well known to the Foreign Office, which had passed on to it on many occasions the complaints of the Chinese authorities and also of the Hong Kong government and the British trading communities of its failure to proceed with construction. The reply consistently given was that the reluctance of the London money market to invest in Chinese railways made it impossible to float the loans necessary to finance construction.

By 1904 official impatience was mounting. Earl Percy, the vigorous parliamentary under-secretary, who was particularly interested in the Far East, was insistent for pressure on the corporation to carry out without further delay its agreements, particularly that for the most important of the Yangtze contracts, the Shanghai-Nanking line. The corporation, he urged, should be told that the government could not

---

[32] Treasury Papers, TI/9736/8091/1901, minute on FO to Treasury, 20 Aug. 1901; FO 800/119, Satow to Lansdowne, 19 Dec. 1901; FO 800/120, Satow to Lansdowne, 11 Jan. 1904.

possibly acquiesce in the permanent blocking by a single syndicate of all British railway enterprise in China.

The corporation at this point asserted eagerness to issue the Shanghai–Nanking loan but found difficulties continually being raised by the director-general of railways, Sheng Hsuan-huai. When by July 1904 these were resolved and the issue was authorized by the Chinese authorities, the corporation claimed that the market had become hesitant, and asked that a letter in which the Foreign Office had welcomed the news of authorization and had looked forward to capital being available for what it described as 'this important project' should be included in the loan prospectus.

To assent meant that the government would assist in ensuring a possibly successful loan issue and thus further the financial interests of the corporation. Yet, where Salisbury and Hicks Beach would have been reluctant, Lansdowne granted the request immediately, merely requiring the corporation not to state in the prospectus that they were authorized to publish the letter. In fact the issue was a failure, to the bitter disappointment of the Foreign Office.[33] The affair gave some justification for the past inactivity of the corporation. It reacted, too, upon a newer and much more ambitious project, where again the driving force came not from the British financiers but from the Foreign Office: a major railway through the Yangtze Valley to Szechwan.

---

[33] FO 17/1655, memorandum by Campbell, 19 May 1904; FO 17/1656, BCC to FO, 12 July; FO to BCC, 13 July 1904. The loan contract for the Shanghai–Nanking line had been signed in July 1903 (MacMurray, 1, pp. 387–402). Earl Percy succeeded St John Brodrick as parliamentary under-secretary at the FO in Oct. 1903.

3

The Hankow–Szechwan Project

THE desirability of a system of communications that would open Szechwan to British trade was well recognized, but schemes for a railway from Burma to Yunnan and ultimately to Szechwan had never won the support of the British government or the government of India. There had been no change in the official attitude even when the Yunnan Company's surveys found a practicable route, for it was plain that it would be arduous, expensive and unremunerative. By 1903, however, though there was little concern about the French railway from Indo-China into Yunnan, which was making slow progress, there was awareness of the activity of rivals in Szechwan—not only French, but German and Japanese as well. It was clear too that quite apart from commercial factors, the political interest of China in binding the western provinces to the main body of the country was likely in time to bring an east–west railway along the Yangtze Valley. It was the aim of British policy to ensure that so important an artery should not be under the control of a rival power, which in addition to the rewards from its financing and construction, would gain entry into the western Yangtze area and a possible means of hampering British trade as well as expanding its own. If China could build this and other arterial lines herself, well and good. It was the prevailing view of the Far Eastern Department of the Foreign Office that the extension of the railway system of China was in the interests of British trade, but it was generally felt to be essential that vital lines were not constructed, and therefore possibly controlled, by rival powers wedded to exclusivist economic policies.

The Peking–Hankow (Luhan) line was regarded as a very serious threat, because the contract for it had gone to a Belgian group in which French financial interests were considerably involved. In fact it appears that overall control and management of the line, now under active construction, were retained by the Belgians,[1] but in British eyes

---

[1] Kurgan-van Hentenryk, *Leopold II*, pp. 636–52. Relations between the French and

it constituted a penetration into the Yangtze by France. It was therefore the British aim to hamper it as much as possible, and in particular
to prevent it from pushing out branch and link lines; or to secure
Chinese or British control over such branches.

Early in 1903 the possibility of a major stroke emerged from efforts
made by the Pekin Syndicate to obtain a concession for a line to
connect its mines in Shansi with the Yangtze. The matter had been
under discussion at intervals since 1899 but the Chinese authorities
had continued to oppose the concession because, they maintained, the
proposed line would compete with the Peking–Hankow line, which
they were committed to guarantee. Hence, while recognizing the
justice in the syndicate's claim for a railway from its mines, they
wished to link this with the Peking–Hankow route as far as possible.
In February 1903, in an effort to reconcile the conflicting interests,
Sheng Hsuan-huai, the director-general of railways, proposed that the
syndicate agree to run its traffic over the Peking–Hankow line as far as
Sinyang, in return for a line from Sinyang to Pukow. The syndicate's
agent George Jamieson, a former consul-general, whose appointment
had been approved by the Foreign Office, thought this an unsatisfactory solution but then, he reported to the legation, Sheng made

a sort of suggestion that we might be able later on to extend the Pukow–
Sinyang line on to Sianyang and eventually to Szechwan. He knew that we
were anxious to secure the Szechwan line but remarked that there were other
applicants for that, not English.

Townley, chargé d'affaires at Peking during Satow's absence on leave,
at once appreciated the significance of Sheng's hint on the Szechwan
line.

The commercial results to be obtained by such a line are perhaps prob-
lematical . . . but its political and strategic importance is undoubted. It will
provide a valuable rival to the French line from Kaifeng to Sinanfu via
Honanfu which is to be constructed as a branch line of the Luhan line as soon
as the main line is completed.[2]

Belgians were strained. The French had provided the bulk of the capital and sought
more power in the railway.

[2] FO 17/1597, Townley to Lansdowne, 10 Mar. 1903. The Pekin Syndicate's
projected line was to run from Tsechow to Pukow. Jamieson had been appointed to the
board of the Pekin Syndicate in 1899 with the approval of the FO. F. A. Campbell
commented that his appointment would be an advantage to the FO. Jamieson 'would
help to keep the syndicate in the way they should go'; see FO 17/1402, minute on Neel

Whatever prospects there were of obtaining the concession clearly depended in the first instance, Townley pointed out, upon agreement between the British and Chinese Corporation and the Pekin Syndicate as to the Pukow–Sinyang line, for which the corporation had been granted a concession in 1898. His advice was quickly acted upon, for the significance of a Szechwan line was already accepted by Lansdowne. The primary interest of the Foreign Office was political; the means at its disposal were the corporation and syndicate, and these it was prepared to use. William Keswick was summoned to see Campbell and told that Lansdowne was of the opinion that some arrangement between the two groups was highly desirable in order to end the existing deadlock. This was followed by written communication to both groups, setting out Townley's suggestion for a possible compromise between them. When the syndicate showed some hesitation it was told:

Lord Lansdowne cannot too strongly impress upon the Syndicate ... the importance of an agreement being arrived at without loss of time and of the agents in China of the Syndicate and Corporation being instructed to co-operate in the negotiation with the Chinese authorities. Otherwise it is clear that H. M. representatives at Peking will experience great difficulty in according any effective support to the British interests concerned.

This plain indication of official wishes brought a successful conclusion to the discussions between the groups, which had been lagging. Lansdowne had no legal power to oblige them to reach agreement in the national interest but the tone of the Foreign Office could hardly be ignored by enterprises that in the future would from time to time inevitably have to look to the legation in Peking.

What now rapidly emerged from the negotiations was an agreement between the groups more satisfactory perhaps than was expected by the officials, for in addition to covering the Pukow–Sinyang line it was to provide that all concessions for railways north of the Yangtze 'hitherto obtained or yet to be obtained by the British and Chinese Corporation Ltd. and by the Pekin Syndicate Ltd. shall be considered as joint, that is are to be financed, constructed, and worked on equal terms by the said two parties'. Furthermore, a fusion of the two groups

(India Office) to Campbell, 27 Mar. 1899. The agent of the BCC at this time, Byron Brenan, was also a former consul-general. There were to be other instances where former members of the foreign service took posts with the corporation.

into one concern was foreshadowed. At the same time the agents of the groups were instructed to apply jontly for three lines, including the Pukow–Sinyang line with an extension to Chengtu in Szechwan.[3]

When, however, Townley formally applied on behalf of the two groups for the Szechwan line, he met resistance. Several influences were working on the Chinese government. There was undoubtedly resentment at the failure of the British companies to exploit concessions already held by them, thus hampering the progress of Chinese commerce. There was also disinclination to see a line recognized as desirable and important falling into the hands of one national group of foreign capitalists. This attitude was exploited by American interests working through Conger, the United States minister. The most pressing political consideration for the Chinese authorities was the growing resentment in the country against the grant of any railway concession to foreign interests. The rising voice of provincial feeling called for China herself to build her railways, so as to keep control of the great new arteries (and the profits to be made from their construction and operation) in her own hands.

When a preliminary and informal agreement was eventually secured by Townley on 9 August 1903 it reflected these trends. The Szechwan railway was to start from Hankow, not Nanking as the British groups had wished; it was to be built by China if possible, but if sufficient Chinese capital were not forthcoming China would turn to British and American sources. The inclusion of America meant that the prospect of an entirely British line into Szechwan was lost, but it was accepted by the British on realistic grounds. The Chinese authorities, who wanted the railway built and who understood that despite popular clamour there was little chance of the necessary capital being raised in China, were clearly decided that American participation was in China's interest.

Lansdowne in fact welcomed the prospect. From the outset of acute Great Power rivalry in China, Britain had looked for American activity in a common policy. Now, in the summer of 1903, with the return of tension in Russo-Japanese relations, British apprehensions about the integrity of China were considerable, and new approaches were being made for American political support. The alliance with Japan had been intended as a political weapon to restore a balance of power in

---

[3] FO 17/1617, memorandum by Campbell, 20 Mar. 1903; FO to BCC, 24 Mar., to Pekin Syndicate, 4 Apr.; BCC and Pekin Syndicate to FO, 9 Apr. 1903.

the Far East. The British had little confidence in Japanese military capacity and felt growing alarm at the dangers looming, either of involvement in conflict or of renewed isolation in the event of a Russo-Japanese *rapprochement*. In these circumstances Lansdowne and Balfour were looking to the United States, and acquiescence in American participation in the Szechwan railway was a timely gesture. There were no objections from the British groups to the inclusion of an American interest, but the agreement stipulated that British capital was to take a larger share than American, and that the Americans were not to have the power to alienate their share to the subjects of any third power.[4]

The significance of the agreement was not exaggerated. Townley regarded it as no more than a rough sketch on which future negotiations could be based and in which desirable modifications could be introduced, but it did give British interests a contingent claim to the Szechwan line and as such was of great value, not least as a means of blocking rival applications. It was this that was found particularly satisfying in the Foreign Office, even though the agreement was not embodied in any formal exchange of notes.

The impact of the Townley agreement was at once appreciated by the French, who recognized it as an important success for the British. Before its conclusion the prospect of a Szechwan railway constructed under British direction had aroused their concern. In Peking, French representatives mingled suggestions for Anglo-French combination with threats to offer strong opposition unless concessions were made to give France the share in the railway to which it was asserted she was entitled under Article IV of the Anglo-French agreement of 1896. At the same time an approach was made to Carl Meyer, chairman of the Pekin Syndicate, with a view to making the line an Anglo-French undertaking. The British groups reported these approaches to the Foreign Office, seeking guidance as to the reply to be made.

It is clear that among British officials, though it was recognized that the French could create many difficulties for Britain in China and that

---

[4] FO 17/1603, minutes by Lansdowne on Townley to Lansdowne, 20 July and 10 Aug. 1903. The provision against alienation was a safeguard against a repetition of the sale by American interests of the bulk of their stake in the Canton–Hankow contract to a Belgian syndicate supported by French banks. See minute by Langley on Townley to Lansdowne, 20 July 1903, and W. R. Braisted, 'The United States and the American China Development Company', *Far Eastern Quarterly* 6 (1952), pp. 147–65. For Lansdowne's approaches to the United States in 1903, see Monger, pp. 123–32.

perhaps ultimately it would be necessary to come to terms with them, there was no enthusiasm for co-operation at this stage. Lansdowne, though not opposed in principle to French participation, was not in any way inclined to take steps to bring it about. The matter had been considered before the visit of Delcassé, the French foreign minister, to London in July 1903, and Lansdowne had then decided that for the present it would be better to try for an all-British east-and-west trunk line. After the conclusion of the Townley agreement he commented, 'We are I understand committed to the policy of American cooperation for the Szechwan line and I do not see how we could now take up the idea of bringing in the French, but we may have to make terms with them.'[5] Though the power of the French to obstruct the Szechwan project was recognized, there was thus no eagerness in the Foreign Office in the summer of 1903 to admit them to participation.

French overtures continued, though indirectly. No mention of China issues appears to have been made by Delcassé during his visit to London, or by Paul Cambon, the French ambassador in London, in the subsequent conversations in August during which the basis was laid for the negotiations that were to end in the Anglo-French agreement of April 1904. Though on both sides the danger of a Russo-Japanese conflict in which France and Britain might become involved was a compelling influence in drawing the two countries together, Delcassé might well have felt that the Far East was a zone in which in the existing tension it was particularly necessary to move carefully. He himself, as minister for foreign affairs, seems never to have shown much interest in China or to have regarded the French stake as of more than limited significance. At the same time he could not afford to ignore the pressure of those who saw China as a field for advance. The foundation in 1901 of the Comité de l'Asie française indicated that in the infuential colonial group, interest in Asia was high. The successful opposition of the colonial group to what was held to be his too-yielding policy towards Siam in the treaty of 1902 was a warning that neglect of France's interest in Asia could involve him in political danger. Hence, while he did not choose for the moment to raise the Szechwan railway issue officially, Delcassé evidently did not discourage efforts to bring the British to agreement, and activity was maintained in Peking and London to this end. In Peking an applica-

---

[5] FO 17/1618, memorandum by Campbell, 26 June 1903; minutes by Campbell and Lansdowne on Hongkong Bank to FO, 21 Aug. 1903.

tion by French interests for a line to Szechwan was refused by the Chinese, and in London an approach to the Foreign Office—a clear recognition of where the power of decision lay—was made on behalf of a French financial group, which included 'all the best people in Paris', by Sir Vincent Caillard, a director of the National Bank of Egypt. He wished to know whether British interests would join in building a railway from Ichang to Wanhsien (about halfway to Chungking), with eventual extension to Chengtu, the capital of Szechwan. The French thought this much better than opposing each other with the result that neither would get anything. Caillard indicated that 'were the railway to be agreeable to British interests . . . capital would be forthcoming without difficulty.' The British position had not changed, and with Lansdowne's approval Caillard was given 'a dilatory answer', which left the way open for possible inclusion of the French at some future time.

It soon became clear, however, that a serious counter-move was, in fact, in preparation in Paris. A syndicate was formed under the auspices of the French government to obtain a concession for the scheme outlined by Caillard. A second French scheme, for a line from Chengtu to Wanhsien, was also mooted. This was ominous. 'The grant of such a concession', Langley of the Far Eastern Department observed, 'would be disastrous to our Szechwan line, the object of which is to tap the rich province of Szechwan and the Szechwan terminus of which would be Chengtu.' At the same time a detailed French–Chinese agreement was concluded, complementary to an earlier concession in principle of April 1898, for the Tongking–Yunnanfu railway, the ultimate purpose of which was assumed to be strategic—to bring not only Yunnan but Szechwan, too, into the French sphere.[6]

Apprehension as to the aims of France was heightened in December 1903 by the terms of a report prepared by Lieut.-Colonel Manifold, who had carried out preliminary survey work in south-west China and was now about to return there for a more thorough survey of the Szechwan route commissioned by the British groups. He judged the French line under construction from Tongking to

---

[6] FO 17/1621, memorandum by Campbell, 2 Oct. 1903, with minute by Lansdowne; Caillard to FO, 5 Oct. 1903; FO 17/1601, Satow to Lansdowne, 4 Nov. 1903, with minute by Langley. On Sir Vincent Caillard, see D. J. Jeremy, *Dictionary of Business Biography* (London, 1984–), 1, pp. 564–8. On Delcassé's position, see C. Andrew, *Théophile Delcassé and the Making of the Entente Cordiale* (London, 1968), pp. 256–8.

Yunnanfu a serious threat but indicated counter-measures that could thwart the French. He accepted the value of the Hankow–Szechwan project but suggested that since this would take about fifteen years to lay, more immediate measures were advisable in view of the progress of the French line from Tongking, which was undoubtedly to be prolonged into Szechwan. His suggestion was for a railway from Chengtu to Chungking, which would anticipate French schemes and establish British commercial and political influence in the upper Yangtze on the basis of a profitable commercial undertaking, and which would gradually be extended to meet the line coming up from Hankow.[7]

Manifold's report, together with knowledge of French projects and the necessity for an immediate counter to them, reawakened official interest in a Chengtu–Chungking line, as had been discussed during the Yunnan Company's surveys. Campbell saw possibilities in Manifold's argument. He was supported by Earl Percy, who accepted the view that the best course for the British was to start work, if possible, in the Szechwan basin. The Foreign Office had already supported the project for a detailed survey of the Hankow–Szechwan route by persuading the government of India to lend the services of Manifold and another officer and to supply native surveyors. The necessary scientific instruments were to be lent by the state, and the pay of the officers was to be met from official funds. Now, presented with the prospect of a more rapid means of securing a position in Szechwan, it was the officials who initiated measures for speedy action.

As regards railways, it struck us here on a perusal of Col. Manifold's report that if our railway via the Han river is to take 15 years to build (and if in the hands of Keswick and Co. this may be extended to 150) that the French may well be found in possession as they are really keen about it. Lord Percy was very hot on our doing something, as in Parliament and the press they are always wanting to know why it is that not a sod is turned of any British line while Germans and French find no difficulty in getting money and going ahead. So we called a meeting at which Lord P[ercy] presided, and Cameron, Keswick and Carl Meyer attended . . . I put it pretty straight to them. If we get the concession can you get the money, otherwise it's no use wasting our time and that of the minister and public funds in telegraphing. They said they certainly thought they could, *for a light line*. Nous verrons.[8]

---

[7] FO 17/1653, memorandum by Manifold for India Office, 10 Dec. 1903.
[8] PRO 30/33/7/4 (Satow Papers), Campbell to Satow, 26 Feb. 1904.

The meeting, on 6 February 1904, took place as the negotiations for association between the British and Chinese Corporation and the Pekin Syndicate were reaching their conclusion with the registration in January 1904 of Chinese Central Railways Ltd. To the new company the corporation sold its rights in the Pukow–Sinyang and Tientsin–Yangtze concessions and the full benefit of its pending negotiations respecting the Sinyang–Szechwan line. The syndicate similarly sold its benefit in the negotiations for the Sinyang–Szechwan line, and the two groups undertook from the date of the agreement between them and Chinese Central Railways, 19 February 1904, 'not to negotiate, except for and on account of the Company, for any railway or scheme for the construction of any railway in the area bounded on the north by the Province of Shantung, on the south by the Yangtze-Kiang, on the East by the sea and on the west by the Western border of the Province of Szechwan'. The syndicate's railway to the Wei River was specially excluded from the agreement.

It was therefore in the name of Chinese Central Railways that Satow was instructed to press the Chinese government for a railway from Chengtu to Chungking, or at least for a promise that no other power be allowed to construct the line; and that whenever China wished it built and could not raise the money herself, she would invite the assistance of British capital. The object was clearly indicated by Percy to Lansdowne—to block a possible French demand for the concession. The moment seemed favourable

as the B. and Ch. Corpn. have temporarily squared the Belgians, and in view of the Russo-Jap war China will probably be anxious to stand in our good graces. At all events it seems worthwhile to try. With the Nanking–Shanghai and the Chengtu–Chungking lines in our hands we shall have definitely earmarked the Yangtze valley as our 'sphere'.[9]

The British attitude supports the view that the negotiations in progress with France on colonial issues had a limited object: the settlement of specific and troublesome matters where equitable bargains were felt to be possible and desirable. China was clearly not regarded as one of these areas, and the British intended to block French penetration into the upper Yangtze. France was still seen as a rival threatening British interests in southern and central China—and

---

[9] FO 17/1653, memorandum by Percy, undated, with approval by Lansdowne, 6 Feb. 1904; FO 17/1640, Lansdowne to Satow, 20 and 23 Feb. 1904.

possibly as a rival who in the event of a Russian victory against Japan might be drawn into a new forward policy.

The Russo-Japanese war brought a major element of uncertainty in which the Prime Minister, Balfour, saw dangers for the integrity of China. He thought that Russia, if convinced she could defeat Japan, would pick a quarrel with China in order to be able to insist on the surrender of Manchuria. The question had been raised by the Americans with the British government. Balfour now wondered how much the Americans were prepared to help to prevent that. If they would depart from their tradition so far as to suggest an alliance to preserve the integrity of China by arms if necessary, it would open a new phase in world history.[10] Balfour was not too sanguine about the prospects of American co-operation, nor did he regard the situation as urgent, but clearly it was to American support that he looked to maintain the territorial *status quo* in China. For this reason alone, association with American business was desirable; and where it was already provided for, as in the Szechwan line, it would be politically unwise to disturb it—certainly in order to replace it by French interests at a time when it seemed likely that France's ally would again threaten the integrity of China.

The tendency in official circles to encourage American and discourage French participation in the Szechwan railways scheme was further illustrated in the Chengtu–Chungking project. Though Satow's application for a concession of the line was rejected, this caused little dismay. The immediate object had been to block the French, and this was secured by the Chinese decision that a Chengtu–Chungking line would form an integral part of the Hankow–Szechwan scheme; and since this was to be financed by Chinese capital, no application from foreign interests could be entertained. As, however, there was already an undertaking in the Townley agreement that if China were unable to finance the Hankow–Szechwan line she would apply to British and American capital, the possibility of a British interest in the Chengtu–Chungking line remained.[11] It was the view of Satow, adopted by the Foreign Office, that the proposed association of American and British capital should extend to the Chengtu–Chungking line. The inclination of Chinese Central Railways, however, was towards co-operation with French interests rather than American.

---

[10] Balfour papers, BL Add. MSS 48728, Balfour to Lansdowne, 11 Feb. 1904.
[11] FO 17/1636, Satow to Lansdowne, 1 and 2 Mar. 1904; to Campbell, 10 Mar. 1904.

They wanted to get the Szechwan railway built and they knew that the French group, which was renewing its overtures, had access to considerable capital resources.

Nevertheless it was the official view that prevailed. In face of a clear indication of Foreign Office preferences, Chinese Central Railways withdrew from the position that the Chengtu–Chungking railway was a local and not a main line (and thus exclusively a British enterprise) and concurred in the decision to present the scheme to the Chinese, if opportunity arose, as one in which British and American capital might participate.[12] Even so, the situation was not reassuring. There seemed to be little prospect that the Chinese company to be formed by the viceroy of Szechwan to build the railway with Chinese capital would in fact succeed. Satow reported the opinion of a high Chinese official that the necessary funds would not be forthcoming: 'No Chinese would be induced to take shares in an undertaking which was to be managed by officials'—a view confirmed by Hosie, the British consul-general in Chungking. The danger was that the Chinese, if they organized a company and failed to raise the money locally, might then turn to British sources. This could lead to an embarassing situation, for the corporation, in view of the attitude of investors, would find it difficult to raise funds in the money market.

Yet the corporation and the new group continued to have official support, for as Campbell put it, 'the Corporation has been dilatory and slack but they are substantial people who it is proposed to support and who else is there?' When information was received of a projected new syndicate to include the banking firms of Erlanger and David Sassoon and Company, it was hailed by Campbell. 'It would be a great thing', he minuted, 'that we should not have to depend entirely on the Br. & Ch. Corporation and the Pekin Syndicate as regards railways in China.'[13]

The much criticized corporation and syndicate were obviously well aware of the necessity to rehabilitate themselves and put their joint concern, Chinese Central Railways, in a position in which it would clearly be able to finance construction work on railway concessions that fell to it. Yet the root cause of earlier difficulties still remained: the reluctance of the London market to invest in Chinese railways. This

[12] FO 17/1654, Chinese Central Railways to FO, 17 Feb., 7 and 8 Mar. 1904; FO to Chinese Central Railways, 15 Mar. 1904.

[13] FO 17/1637, minute by Campbell on Satow to Lansdowne, 11 Apr. 1904; FO 17/1640, minute by Campbell on FO to Satow, 23 June 1904.

situation was largely a consequence of the *laissez-faire* attitude traditionally adopted by British governments to the operations of British capitalists abroad. The position was clearly set out by Carl Meyer in April 1904 in an opinion requested by the Foreign Office following a suggestion from Satow that China might construct railways with her own capital, at least in the initial stage, and then mortgage them to foreign lenders, on lines of the Northern Railway extension loan agreement of 1898. It would be impossible, Meyer stated, to find British capital for Chinese railway construction if there were an idea that the managements of the railways would be vested in Chinese hands. 'It is a fact that there is a very limited investing public in this country for Chinese railways and unless one is able to make out that the security is undoubted and is under European control, it would be useless to appeal to the public at all.' Meyer, who was connected with Rothschild interests and was a member of the London committee of the Hongkong Bank and of the National Bank of Egypt, was well informed on the attitude of the City. He went on to comment on the methods of continental groups, which included bribery, and concluded that, while these would not commend themselves to British views on promoting railway and other industrial schemes, foreign competitors nevertheless received strong support from their respective governments.

It is unfortunately true that British syndicates are a good deal handicapped in their endeavours to compete with the foreigner and that their efforts to create an interest in the circles of English capitalists proportionately to the preponderating influence which English trade in China enjoys over that of other nations have not hitherto been very successful.[14]

The continental groups enjoyed other advantages in addition to the support of their governments. In contrast with the individuality and independence of the British investor, his continental counterpart (certainly in France) was very much influenced by the attitude of the deposit banks, which canalized the savings of their customers into investments chosen in effect by the great banks, all of which were closely linked. Furthermore, since prevailing interest rates in the French capital market were lower than elsewhere, there was an obvious incentive to lend abroad where higher rates could be obtained. The French market had varied in its attitude towards invest-

---

[14] FO 17/1655, Meyer to FO, 29 Apr. 1904.

ment in China. In 1899 Paul Cambon had noted with surprise the large amount of French money staked in the Yangtze Valley, but there were indications that government pressure had been necessary to bring about this result.[15] By 1904 the position had changed. French banks, reflecting the new interest in China as a land of opportunity, were evidently eager to participate in the Szechwan railway.

Since the distaste of British investors for Chinese railway loans was shared by Americans the British groups could expect little from association with American interests, whereas co-operation with the French with their ready sources of capital would enable loans to be floated successfully and profitably. In the light of the economic interest of the British groups, the attraction of the overtures that continued to come from France was obvious. The strength of the British position rested on the contingent concessions that enabled them to block the French. The French had abundant capital resources for use in China. 'The French', Satow reported in July 1904, 'have actually been offering large sums for the construction of the Szechwan–Hankow railway when we could not get a penny even if we had a concession in our pocket.'[16] Moreover, the French also had a diplomatic weapon: their right under the Anglo-French agreement of January 1896 to equality of treatment with Britain in Yunnan and Szechwan. This, as Earl Percy recognized, was a right that could cause serious difficulty for British hopes in Szechwan.[17]

The position in the summer of 1904 was one of stalemate. Each side was able to obstruct the other but neither could make progress. The British recognized the desirability of a Hankow–Szechwan railway, and perhaps recognized too that its construction was so obviously in the interests of China that it was likely to be built. Their blocking agreements were assets that must waste, if slowly. To admit the French to partnership would be to let them further into the Yangtze Valley and to permit them, with their existing interests in the Peking–Hankow and Yunnan lines, to assume a very significant influence in the railway communications of China. To persist in opposition without the financial strength to undertake construction if the Chinese

[15] *DDF* 1st series, 15, no. 164, Paul Cambon to Delcassé, 2 May 1899; no. 201, Pichon to Delcassé, 3 June 1899, with annotations by Delcassé.
[16] FO 17/1655, Hongkong Bank to FO, 24 June 1904, with enclosure; FO 17/1638, Satow to Campbell, 28 July 1904.
[17] When the British turned to consider developing railways in Szechwan, the reciprocity clauses of the Anglo-French agreement of Jan. 1896 became a handicap.

turned to foreign assistance, as they were increasingly likely to, was to hinder the interests of British commerce in China as a whole (which would benefit from improved railway facilities) and still further to damage the standing of British enterprise. The logic of facts pointed towards co-operation with the French, particularly in view of the improvement in Anglo-French relations generally, symbolized by the agreements of 8 April; but it was a logic which the Foreign Office was less ready than the British financial concerns to recognize.[18]

[18] This and the following chapter are for the most part drawn from my article, 'The Origins of British Financial Co-operation with France in China, 1903–6, *EHR* 339 (1971), pp. 285–317. See also D. Mclean, 'Chinese Railways and the Townley Agreement of 1903', *Modern Asian Studies* 7 (1973), pp. 145–64.

4

The Anglo-French Agreement

THE lack of response to their various unofficial overtures evidently determined the French to raise the question at government level. On 10 August, Cambon proposed to Lansdowne a basis for 'a mutually advantageous arrangement' that would end a good deal of unnecessary competition. He made three suggestions: that the British should withdraw opposition to the projected line between Paotingfu and Tientsin, in return for which the French should cease to oppose the proposed extension of the Shanghai–Nanking line to Sinyang or some other point on the Peking–Hankow railway; that, whereas the Pekin Syndicate was now opposing the construction of a French line from Hankow to Szechwan because they wished to obtain a concession for a line parallel to it but further north, the two sets of promoters might combine and either divide the projected line or build it conjointly, neither of them being able to undertake the work alone; and that a loan of £2 million for Siam should be provided jointly by the Hongkong Bank and the Banque de l'Indo-Chine.[1] Clearly the French were eager to establish co-operation and saw an opportunity in the existing stalemate to gain their point. There was an obvious prize to be won, and judging the situation shrewdly they saw that internationalization was their best tactic. Perhaps, too, they saw association with Britain as insurance against a victorious Japan, of whose ambitions they were very much afraid, or a triumphant Russia, of whose cavalier attitude France had long experience.

Cambon's *démarche* led to a thorough re-examination of the issue in London. The proposed joint loan to Siam raised no problems, for the Hongkong Bank was ready to co-operate with the Banque de l'Indo-Chine, and Lansdowne had for some time been ready to approve such a project. On the larger matter of the Hankow—Szechwan railway, where the facts as presented by Cambon were questioned, there was less enthusiasm. Langley remarked that 'we

---

[1] FO 27/3663, Lansdowne to Monson, 10 Aug. 1904.

and the French can make it very difficult for one another to get any concessions through in China, but the present offer does not strike one as a very generous one . . .' The parliamentary under-secretary, Earl Percy, was markedly cool. He was very conscious of the provisions for equality of rights in Yunnan and Szechwan included in the 1896 treaty, and thought that 'no violation of that treaty would be entailed by the concession of the Szechwan line to us if we left Yunnan to the French'. He was inclined to favour that solution, 'though India would not like it'. Failing that, he saw nothing for it but a settlement on the lines proposed by Cambon, but it must be equitable and 'Yunnan must be dealt with *pari passu* with Szechwan. We cannot give France a joint share in the latter as well as a monopoly of the former.' There was another possibility—to wait for the close of the Russo-Japanese war,

come to an understanding with Japan on the whole question of the opening up of China and having got her influence at Peking on our side, make an arrangement with France on our own terms. If the Szechwan line is not to be British I should prefer a British–French–Japanese–American railway to a railway controlled by France and ourselves alone. In fact, I do not feel at all sure that an internationalized railway in which Japan had an interest would not serve our purpose better than a British–American one. The Yanks will never take and cannot take active steps to defend concessions in the interior any more than we can—and from a financial point of view, the more powers have a hand in the business the more likely it is that the line will be built in a reasonable period.

Percy was alone in advocating association with Japan in an internationalized line rather than with France only. Lansdowne 'thought there was a good deal of force in M. Cambon's contention' as to the desirability of co-operation, and Chinese Central Railways were informed of the French proposal and asked for their views in terms that clearly indicated his sympathetic attitude. 'With regard to railway construction in Szechwan, it appears to Lord Lansdowne hardly likely that the necessary capital could be raised in this country even if a definite agreement could be secured in face of the strenuous opposition from the French government which such a project would have to encounter'.[2]

British policy was thus moving towards change, but the stimulus

---

[2] FO 27/3663, memoranda by Percy, Langley, and Campbell on draft of Lansdowne to Monson, 10 Aug. 1904; FO 17/1656, FO to Chinese Central Railways, 30 Aug. 1904.

was political; the wish not to rebuff an official overture from France influenced Lansdowne more than the inclinations of the financiers. For years French attempts at infiltration into what were regarded as British preserves in China had been resisted, and all suggestions of association with French interests had been discouraged by the Foreign Office. Indeed, the aim of the Townley agreement, as of the application for the Chengtu–Chungking concessions, had been to a large degree to thwart French efforts. American participation had been accepted, in fact welcomed, by the Foreign Office on two counts: that it would ease negotiations with the Chinese authorities; and that it would strengthen bonds with the United States, which shared the British aims of preserving the integrity of China and the open door for trade. But any arrangement admitting the French into the heart of the Yangtze was likely to provoke fierce opposition from those who saw in France with its exclusivist economic policies a dangerous competitor.

These considerations were certainly clear to Percy, who did not see in Cambon's proposals 'any prospect of an arrangement which will not practically mean our giving everything and the French nothing, and if we announce any such arrangement to the House of Commons on the top of the Anglo-French agreement, I feel convinced that it will be profoundly unpopular'. Lansdowne, however, was not to be shifted. Now that France had put forward officially a definite basis he was ready, if without enthusiasm, to undertake a negotiation that must result in a French advance. The object of British policy, hitherto, had been negative: to block rivals, particularly the French. Official opinion had been content to wait for the Chinese self-help railway movement to work itself out while stimulating the British groups to organize in readiness—all the more so because of awareness that for the time being it would be difficult to float a loan in London. Percy, indeed, still held that to wait until the financial situation improved would make the British position stronger in any negotiations that might be necessary, but Lansdowne now argued that the construction of railways was of first importance.

There are no doubt obvious objections to French co-operation within the Yangtze Valley, and it is quite clear that without some such co-operation these lines are not likely to be built. The question seems to me to be whether we desire that they should be built or not. I have always understood that we regarded it as all important that the rich province of Szechwan should be opened up to British trade, and if this view prevails we have to consider whether we would rather have an international railway or no railway at all. We ought, however, certainly as Sir Ernest Satow proposes, to bring in the American element if it will come. The real difficulty is to ascertain whether French or American money will really be forthcoming. Unless their financiers are more courageous than ours, this seems to be at least doubtful.[3]

The reluctance of the London capital market to invest in China was much in Lansdowne's mind. He had been impressed by the poor success of the loan for the Shanghai–Nanking railway 'which showed how difficult it is for this country to undertake alone the construction of railways in China'. The failure of this loan was a setback deeply felt in the Far Eastern Department of the Foreign Office, for official help had been constant in endeavouring to further the railway, which was judged to be an essential element in maintaining British commercial predominance in the Yangtze delta. Campbell lamented:

We have given strenuous backing, spent thousands of pounds of public money on telegrams, have bullied the Chinese to a considerable extent even, and when at last the result of all this we have secured concessions, the great British public won't put a shilling into it. What could be more disheartening than the fiasco of the Shanghai–Nanking loan . . .?[4]

The issue of the loan had in fact been badly timed because, in addition to the countinuing impact of the Boxer Rising on British investors, there was now the uncertainty created by the Russo-Japanese war. The increasing signs of Chinese determination to secure greater control over railways was an additional reason for caution. Though the terms of the Shanghai–Nanking contract still provided for a degree of British control greater than the Chinese wished, their pressure in the negotiations to decrease it, together with evidence of their success elsewhere, could not have been without effect. In the administration of the Northern Railway, Yuan Shih-k'ai as viceroy of Chihli had worked successfully to diminish the British role. He had made himself sole director-general and all the personnel, European and Chinese, obeyed him absolutely. The British engineer, C. W. Kinder, who had directed the construction and operation of the railway, had become a mere engineer-in-chief with no authority.[5]

[3] FO 17/1656, minute by Percy on Chinese Central Railways to FO, 21 Sept. 1904; FO 17/1641, minute by Lansdowne on Satow to Lansdowne, 27 Sept. 1904.

[4] FO 27/3663, memorandum by Campbell, 16 Aug. 1904; PRO 30/33/7/3, Campbell to Satow, 9 Sept. 1904.

[5] G. Kurgan-van Hentenryk, *Jean Jadot: Artisan de l'expansion belge en Chine* (Brussels, 1965), pp. 119–20.

Whatever the reasons, the disappointment over the Shanghai–Nanking loan—a line generally regarded as likely to prove the most profitable railway enterprise in China—carried ominous implications for officials as well as financiers concerned with enterprise in China. Unless new sources of capital were tapped, much of the potential British railway stake in China might pass entirely into other hands, for Chinese resentment at the terms of the preliminary contracts secured during the battle of concessions in 1898 was equalled by anger at the failure of British enterprise to proceed to negotiation of final contracts. China wanted the railways built, so did the Far Eastern Department; but the department wished to ensure the maintenance of a preponderant British presence. In these circumstances the case for a partnership with other powers in which Britain would have a controlling share was very strong. Satow himself, not hitherto favourable to association with the French, now recognized in principle the advisability of co-operation, given safeguards to maintain British primacy. It was also true that the British position in the Chengtu railway was 'delicate', for if the Chinese, egged on by the French, decided to ask for a British loan, the money could not be raised and the French might then be able to step in. Nevertheless Lansdowne's emphasis now on the need for construction of the Szechwan railway was significant. There is no indication that up to this time he had not approved the 'waiting' policy, and a year later he was to write:

I have thought for some time that European promoters have been attempting too much. The map of China is hatched all over with railway lines, for one quarter of which capital could probably not be provided if the whole of the concessions were to be sealed tomorrow. I shall not, therefore, break my heart if we do not make much advance with such vast schemes as the Szechwan–Hankow or the Yunnan-fu–Chengtu lines.[6]

It would seem to be Cambon's overture that made Lansdowne more open to arguments from Campbell justifying a more positive response to the French. The situation in the capital market and in China, as Satow's attitude showed, justified at least an examination of the French proposals, but it is likely that Lansdowne in the summer of 1904 was also guided by considerations of general policy. Since April 1903 Britain had drawn closer to France, and the agreement of 8 April 1904 had settled a number of contentious issues in Anglo-French

[6] PRO 30/33/7/4, Lansdowne to Satow, 2 Oct. 1905.

relations. At a time when friendship seemed more necessary than ever China remained an area where friction was likely to revive. If expert British opinion was now coming round to believe in the possibility of a Japanese victory, Lansdowne and Balfour retained all their apprehensions of Russia. France therefore continued to be important as a bridge to agreement with Russia, and, if in association with Britain in China, as a moderating influence upon a victorious Russia. There was also uncertainty about Japan. Percy felt that the Japanese, if not brought into an arrangement with France, should at least be taken into British confidence. 'They will have the greatest influence in Peking in the future and it would be well to make sure that they are friendly.' Campbell opposed the inclusion of the Japanese.

I doubt if this is practicable at present. Heaven knows how long the war will last and though, of course, we could tell the French that the whole question must be postponed till after the war, I am not sure that this is very desirable in itself. If the Japanese are victorious they may well want more than we are prepared to concede and be troublesome generally.[7]

Campbell evidently foresaw that the maintenance of the overriding aim of British policy, the integrity of China, might well meet difficulties after the war in face of the victor, be it Russia or Japan. The 'American mirage' was still pursued, and it was clear that Lansdowne would insist on the way being left open, should American interests wish to take it, for their participation in any agreement on the Hankow–Szechwan railway; but it was recognized that the likelihood of active involvement of the United States was remote. Agreement with France would at least give the prospect of some support in an uncertain future. Moreover, since the French government was ready for agreement and so were the British groups, it may have been felt unwise for the British government to appear as the sole obstacle.

These decisions were taken on grounds of national interest as judged by the Foreign Office, which had exercised overriding control throughout the development of the Hankow–Szechwan project. Townley had grasped the opportunity offered by the hint from Sheng Hsuan-huai, the director-general of railways, and had gained the contingent undertaking. The Foreign Office had brought the two British groups together and its attitude had governed the question of

---

[7] FO 17/1636, minute by Percy on Satow to Lansdowne, 29 June 1904; FO 17/1656, minute by Campbell on Chinese Central Railways to FO, 21 Sept. 1904.

co-operation with the French: political, not financial interest had dominated. Nevertheless the policy adopted was welcome to Chinese Central Railways, which speedily arranged a meeting with the powerful French syndicate grouped around the Banque de l'Indo-Chine.

As the Foreign Office was aware, contacts between certain members of the British and French groups had existed for some time, but it appears that they were of longer standing and closer than was known at this stage. Indeed, it was later claimed by the French that their group, through its relations with the Pekin Syndicate, had been instrumental in bringing about the agreement between the syndicate and the British and Chinese Corporation. It may have been the financiers, British and French, seeing in co-operation the way to lucrative business, who persuaded the French government to raise the question in London. At all events the development was clearly to their liking as they now prepared for negotiations. These, however, were to be within a framework of conditions proposed by the Foreign Office on the basis of recommendations from Satow, who thought that the British negotiating position was strong enough to allow them to impose their terms. Acceptance by the French of American participation was, he held, an essential requirement, and further, British interests must be secured. Specifically, he proposed that if a concession were obtained from the Chinese, any international company formed should provide against the passage of political control into the hands of another power in consequence of the transfer of shares, and the board of directors should consist of equal numbers of the three nationalities without regard to the proportion in which the shares or bonds were held. There should be a similar arrangement in respect of employees, and orders for material and rolling stock should be divided in equal proportion. The chief engineer should be British.[8]

These conditions were communicated to Chinese Central Railways and were subsequently discussed with its representatives by Campbell and Percy in preparation for the conference of the British and French groups. Clearly the Foreign Office intended to exercise close control over the nature of any association that might emerge. Little effort was made to hasten the negotiations on the British side, though the French government showed concern as time passed without result. Finally, in March 1905, Carl Meyer, on behalf of Chinese Central Railways,

---

[8] FO 17/1641, Satow to FO, 27 Sept. 1904; FO 17/1656, FO to Chinese Central Railways, 4 Oct. 1904.

submitted a draft agreement to the Foreign Office—in his view, 'the best terms that could be obtained'. The French group, he reported 'are very dependent on their government and M. Delcassé objects to anything which obviously and on the face of it, gives us a position of advantage over the French . . .' The draft provided for a comprehensive Anglo-French partnership for all the objects of Chinese Central Railways: it was not an *ad hoc* agreement limited to the Szechwan railway, but was to apply to all railway business north of the Yangtze. Although it gave the British group half the directors and the chairmanship, and met the requirements for the purchase of materials and recruitment of employees, it by no means fulfilled the conditions laid down by the Foreign Office. A small proportion of shares was to be allocated to American interests but there was no provision for giving them a share in the control if they did come in; if they did not, additional shares were to go to the Belgian group, who initially were to have a $7\frac{1}{2}$ per cent participation, as were the Americans. Further, there was no stipulation that the chief engineer should be British because, Meyer explained, it has been agreed that the line to Szechwan should be constructed in two sections, one British and one French, and each would have its own chief engineer.

On one point there was complete agreement in the Foreign Office; the way must be open for American participation in construction and control of undertakings as provided in the Townley agreement. Lansdowne had always sought to work with the United States, and though he found American diplomacy a little irritating he was especially anxious, at a time of critical importance in the Russo-Japanese War, to keep on close terms. Following receipt of the draft agreement, Sir Mortimer Durand, the ambassador in Washington, was instructed to sound the president as to the probability of participation by American capitalists in the proposed group. His reply indicated that the State Department intended to assert the American right to participate, but when, later, a definite inquiry was made, it turned out that American financiers were not interested. This was readily accepted by the British group, who had observed that they 'do not consider American co-operation essential from the point of view of finance, inasmuch as the English and French markets combined will in their opinion, be sufficient for raising the capital'. Their attitude was not surprising as the British element had never been eager for American participation, while French sources had on several occasions been reported as hostile to the expansion of American interests in China. Lansdowne may have regretted the failure of the State Department to encourage American finance but his approaches had shown British good faith.[9]

The American question thus solved itself, but other aspects of the draft agreement provoked lively discussion. Percy, now engaged in a vigorous campaign to persuade Balfour and Lansdowne to renew the Anglo-Japanese alliance, took the opportunity to repeat his plea for Japan to be brought into association in railway enterprise in China. He had come reluctantly to accept the case for Anglo-French partnership in principle, but he sharply attacked the draft. He thought it 'a very wide departure from the scheme originally contemplated.' It did not take sufficient care of British interests, and through the provision for separate construction it admitted the French to a position from which, if they were to build the Szechwan end, 'they will be in a fair way to 'Frenchify' the Eastern as well as the Southern approaches to the upper Yangtze basin and if they built the eastern half it will be in the heart of the British sphere'. As to the question of the chief engineer, while he did not care how the point was made, 'I do regard it as vital that we *should* assert unmistakably the predominance of British or Anglo-Saxon interests in this region. If we cannot secure this I should drop the idea of co-operation altogether.'

Campbell, though not satisfied with the terms, was ready to defend them. He denied Percy's claim that concessions to the French would allow the Germans to claim a share in construction of Yangtze lines, because there was an agreement limiting them roughly to the basin of the Yellow River, and pointed out that the operations of Chinese Central Railways were confined to the north of the Yangtze. True, this would give the French some part in the Tientsin–Pukow line, which was now Anglo-German, and in the Pukow–Sinyang line, 'which our people appeared to have given up the idea of constructing'. He could not refute Percy's point that, if the British group revived the Pukow–Sinyang scheme because they could draw on French capital, 'the position will surely be that the French will obtain a footing in practically the whole length of the Yangtze valley'. The basis of his position was

that an Anglo-French railway was better than no railway and that this was the only alternative. But if such a scheme as is here proposed w[oul]d be subject

[9] FO 17/1763, papers communicated by Meyer, 13 Mar. 1905, Lansdowne to Durand, 22 Mar. 1905; Durand to Lansdowne, 29 Mar. and 30 Sept. 1905; Chinese Central Railways to FO, 21 July 1905. The final agreement allowed American participation if taken up within one year (MacMurray, 1, pp. 535–6).

to violent criticism and be very unpopular, then I suppose it must no railway unless by chance better terms could be squeezed out of the French.[10]

At Percy's wish the general question of policy was put to Lansdowne. The outcome of the discussion, followed by a meeting between Campbell, Percy, and Meyer, was a decision to recommend to Lansdowne acceptance of the Anglo-French agreement subject to satisfaction on two points: first, that the British section of the Hankow–Szechwan line should be fully equal in length to the French; and second, that the French should agree that any prolongation of their line to Yunnan into Szechwan should be a joint Anglo-French affair.

These points, together with an indication that there should be an adequate place for American participation, were put to Cambon on 5 May. Two days later Meyer reported that the French group, which was very anxious to conclude as soon as possible, was ready to satisfy the British conditions. It soon became evident that the French government was less yielding, but Lansdowne held his ground and on 15 July received the desired assurances including a specific pledge that, if a railway were built from Yunnan-fu to Szechwan, its construction and management would be undertaken by the joint Anglo-French association known as Chinese Central Railways.[11] When the problem of American participation was removed, the groups reached agreement on 2 October 1905. Wrangling had continued, however, between the governments as to the distribution of power in the revised constitution of Chinese Central Railways, the French objecting in particular to the provision that the president of the board of directors (above the London and Paris committees) who was to have a casting vote, was always to be British. Campbell, who believed that the Szechwan railway was necessary in British interests, was ready to give up the casting vote rather than jeopardize the scheme. 'The main thing to bear in mind', he remarked, 'is that we want the French money and that the French will not join unless on absolutely equal terms with us.' Lansdowne, however, had never admitted the principle of equal treatment for the French and refused to give way, remarking, 'while the French

[10] FO 17/1763, minutes by Percy and Campbell on papers communicated by Meyer, 13 Mar. 1905; Balfour Papers, BL Add. MSS 49747, Percy to Balfour, 13 and 18 Jan. 1905.
[11] FO 17/1763, memoranda by Lansdowne and Campbell, 4 May 1905; Meyer to Campbell, 7 May 1905; memoranda from and to French Embassy, 9 and 15 May 1905; Lansdowne to Bertie, 15 July 1905; FO 27/3703, Lansdowne to Bertie, 5 May 1905.

bring in part of the money, the British bring in everything else inclusive of the good will of the Chinese authorities'.[12]

While this matter was still under discussion there emerged a large issue—the financing of the Hankow–Canton railway—in which the British in the summer of 1905 had brought off a *coup* by securing from the Chinese a pledge of preference for British enterprise over foreign rivals. The success was noteworthy on two counts: because it seemed to establish a hold on a major route, and because it was obtained not in response to pressure from commercial interests but by official initiative involving the use of funds under government control.

The Hankow–Canton concession had been awarded in 1898 to the American China Development Company (ACDC). The British and Chinese Corporation had initially entered in 1899 into a working agreement with the American company in which each partner was to take a half share in all future business in China, this to include the Hankow–Canton line, and the line projected from Canton to Kowloon for which the corporation secured a preliminary agreement in March 1899, but not the concessions that the corporation had already obtained. The actual investment by the corporation in the ACDC, made in 1900, was small however. By the end of 1900 a large interest in the ACDC had been sold by the Americans to a Belgian group with French associates dominated by King Leopold II. One consequence of this was the withdrawal of the corporation. It was offered a new participation if it was prepared to bear 50 per cent of the preliminary expenses of construction of the Hankow–Canton railway. This it declined since it lacked the funds to make the required immediate payment. Further, because of the slump in the capital market, it was felt unwise to participate in an enterprise where it was not possible to estimate the costs.

The withdrawal of the corporation was amicable. It informed the Foreign Office that it was not influenced by hostile intentions and that it did not wish for government intervention to protect its interest in the Hankow–Canton line. The Foreign Office seems for some time to

[12] FO 17/1763, minute by Campbell on Satow to Campbell, 1 June 1905, and on memorandum from the French Embassy, 14 Aug. 1905; memorandum by Tyrrell, 18 Aug. 1905; Lansdowne to Cambon, 13 Sept. 1905. Lansdowne's remark reflected the view of Satow (to Campbell, 1 June 1904), who thought the French contribution 'vastly unequal'. Meyer indicated that if Lansdowne wished the British group to give way on political grounds they would, but they would certainly not do so from a business point of view; memorandum by Campbell of interview with Meyer, 4 Sept. 1905; MacMurray, I, p. 534.

have been little concerned about the line and the Franco-Belgian presence in it, although British publicists in China saw the alarming prospect of French influence (and Russian too), already established in the Peking–Hankow railway, extending over the whole of the artery from Peking to Canton. Despite the alarms, the fact was that very little progress was being made with construction. This was largely the consequence of friction between the Belgians and the French Foreign Ministry. Delcassé was determined upon absolute equality between French and Belgian interests in the enterprise. King Leopold was equally determined to maintain the dominant position he had secured from the Americans. Hence access to the Paris capital market was blocked, and the funds necessary to press ahead with construction were not forthcoming.[13]

The Hong Kong government, however, was early concerned by the French presence. The prolongation of the line to Kowloon would strengthen the colony's position as the entrepôt of southern China, and the colony itself had undertaken to finance the section from Kowloon to the Chinese border. Both the delay in construction and still more the prospect of the Hankow–Canton line under other than British direction disquieted opinion in the colony—all the more so as American voices were raised from time to time in favour of the line terminating in a new port to be built at Whampoa rather than at Kowloon. It seems that there was little actual prospect of this, but uneasiness in the colony was to remain as long as the interests of rivals appeared to be in a position to shape the development of the railway.

To the British community, the way out seemed to be through direct involvement of the British government in the railway, a course urged from 1899 by the China Association and raised once more by the colony in February 1904. Campbell's minute reiterated the government's attitude. 'There has never been any question of HMG acquiring an interest in the Hankow–Canton railway and there is no prospect of such a proposal being entertained by the Treasury.' A later request from Hong Kong that steps be taken to stop the transfer of control in the ACDC and therefore in the railway to the Belgians led him to remark, 'We have enough to do to retain the concessions we have got without trying to obtain the cancellation of those given to others'. The fact was that the lack of support in the market held back advance.

[13] Kurgan-van Hentenryk, *Leopold II*, pp. 227, 436–8, 457–61; FO 17/1500, BCC to FO, 4 Feb. 1901.

Much as we should like to see the Hankow–Canton railway in British hands again—for we once had a $\frac{1}{2}$ share . . . There is no money here or in America for investment in Chinese railways with or without the benevolent interest and support of the British and American governments. The Hankow–Canton line can hardly be compared with the Shanghai–Nanking—the latter being generally acknowledged to be the best thing in Chinese railways, far and away.

We blessed the concern and allowed the official blessing to be printed with the prospectus, indeed it was written for that purpose. Yet the loan was a ghastly failure.[14]

By the summer of 1905 attitudes had changed. Partly in response to the widespread rights recovery movement, partly to the campaign waged by G. E. Morrison, *The Times* Peking correspondent, and others who argued that the Belgians would allow France and Russia to infiltrate the Hankow–Canton line, the Chinese at the end of 1904 had given notice that they would annul the ACDC contract for the line. Leopold attempted to avert this by returning control to American interests, but the banker, J. P. Morgan, who headed the American group, judging, in face of all the difficulties (particularly the temper of the Chinese) that the contract was not a sound business proposition, determined to sell out to the Chinese.[15] Chang Chih-tung, viceroy of Wuchang, and the viceroy of Canton, through whose provinces the line would pass, were eager to buy but lacked the funds and could not raise them from Chinese sources. Chang, who had been given charge of the Hankow–Canton project by the Chinese government, approached Fraser, the British consul-general at Hankow, for a loan on the security of the opium revenues of Hupeh and Hunan to make the purchase, but insisted that the purpose be kept secret. There were competitors for the loan, Japanese and German, Fraser reported, who were making tempting proposals. Chang, however, wished to borrow from the British—but not from the Hongkong Bank because of its relations with the Deutsch-Asiatische Bank and the presence of a German on its directorate. Satow, in telegraphing the proposal, noted that the other British bank in China, the Chartered, while a sound establishment, had hitherto done little government loan business. Clearly he and Fraser saw the opportunity as one to be taken, Fraser

---

[14] FO 17/1762, Colonial Office to FO, 4 Feb. 1904; FO to Colonial Office, 16 Feb. 1904; CO to FO, 22 Apr. 1904 with minute; memorandum by Campbell, 20 Oct. 1904; Scott (consul-general at Canton) to Lansdowne, 1 June 1905.

[15] Kurgan-van Hentenryk, *Leopold II*, pp. 509–50; E-tu Zen Sun, pp. 74–83.

suggesting it would be worthwhile for the British government to advance the money to the viceroy.

Satow's telegram posed tricky problems. One was that the secrecy demanded by Chang as to the purpose of what would be a considerable loan would make it difficult to raise funds in the market. The other was the veto on the Hongkong Bank. Campbell agreed that the Chartered Bank might be approached, 'but considering our very friendly relations with the H & S Bank I should not myself like doing this without saying anything to the latter'. He proposed explaining the difficulty to the bank and hearing its views. Lord Percy saw a way around, suggesting that the Hong Kong government borrow the money from the bank and lend it to the viceroy. The Colonial Office, accepting the idea of an indirect loan, suggested a means that made recourse to the bank unnecessary: the sum needed by Chang, now £1.1 million because the Canton viceroy was unable to provide the contribution he had promised, should be advanced as a loan to the government of the colony by the Crown Agents for the Colonies. This was adopted, but because technical difficulties prevented the Crown Agents from making a transfer at short notice when Chang was faced with a demand to make the first payment in New York more quickly than expected, the Hongkong Bank was called upon to lend him £400,000 of the total loan. This sum was repaid to the bank by the Crown Agents.[16]

The readiness of the British authorities to meet Chang Chih-tung's requirements through the use of funds under official control was a rare instance of financial involvement by the government in railway enterprise outside British territory. It was a response to an unexpected opportunity grasped by British officials in China and in London and made without prompting from British financiers, who were kept in ignorance as Chang had requested. 'It is hoped', noted Campbell, 'that the loan will get us control of the Hankow–Canton railway', and with its conclusion steps were taken to secure a position for British finance and industry in what the Foreign Office had now come to accept as a railway project important for British interests south of the Yangtze. Fraser had suggested that the viceroys be asked that in case foreign capital and engineers should be needed within the Hukuang

[16] FO 17/1762, Satow to Lansdowne, 7 June 1905, with minutes by Campbell and Percy; Lansdowne to Satow, 30 June 1905; Colonial Office to FO, 9 and 15 Sept. 1905; Crown Agents to Colonial Office, 9 Oct. 1905; PRO 30/33/7/4. Campbell to Satow, 28 June 1905.

and Kwangtung provinces for railway purposes, first option of supplying them should be given to Britain. With the authorization of the
loan, Satow and the governor of Hong Kong, Nathan, were told that it
was desirable to secure assurance along these lines together with a
pledge that Chang would not part with the shares without British
assent, but it was left to their discretion 'to secure as much as possible
for British commercial interests'. In September, when he completed
the loan agreement with the government of Hong Kong, Chang
acknowledged in a pledge to Fraser the assistance from the British
authorities that had allowed China to redeem the Hankow–Canton
railway.

> As regards funds for the future construction of the Canton–Hankow railway,
> in case it is necessary to borrow abroad in addition to the amount China may
> herself provide, the first application shall be made to England, and if the
> British tender is, as regards interest and issue price, equal to the tenders of
> other countries, British financiers shall have the first option of undertaking
> the business; if in the above and other respects the tenders of other countries
> are fairer and more favourable than England's, China will be free to choose
> the fairest and most favourable and make other arrangements for borrowing.

If a British loan were made, British suppliers of construction
materials and machinery were to receive a similar preference. The
same system in respect of loans and materials was to apply to other
railway construction enterprises within Hupeh and Hunan. As to
engineers, one-half would be drawn from the nation providing the
loan, the other half would be Japanese.[17]

Though this undertaking, which bound the viceroy and governors
of the provinces of Hupeh and Hunan, was not as tightly drawn as no
doubt the British authorities would have wished, it did appear that by
its action the government had put British enterprise in a favourable
position to secure the two loans Chang was now reported to be seeking: £2 million for the building of the Hupeh section of the Hankow–
Szechwan line and £3 million for the Hankow–Canton line. In the
first of these it was accepted that French interests would be involved
through their approaching agreement with Chinese Central Railways;
the second, however, was intended to be a purely British loan through
the British and Chinese Corporation. Satow was advised of the

---

[17] FO 17/1762, Satow to Lansdowne, 22 Sept. 1905; MacMurray, 1, pp. 528–31; E-tu
Zen Sun, pp. 82–3, who notes that Kwangtung was omitted from the pledge on the
insistence of its viceroy.

distinction between the loans and told it seemed important that the two lines be dealt with separately.[18]

The first attempt to cut into hopes of an entirely British operation came, however, from the Germans. The Deutsch-Asiatische Bank entered the field, asserting that for the British group to seek the loans on its own account would be a violation of its agreement of 1895 with the Hongkong Bank to share all bank business. This claim was of doubtful validity in respect of a loan for railway construction, but the agreement was the reason why the Hongkong Bank had been bypassed in the arrangements for the repurchase by Chang of the American shares. As it was, the bank was well placed to reject the German demand for participation. The existence of the British and Chinese Corporation and Chinese Central Railways enabled it, in face of German protests, to deny involvement and to present the railway syndicates as entirely independent concerns. This was legally accurate but was in fact, as the bank recognized and the Foreign Office understood, a transparent fiction. The bank reported that Chinese Central Railways was seeking the Hankow–Szechwan (Hupeh section) loan for which the Germans had already made a bid.

As Mr. Hillier [the Peking agent of the bank] is in the best position for negotiating such business, the Central Railways will officially request us to allow him to act as their direct negotiator as soon as they can get a Board Meeting to arrange this . . . Mr. Hillier's negotiating on behalf of the Central Railways will no doubt be criticized by the Germans as an evasion of our agreement to act on joint account with them in all bank business, but we will endeavour to keep the point as clear as possible that in his negotiations he does not represent the Hongkong and Shanghai Bank, but represents other interests entirely.

Similar tactics were adopted when the French group, now partners in Chinese Central Railways, raised the matter of the Hankow–Canton loan. There was of course a long-standing French interest in the project through participation with the Belgians in the original concession, and France was not now minded to abandon it. The first approach was made by Simon of the Banque de l'Indo-Chine, who wrote to Townsend of the Hongkong Bank that the French government, having learnt that the Hongkong and Deutsch-Asiatische banks were disposed to advance £3 million for the construction of the line,

[18] FO 17/1762, memoranda by Campbell, 20 Aug. and Tyrrell, 24 Aug. 1905; FO 17/1763, Lansdowne to Satow, 15 Sept. 1905.

'has the utmost desire to see the French banks participate in this business which was formerly pursued by a Franco-Belgian group. I was recently summoned to our Foreign Office where I was instructed to attend to the matter.'

Townsend's reply of 4 October was submitted in draft to the Foreign Office; on Campbell's suggestion, reference to a desire to keep the Hankow–Canton line as a British enterprise was omitted. Townsend followed the same tactics as with the Germans over the Hankow–Szechwan loan, disclaiming any permanent connection of the Hongkong Bank with the business and adding:

I understand, however, that the British and Chinese Corporation is carrying on negotiations in China with a view of supplying funds for the construction of this railway. This corporation issues its loans, if obtained, through the Hong-kong and Shanghai Bank, but otherwise we have no connection with it and it will be necessary for you to apply to that corporation should you desire any participation.[19]

This the French did, but they also took political action. In Peking, the Belgian minister was supported by his French colleague in efforts to claim prior right to the concession, while on 18 October Cambon raised the question with Lansdowne, emphasizing his regret that the British group, according to his information, had applied to the Deutsch-Asiatische Bank rather than to the French group for capital to finance the line. On 5 November, a French note urged that Chinese Central Railways should participate in the Hankow–Canton project. Making it clear that the French regarded the matter as a test of the sincerity of British support for the Anglo-French financial entente in China, it asked that the Foreign Office use its influence to remove the opposition of William Keswick, chairman of the British and Chinese Corporation.[20] At the same time French and German protests in Peking succeeded in persuading the authorities to forbid Chang Chih-tung to borrow. Although the viceroy promised that if a foreign loan should be authorized he would stand by his pledge to the British, it seemed clear that in the face of further opposition it would not be possible to maintain this advantage; and there was the continuing problem of the London capital market.

---

[19] FO 17/1762, Townsend (Hongkong Bank) to Campbell, 8 Sept. 1905; Townsend to FO, 3 Oct. 1905; Townsend to Simon, 4 Oct. 1905.
[20] FO 17/1762, Lansdowne to Bertie, 18 Oct. 1905; Satow to Lansdowne, 25 Oct. 1905; note from French Embassy, 5 Nov. 1905. The British group had not, in fact, approached the Deutsch-Asiatische Bank.

By November, opinion was moving to acceptance of French participation. Lansdowne was not ready to take the view advanced by the
French group and the Pekin Syndicate that the principle of Anglo-
French financial co-operation embodied in the Chinese Central Railways agreement applied to all railways in China, a principle that he
thought might prove inconvenient in the future. He recognized, however, the case for French participation in the Hankow–Canton line,
since this 'would appear to afford the only means of overcoming the
opposition on the part of the Chinese government to the construction
of the line at all in the immediate future'. The men on the spot, Satow
and the governor of Hong Kong, were both opposed. Satow urged that
French advances should not be accepted, at least until the French
government had given way on the question of the chairmanship of
Chinese Central Railways; and further, he argued, as a matter of
tactics, since Britain had so many other railways in hand, the
Hankow–Canton could be allowed to sleep for a while. Lansdowne
accepted Satow's views on tactics but not on the question of admission
of the French, but felt that he could not take a decision opposed to the
minister's view when the government was about to resign. The intention of the Far Eastern Department was evidently to draw the matter
out, as Satow had suggested, but the ground was cut from under the
feet of the advocates of delay by the unexpected action of the British
and Chinese Corporation in arranging matters directly with the
French group before a final decision had been taken in the Foreign
Office as to the admission of the French.[21]

Since the French group informed their government of the settlement, the Foreign Office had to make the best of the situation and
accept French participation rather more easily and quickly than had
been intended. All that could be done was to ensure that the chairmanship of the new company to be formed (with casting vote), as well
as of Chinese Central Railways, remained in British hands. There was
some further delay while the governments satisfied themselves that
Article 10 of the agreement of 2 October providing for a French
interest in Chinese Central Railways did not commit them to similar
constitutions in respect of subsidiary or associated enterprises in
which the company might engage, except for the company to be

---

[21] FO 17/1762, Satow to Lansdowne, 3 Nov. 1905; FO to Colonial Office, 20 Nov.
1905; memoranda by Campbell, 11 and 27 Nov. 1905; Colonial Office to FO, 29 Nov.
1905, with minute by Campbell; Satow to Lansdowne, 5 Dec. 1905; memorandum by
Campbell, 21 Dec. 1905; Campbell to Keswick (draft) 25 Dec. 1905.

formed to build the Szechwan line itself. Finally, the French government being assured that the constitution of subsidiaries would reflect the predominance of French interests where appropriate, an exchange of notes on 5 and 19 April 1906 registered the two governments' approval of the agreement of 2 October 1905 and their intention to uphold the partnership in so far as it did not conflict with the fundamental interests of either government in China.[22]

The French had thus made a considerable advance. At a time when their position seemed to be seriously weakened by the defeat of Russia, which threatened to impair their ability to obstruct plans, they had succeeded, with British acquiescence, in making an important advance in the Yangtze area in the significant field of railway finance and construction. Not only had they acquired a place in the Hankow–Szechwan project, they had also regained participation in the enterprise that the British, having accepted French partnership, had nevertheless intended to keep as their preserve: the Hankow–Canton line.

The change in British policy from rivalry with France to partnership was influenced by the local situation in China as well as by considerations of general policy. The overtures came from the French side in consequence of the Townley agreement. That agreement was seen by Townley and Satow as a successful stroke against French ambitions; and Satow, except for a momentary acceptance, remained opposed to the admission of French interests into British preserves. Campbell, the leading official advocate of co-operation with the French, was obviously keenly alive to considerations of the China trade. He was consistently eager, in the general interests of British trade, to get railways built; and he was much impressed both by the power of the French to obstruct British schemes and especially by the resources of the Paris capital market—which co-operation would make available for lines that would otherwise not be built, at least by British enterprise. Campbell was also alive to broader political factors. In 1903 it had not been felt necessary on political grounds to make a gesture by accommodating the French in China. By the end of 1905,

[22] FO 17/1762, correspondence communicated by Keswick, 19 Dec. 1905; PRO 30/33/7/5, Campbell to Satow, 1 Dec. 1905, 12 Jan. 1906; FO 17/1762, Addis to Francqui, 20 Dec. 1905; FO 405/165, FO to BCC, 6 Jan. 1906; FO 371/25, memorandum to French Embassy, 21 Jan. 1906; Paul Cambon to Grey, 5 Apr. 1906; Grey to Cambon, 19 Apr. 1906.

however, in commenting on the Hankow–Canton question to Satow, Campbell was emphasizing general considerations.

Is it desirable from the Entente Cordiale standpoint to put the backs of the French up by such a show of want of confidence as a refusal must entail? We have to consider our relations with France all over the world and not in China only. I had some talk with Lord L. this afternoon on the subject, and though he said nothing definite, this was, I should say, the view he seemed to take.[23]

It does appear that Lansdowne was more impressed by the general desirability of remaining on close terms with France than by arguments as to the necessity of Chinese railways. If at one point he was sufficiently influenced to accept that the building of the Hankow–Szechwan line was of overriding importance, he did not maintain that attitude. Further, he was ready to accept Satow's suggestion that the Hankow–Canton project be allowed to sleep for a while. But once having agreed to the idea of partnership with France he did not depart from it.

That the new partnership was not intended on the British side to be part of a complete recasting of relationships in China in conformity with changing alignments in Great Power relations seems to emerge from examination of modifications in 1905 of the links between the Hongkong and Shanghai Bank and the Deutsch-Asiatische Bank. In fact, this change was in no way encouraged by the Foreign Office; on the contrary, it was regarded without enthusiasm by Lansdowne and his advisers. The connections between the banks were twofold: the agreement of 1898 between the German group and the British and Chinese Corporation establishing respective zones of operation for loans directly related to railway construction; and the earlier agreement of 1895 for sharing administrative loans. The railway agreement had not prevented subsequent friction between the parties, but it was the 1895 agreement that now concerned the Hongkong Bank. The existence of this compact had been forgotten in the Foreign Office, where casual reference to it by the bank in January 1905 caused surprise. In April, C. S. Addis, now joint manager with Townsend of the London office of the bank, inquired what view the Foreign Office would take of the bank's giving notice to the Germans to terminate the agreement. He remarked that it had been most loyally observed by the Germans, though since the indemnity loans of 1896 and 1898 only one

---

[23] PRO 30/33/7/5, Campbell to Satow, 1 Dec. 1905.

loan falling within its terms had been arranged. Now, since the political situation in relation to Germany had so much changed, he wondered whether it might be desirable to work with the French instead.

Lansdowne saw no reason for a break with the German syndicate: 'To pick a quarrel with them (and therefore with the German government) *à propos de bottes* would to my mind be unjustifiable. Unless there is some good reason for a dissolution of partnership I venture to think that Mr. Addis had much better leave the matter alone.'[24] When, however, Addis reported the opinion of Hillier in Peking that the alliance with Germany was a handicap to the bank in seeking business in China, Lansdowne agreed that it should approach the Deutsch-Asiatische Bank for modification of the agreement, but requested consultation if the denunciation of the 1895 agreement was contemplated. Then, when the loan to Chang Chih-tung for the purchase of the American interest in the Hankow–Canton railway was under discussion, came a further incentive: because of its association with German interests and the presence of a German on its board, Satow refused to give Hillier any information about the transaction. The Foreign Office regarded this as a special case, but did not deny that similar instances might occur under the agreement of 1895. This clearly supported the bank's argument that the German link providing for joint negotiation and signature of loan agreements was a serious obstacle. However, the Hongkong Bank in discussion in October 1905 with its German partner did not press for termination. What emerged was a modified arrangement that waived the provision for joint negotiation and signature of loans within the scope of the 1895 agreement where such provision might prejudice business, and allowed either bank to negotiate such loans with or without notice to its partner. It preserved all other rights of participation to the partner. Campbell thought that this was 'much better than the alternative of breaking off altogether with the Germans', and Lansdowne agreed that there was no ground for objection.[25]

Acceptance by the British of French participation in the Hankow–Canton railway was a sign that at the end of 1905, association with

---

[24] FO 17/1687, memorandum by Campbell, 4 Apr. 1905; Addis to FO, 7 Apr. 1905, with minutes by Campbell and Lansdowne.

[25] FO 17/1689, memorandum by Langley, 28 July 1905; FO to Hongkong Bank, 28 July 1905; minutes by Tyrrell and Campbell, 2 and 4 Sept. 1905; FO 17/1690, minutes of a meeting between representatives of the Hongkong Bank and the Deutsch-Asiatische Bank in Brussels, 4 Oct. 1905.

France was more necessary on general political grounds than in 1904. The defeat of Russia by Japan was at first hailed in Britain as a great gain; within a few months it was clear that the beneficiary was Germany, and that Russia was an essential element in the European balance of power. The Moroccan crisis emphasized the realities of the situation still further, and the strengthening of the entente by a partnership with China even at high cost to British aims was clearly judged desirable. In bringing this partnership into being, the resources of the French capital market were of obvious importance. Money was the great positive contribution that the French could bring; it is open to question whether without it the entente would have extended to China. With it, the French government—closely controlling its financiers, less complaisant than them and determined that France should secure a presence and not merely a financial participation in major enterprises; and benefiting, too, at the end of 1905, from the British desire for a closer relationship in general policy with France—was able to achieve a significant advance.

In this change of direction by Britain in China, the British enterprises (the Hongkong Bank and its affiliates, and the Pekin Syndicate) had been willing instruments; indeed, they had initially shown greater eagerness than the Foreign Office for links with the French. Throughout the negotiations they had responded to official wishes, embracing the details as well as the broad lines of the British negotiating position;[26] and in consequence a still closer relationship than had hitherto existed had been established. This relationship marked a movement by Britain in the direction of a continental-type association between government and finance, for the government was now formally bound through the agreement with France to support the British groups—the British and Chinese Corporation and Chinese Central Railways—in the railways covered by the Anglo-French agreement.

---

[26] Save for the premature agreement to admit the French group to the Hankow–Canton scheme.

5

The Anglo-French Partnership, 1906–1907

THE Anglo-French combination had come into being at a time when the conditions in which foreign enterprise operated in China were undergoing significant change; indeed, it was to some extent a response to the change. The most important factor in shaping the new scene was the defeat of Russia by Japan. Since 1895, when China's weakness had been starkly exposed by the Sino-Japanese war, she had been the arena of competition between powers seeking to carve out areas of exclusive privilege and control. While this was achieved mostly by peaceful penetration, there was also the threat and indeed the experience of territorial loss under the transparent guise of lease arrangements and special privileges. Japan's victory in 1905 marked another watershed, as significant as her earlier success in 1895. After 1905 came a period in which international rivalry gave way gradually to international co-operation, bringing about in 1909–10 the formation of the first China consortium linking British, French, German, and American banks in agreements, acquiesced in by their governments, embracing railway and administrative loans to China.

The emergence of co-operation in place of competition was in essence the result of adaptation by the European financial groups and their respective governments to the new situation in China. In this the Russo-Japanese War was a central factor, most of all in that it exhausted both combatants so that neither was able for some years to play a dominant role in Far Eastern politics. Though Russia did not abandon the position in Manchuria that remained to her after the Treaty of Portsmouth, both military weakness and the changed direction of policy under Isvolsky ensured that her aims became essentially defensive: to retain what she still had rather than to pursue the expansionist goals of the period before 1905. As for Japan, her ability to exploit victory was seriously limited by economic weakness. The war had put an immense strain upon her financial resources, so much so that her aims were perforce confined to the consolidation of the gains that victory had brought. A forward policy in China proper was beyond her capacity; the difficult tasks of economic recuperation coupled with apprehension (exaggerated, but certainly felt) as to Russia's aims imposed caution. Economic expansion in areas other than Manchuria was desired and to a limited extent achieved, but it was not until the revolution of 1911 and its aftermath that Japan made a serious bid for a key position in the Yangtze Valley.

A situation that neutralized the two powers with ambitions to dominate China promised much more congenial conditions for those whose interests were essentially economic rather than territorial. This was certainly the position of Britain; governments in the preceding ten years had looked anxiously at what seemed to be the impending disintegration of China, well aware that British commercial interests could not be safeguarded by British power because scarce military resources could not be stretched to cope with a second India. In fact the new situation was to bring its own problems for the trading powers, the consequence of the changing currents in China considerably strengthened as a result of the Russo-Japanese War.

The essential change, apparent well before the war, was the recovery of self-confidence by the Chinese authorities, provincial and central, reflecting a most significant development: the rise of national consciousness. 'China is no longer as ready to submit to all and every demand of the Powers as she was', reported Satow in March 1906, 'and unless she gets another knock-down blow, will in the future be less and less tractable.' He attributed this to the evolution of the international situation culminating in the war, which with the defeat of Russia (the power that posed the most serious threat to China) coupled with the renewal and extension of the Anglo-Japanese alliance, confirmed the belief of the Chinese that they had nothing further to fear. Now, Satow continued, China, relieved of the dread of Russia and with her position consequently improved as regards other powers 'has begun to pluck up courage again, not only to refuse further concessions but also to resume those she made during her period of extreme weakness'. Plainly there were difficulties ahead, most obviously in connection with relations between the Chinese and the foreign communities resident in the treaty ports (especially Shanghai, where Chinese self-assertiveness was found particularly obnoxious), and in the area of major enterprises involving a measure of foreign control, particularly the large issue of railways.[1]

Railways, in which all the foreign powers were involved and in which their rivalry had been most marked were, in the changed conditions, to provide the factors out of which ultimately emerged the four-power banking consortium. The dominant fact in the new situation, presented to Grey in a valedictory despatch by Satow, was the desire of the Chinese, motivated in part by national consciousness and in part by perception of the financial gains to be made (for both the Northern and the Peking–Hankow lines were running profitably), to build and manage their railways themselves in the future, and possibly to buy back those railways managed by foreigners. The Northern Railway, the only line actually in the hands of China, had recently been exceedingly prosperous. During the year ending 30 September 1905 the net profit on the original capital provided by Chinese shareholders and the government, after paying loan and all other charges, actually reached the incredible figure of $47\frac{1}{2}$ per cent. This, of course, Satow observed, made all Chinese connected with railways anxious to secure the profit for themselves instead of sharing it (as in the case of the Peking–Hankow and Shanghai–Nanking railways) with the foreign capitalists. For Satow these facts alone were sufficient to explain the obstacles the British were meeting over the railway agreements, which they had been trying for a long time to get completed. As to the political aspect of railway construction in China—that, in Satow's opinion, had, with the sole exception of the French line into Yunnan, completely disappeared as a consequence of the defeat of Russia. His conclusion from a review of the present situation of the political railways was

that the wisdom of Her Majesty's government in 1898 in refusing to give a guarantee for the construction of railways by British concessionaires, and in confining their action to the support of legitimate private enterprise has been justified by the event; that the policies of 'pacific penetration', 'partition', 'spheres of influence' and 'spheres of interest' are dead; and that if any offer of spare English capital for investment in Chinese railways present themselves they should be regarded as purely commercial undertakings without any political character and be assisted accordingly. It may even seem, on consideration of all the facts, a doubtful policy to insist on holding the Chinese government bound to us for ever by Preliminary Agreements made eight years

---

[1] FO 800/44, Satow to Grey, 31 Mar. 1906.

ago, which either our inertia or inability to procure the necessary capital had hitherto prevented from being carried into effect.[2]

Satow's analysis was part of the advice he presented in the last months of his service to the new foreign secretary, Sir Edward Grey, who took the Foreign Office when the Liberals came to power in December 1905. Satow was trying to provide principles on which Grey could rest his policy and frame instructions for the new minister to China. This was to be Sir John Jordan, who had behind him long years of service in the Far East, latterly in Korea. Jordan was not known personally to Satow (who had suggested other names), but his appointment had been strongly urged by G. E. Morrison, *The Times* correspondent in Peking. During his visit to Britain towards the end of 1905, Morrison had pressed the case for Jordan on officials and on Lansdowne himself. Though the nomination now fell to Grey to make, Morrison's advocacy had evidently made a convincing impression on Grey's advisers.[3] Of these, Campbell, as head of the Far Eastern Department, was most closely in touch with opinions among financiers interested in enterprise in China. He was not impressed by Satow's argument for a relaxation of the degree of control over proposed Chinese railways contained in the preliminary agreements.

With all respect for Sir E. Satow's opinion, I do not believe that capital will be forthcoming for Chinese railways unless the lenders are given at least a considerable share of control. Vague offers may have been made but that is a very different thing from signing even a preliminary contract.

However, Hardinge, the permanent under-secretary and senior official, took a different view. He thought Satow's proposed policy worthy of serious consideration and felt it had 'much to recommend it'. So did Grey:

If 'partition' and 'spheres of interest' are gone for good it must be because the Chinese have both the intention and the power to become masters in their own house. If this is to be so our policy must accommodate itself to a recognition of this fact and our railway concessionaires will have to be told so. The matter must be thoroughly discussed with Sir E. Satow when he comes home and with Sir J. Jordan before he goes out.[4]

---

[2] FO 371/35, Satow to Grey, 16 Apr. 1906.
[3] PRO 30/33/7/5. Grey to Satow, 3 Mar. 1906; Satow to Grey, 4 Mar. 1906; Diary of G. E. Morrison, reel 235, 18, 29 Sept., 2 Oct. 1905.
[4] FO 371/35, minutes on Satow to Grey, 16 Apr. 1906.

Satow's views, reiterated when he returned to London, evidently impressed Grey, and were reflected in the principles on general issues and more specifically on railway matters embodied in the instructions to Jordan that were intended to provide him with broad guide-lines. In these Grey recognized that the old China policy of extorting concessions by pressure and insisting, by force when necessary, upon the letter of them was no longer feasible. It could not in the new conditions be made effective, and could soon be disastrous in face of Chinese resentment 'for it is becoming increasingly evident that foreign trade in China cannot prosper in the face of Chinese ill-will'. Moreover, he felt that a policy of force 'can only be defended with regard to a nation which is incapable of responding to any conciliatory method of keeping its engagements or of taking part in the development of its own resources'. Hence, although it entailed risks, although the Chinese government might mistake conciliation for weakness and seek to take unfair advantage instead of responding with goodwill, this was the course he wished British policy to take. Conciliation would be tempered by firmness where necessary, certainly in ensuring for some time to come that there should be no disturbance or serious change in the administration of the customs, and that China should fulfil in substance all undertakings already given as to concessions. If the Chinese recognized these conditions Britain

will not press the Chinese Government to grant new concessions on terms which are embarrassing to them and will, on the contrary, encourage and welcome her efforts to develop the resources of the country under her own auspices and on terms which would give her the help of foreign capital and experience when required without being derogatory to her sovereignty or her independence.

A sympathetic attitude would also be shown to Chinese efforts to reform their institutions, but Britain would 'unhesitatingly oppose any attempt on their part to interfere with the extra-territorial jurisdiction exercised in China by the Treaty powers'. Yet, while taking an uncompromising stand on extra-territoriality, Grey recognized the problem of the foreign settlements, which 'constitute an *imperium in imperio* in various parts of China which must naturally be regarded with jealousy by the Chinese'. He recognized too, what Satow had stressed: the resistant attitude of the British communities, especially in Shanghai, to the new spirit in China; and accepted that while the Chinese would have to understand that existing rights in foreign settlements must be respected, the fact had to be impressed upon British subjects that these rights 'must be made as little irksome and offensive to the Chinese authorities as possible'.

A conciliatory policy was also to be applied in the important railway question. For the future, Britain would not sympathize with obstruction because expansion of railways was highly desirable in the interests of trade; but if the Chinese could reach agreement with private financiers on the lines of the loan agreement between the British and Chinese Corporation and Northern Railways, the British government would welcome a change that would give China a larger share in enterprises where she herself was primarily interested, provided the terms of the agreement did not conflict with the policy of equal opportunity for the traffic of all nations.[5]

Clearly, though there was no intention of relinquishing treaty rights, Grey accepted the need for adjustment to the currents now running strongly in China. What he now looked to in railway matters was not new in principle in British practice, which had always been essentially commercial in its aim: to secure contracts for loans and construction, not to acquire concessions to own, work, and manage the lines exclusively as was the case with the Chinese Eastern Railway, the German lines in Shantung, and the French lines from Tongking into south-west China. Participation in working lines, at least until the loans financing them had been paid off, was, however, normally insisted on in British contracts. The final agreement for the Shanghai–Nanking line, signed 9 July 1903, had provided for an Anglo–Chinese board to supervise construction and operation, to consist of two Chinese and two representatives of the British and Chinese Corporation together with the engineer-in-chief who was to be nominated by the corporation. The Northern Railway agreement had specified that that line was to remain in control of the Chinese administrator-general so long as the principal and interest were regularly paid. In fact, Chinese authority over the line had been very firmly established by Yuan Sih-k'ai. Nevertheless the agreement of 1898 had asserted an element of British control, for it provided for a British chief engineer and a capable and efficient European railway accountant during the currency of the loan. Further, like the Shanghai–Nanking line, the railway was mortgaged to the lender, the

---

[5] FO 371/35, Grey to Jordan, 7 and 31 Aug. 1906.

corporation, which in the event of default was to take over management.[6] In the new climate in China it was plain that demands for the
inclusion of such provisions, and still more those which gave the
lenders a share in management and operation, as did the Shanghai–
Nanking agreement, would be controversial areas when further contracts came to be negotiated. It was equally plain that the agreement
with the French had limited the freedom of action of the Foreign
Office if it wished to influence the course of negotiation. It tied the
British government in respect of the railways covered by it to the
British group dominated by the Hongkong Bank, and it implied that
policy was to be a joint policy in which French views would have to be
accommodated.

The close association that had developed between the Foreign
Office and the banking group over the preceding ten years, which had
given rise to the belief that the bank was 'the chosen instrument' of the
government, had in fact been the creation of circumstances. By 1898
officials had come to recognize the need for an active policy by the
government in economic affairs in China: the support, even the stimu-
lation, of British enterprise in areas of railway construction and
mining, where rivals backed by their governments were acquiring
advantages because of political support. The Hongkong Bank group
had gained its special position because it was more vigorous and
enterprising in seeking business than others of equal substance, such
as the Chartered Bank, which did not put forward rival proposals, and
altogether more solid than the numerous company promoters of
dubious reputation who plagued officials. There was, in effect, no
other serious British contender for railway business, just as in the
mining field the Pekin Syndicate stood alone. But there had been no
pledge of exclusive support for either the bank group or the syndicate.
The government had remained free to support or not to support.

Now the situation had changed significantly. The Anglo-French
partnership brought a new stage, a formal commitment to exclusive
support of the British and Chinese Corporation and Chinese Central
Railways in the railway projects covered by the agreement of October
1905, subsequently extended to include the Hankow–Canton scheme.
Henceforth the British government was unable to support British
competitors against these concerns. This was a change of considerable

---

[6] MacMurray, 1, pp. 173–9, 384–402.

significance. The government had moved away from the cardinal principle of official impartiality as between competing British enterprises in China towards the continental practice of a politico-economic arm. It had done so in response both to the needs of the China situation and to the exigencies of general policy—the maintenance of the Anglo-French entente. Under Lansdowne, the traditional aloofness in economic matters—still strong, if undergoing modification, in Salisbury's time—gave way to close participation by ministers and officials in shaping decisions on the major question of the Hankow–Szechwan railway. There was evidence, too, in the Shanghai–Nanking railway loan in 1904, of a greater readiness to assist the progress of enterprise outside the agreement with the French.

Before Grey took office the consequences of the link with the French had been made clear to the Chartered Bank, now belatedly showing an interest in railway business. In November 1905 the Chartered Bank, having been refused participation for its clients by the Hongkong Bank in the Szechwan railway, asked for official help in connection with a possible loan to the Wuchang viceroy for a line from Hankow to Ichang. Campbell replied that this line would form part of the Szechwan railway, and the government was bound to support the Anglo-French syndicate formed to construct it under the auspices of the British and French governments. The British government was of course quite impartial between the two banks, but in the circumstances of this particular line he did not see that official help for the Chartered Bank was possible. A year later Jordan was confirmed in his view that he could not support the construction firm of Pauling and Co. in a bid for the Hankow–Canton contract. Official support for any firm other than the British and Chinese Corporation, he was told, would be a breach of faith with the French, and he was advised to recommend Paulings to make contact with the corporation.[7] Situations such as these, a by-product of the association with France in China, promised embarrassment for officials; for exclusive support, though in accord with continental practice, ran counter to views strongly held in Britain as to the proper limits of government action in restraint of free competition.

From the first, Grey was uneasy about commitments that could

---

[7] FO 17/1763, memorandum by Campbell, 2 Nov. 1905; FO 371/20, Jordan to Grey, 13 Nov. 1906, Grey to Jordan, 14 Nov. 1906.

draw political criticism. Association with France was something he was anxious to maintain in the interests of general policy even more than as a response to conditions in China. He was ready to extend it if further foreign support there should be required in future by British financiers. It is evident, however, that it was not his intention to make the Hongkong Bank the sole recipient of official support. When in July 1906 T'ang Shao-yi, who was now coming to the front in Chinese government railway planning, made approaches through the legation in Peking for a large loan for the construction of trunk railways, which he wished to be independent of the Hongkong Bank or at least to be a transaction in which that bank was not directly involved, Grey was at once ready to assist. There was no attempt on the British side to involve the Hongkong Bank, which T'ang disliked because of suspected German influences within it. On the advice of Asquith, chancellor of the exchequer, Grey turned to Sir Ernest Cassel and told him that the Chinese wished to avoid the Hongkong Bank, and that if he needed co-operation it should by preference be French. As Asquith had advised, 'in view of the jealousies that exist among our *haute finance*', Grey indicated that, if others were to be brought in, he would be glad if it were the British Rothschilds.[8]

The project seems to have come to nothing, but the official attitude was significant—not least in its readiness to assist in making capital available for railway construction in China. Construction contracts brought benefits to the enterprises involved, and orders for British industry. While precise stipulations in British contracts that supplies should come from Britain were few, the requirement that the chief engineer should be British was constant. This was the important factor, for whatever the specific terms of the contract as to purchases of material, the source of supply was largely determined by the engineer. Materials for railways constructed by British companies, it is claimed, were purchased exclusively in London without reference to the lowest price on open tender.[9] There were also prospects of profits for the financiers from the successful flotation of loans and the interest to be

[8] FO 371/27, Carnegie to Grey, 27 July 1906; Grey to Carnegie, 30 July 1906; minute by Grey on memorandum by Gorst, 20 Aug. 1906. On Cassel, one of the most powerful financiers in the City, see Jeremy (ed.), *Dictionary of Business Biography*, i, pp. 604–14.

[9] T. W. Overlach, *Foreign Financial Control in China* (New York, 1919), p. 60. The Canton–Kowloon (1907) and subsequent British contracts did give preference to British materials thus underwriting the preference always effectively constituted by the provision in all British contracts for a British engineer-in-chief (FO 371/1617, Jordan to Grey, 1 June 1913).

obtained on them. For the government there were wider factors, which were becoming of more concern. The China trade was expanding as China increased imports, and its place in the overall pattern of British trade was becoming more important.[10] Improved railway communications were expected to lead to still greater expansion in a market in which British exports were now running ahead of imports, reversing the trend before 1900 and promising an increasing surplus on trade account.

The growing significance of the China trade and the recognition of the key importance of railways for its future was the rock on which the Hongkong Bank group's position was founded. Despite the dormant undertakings that it had been unable to finance, the group remained the one sound prospect on the British side—as the Foreign Office had recognized. Exclusive official support for its joint operations with the French group emphasized its standing and brought it into even closer relations with the Far Eastern Department, for exclusive support imposed obligations as well as advantages. The group had to keep the Foreign Office fully informed and pay heed to official advice.

The important role of liaison with officials was filled from 1906 by a vigorous and able personality, Charles Addis, now to begin a distinguished career in international banking, who quickly established good relations with the department. Addis had been marked out by the bank during his service in the Far East. In 1903, when he was sub-manager at Shanghai, Cameron had referred to him as 'exceptionally able and the best man they have got'. His appointment in 1905 as joint London manager of the bank and successor to Cameron as its representative on the boards of the British and Chinese Corporation and Chinese Central Railways had come unexpectedly, as a consequence of Cameron's serious illness, but once installed Addis soon established his command of affairs. His emergence to represent the group at the Foreign Office owed something to the bad impression created there by what were taken to be the devious actions of William Keswick in bringing about, to the annoyance of the Foreign Office, the premature admission of French interests to participation in the Hankow–Canton project. Whatever Keswick's standing in the City, it appears that his reputation among the British business community in China was bad. Satow had already reported criticisms of him and these were shared by Morrison of *The Times*, who gave his opinion to Lansdowne and Earl

[10] Saul, p. 45.

Percy in the autumn of 1905. Percy had asked Morrison not to publish an attack on Keswick saying that 'all our hopes in China' were centred on the corporation and the Pekin Syndicate, and that it would be regrettable if faith in them were shaken by the disclosures contemplated by Morrison. Keswick's action over French participation must have confirmed doubts contributed by Morrison. 'Some say', Campbell told Satow, 'that the old gentleman is not so straight as we have thought.'[11]

Addis lost no time in making his own position clear to Campbell, saying that he, and, he believed, others of his colleagues in the corporation had all along been opposed to French participation in the Hankow–Canton line before being led to give way, on Keswick's assurance (as the result of a personal interview) that the combination was desired by the Foreign Office on political grounds. Now he found that Keswick's interpretation of the interview was not accepted by officials, and he regretted what had been done. 'I need not add', he concluded, 'that our wish on this as on all other occasions is to act in complete conformity to the wishes of the Foreign Office.' Addis's distaste for the partnership with France, which he claimed to have resisted throughout on commercial grounds, was typical of the opinion of the British community in China of which he had so recently been a member, but not of the men with longer and wider experience of the financial world. Cameron, Keswick, and Carl Meyer had all favoured the association, well aware of the resources of capital that the French could call upon. Addis, however, could see none but the political reasons that had been emphasized to the financiers: 'Upon the whole', he told J. O. P. Bland, 'the pressure both under Grey and under Lansdowne has been irresistible.' Addis recognized facts and understood how essential it was to work in harmony with the Foreign Office. 'Ministers come and ministers go', he remarked, 'but the F.O. remains. We could not afford to quarrel with the F.O.'[12] Now, when Keswick had lost official confidence, he came to the front. From this point on it was he who more and more acted for both the corporation and Chinese Central Railways in discussions with officials, though Keswick remained chairman of the corporation until his death in 1912.

---

[11] FO 17/1617, memorandum by Campbell, 27 Mar. 1903; PRO 30/33/7/5. Campbell to Satow, 12 Jan. 1906; G. E. Morrison, Diary, reel 235, 2 Oct., 9 Nov. 1905. On Addis see Jeremy (ed.) *Dictionary of Business Biography*, 1, pp. 13–16.

[12] Bland Papers, vol. 23, box 1 (reel 15), Addis to Campbell, 3 Jan. 1906 (copy); Addis to Bland, 28 Feb. and 28 Mar. 1906.

But Addis was first and foremost a member of the Hongkong Bank. It was the interests of the bank that he represented with the British group and it was those interests that were decisive for him in business matters.

British railway policy had now to be framed with regard to the views of the French as well as to the situation in China. It had soon been made clear that French interests intended to take an active part in the new association. Joint representation of Chinese Central Railways in China had been insisted upon by the French government during the negotiations for the formation of the association, and in May 1906 effect was given to this by the appointment as agents of J. O. P. Bland and Maurice Casenave. The terms of appointment emphasized its joint nature but did provide that, as in the existing business, British interests predominated; and since it was advisable that negotiation be conducted by one person only, Bland, acting in accord with Casenave, should have charge of all the company's negotiations, with Casenave to substitute for him as necessary. A reciprocal arrangement was to operate if business should be undertaken in which French interests predominated. Casenave, formerly attached to the French legation in Peking and now seconded from the diplomatic service, was to become manager of the Banque de l'Indo-Chine there. His appointment, the Foreign Office noted, 'no doubt means that the French government will keep a very careful watch over the company's proceedings.'

Bland's position followed from his appointment in October 1905 as agent for the British and Chinese Corporation. The post was secured for him by Addis, who was to have reason to regret his efforts. The post was necessary, Bland claimed later, in order to end friction between the Hongkong Bank and Jardine, Matheson as joint managers of the corporation in China. Bland had had much experience in China, where he had served for a while as private secretary to Sir Robert Hart and subsequently as secretary of the Shanghai Municipal Council and the Shanghai branch of the China Association, acting at the same time as *The Times* correspondent in Shanghai. Bland was a man of strong views, which embraced a marked suspicion of Japanese and German policy and a hostility to the link between the Hongkong Bank and the Deutsch-Asiatische Bank. He had been a forceful critic of the British and Chinese Corporation and a leading advocate of British predominance in the Yangtze Valley, and was held largely responsible for the pressure that had led to British troops being sent unnecessarily and unwisely to Shanghai during the Boxer

Rising. Satow, who clearly disliked Bland, reported that the hostility of the Shanghai Municipal Council to Chinese nationalism and its tendency to extend its authority reflected Bland's outlook for he 'has practically been the Council'. Satow was very critical of Bland's appointment to the corporation. He recognized his ability and energy but distrusted his views. He thought the appointment 'a corrupt bargain'. Bland was to remain a correspondent of *The Times*. 'He used to attack the corporation but they have made an end of that.' In fact Bland had offered himself for the post and Addis had obtained it for him against the opposition of Keswick, insisting with his fellow directors that Bland was to be free to write for the press if he wished.[13]

Bland's appointment was to be unfortunate for the British group. Though he seems to have got on well with Casenave, his personality was to be a factor hindering agreement with the Chinese. He lacked the qualities necessary in the changed atmosphere in China: tact, readiness to conciliate and compromise, and above all sympathetic understanding of the strong current of nationalism. He had no feeling for the conciliatory element in British policy or recognition of the new spirit among the Chinese, and frequently railed against the Foreign Office and legation for failing to press the Chinese to keep to their engagements.

A further factor soon to become evident as hindering agreement was that the link with the French was to provide the Chinese authorities with an opening for delaying tactics in railway matters. The major British object in 1906 was to encourage construction of the Hankow–Canton railway, for while the Hankow–Szechwan line was potentially profitable there was no question that the Hankow–Canton would directly serve British trading interests in southern China. This was all the more so because of the position of Hong Kong. If the line was extended to Kowloon its trade would undoubtedly benefit, but despite assurances, uneasiness least the terminus be fixed at Whampoa had not disappeared. Partly stimulated by the need to prevent this threat the colony was pressing for construction of the Chinese section of the Canton–Kowloon line, and following its loan to Chang Chih-tung in 1905, expected the contract for the Hankow–Canton railway would go to British enterprise.

<hr>

[13] FO 371/35, Chinese Central Railways to FO, 26 May 1906; FO 800/44, Satow to Grey, 27 Dec. 1905; 19 Apr. 1906; Addis Papers, Bland to Addis, 22 June 1905; Addis to Murray Stewart, 28 Nov. 1905; Pelcovits, pp. 294–9.

By the end of 1906 the Canton–Kowloon contract seemed on the eve of completion, and Chang Chih-tung was again reported to be ready to consider proposals for a construction contract for the sections of the Hankow–Canton and Hankow–Szechwan lines traversing Hupeh and Hunan, the provinces he administered. Chang was an official of great experience who saw railway questions in the context of the national needs of China. He had long recognized the desirability of a railway system that would bind the country together and, equally, the importance of its being in Chinese control. Hence his determination in 1905 to seize the opportunity to repurchase the Hankow–Canton concession. Yet he and other senior officials understood the realities masked by the upsurge of national feeling and the demand that construction and control rest immediately in Chinese hands.

The situation in fact required an equitable partnership between foreign capital and Chinese administration. China needed capital if she were to develop, and it could only come from abroad. Chinese opinion now accepted the need for modernization, and recognized that a railway system was an essential element if China were to follow the example set by Japan, but by and large would not accept foreign participation: the prevailing attitude in the provinces was that China herself must build the lines. The strength of this feeling had to be reckoned with by the authorities, who shared it themselves to the extent that they were determined that any final railway agreements with foreign enterprise should provide for the maximum possible degree of Chinese control. Local feeling led to Chinese railway construction companies being established in a number of provinces, including Hupeh and Hunan, which Chang could not ignore. Even so he appears to have been ready to borrow abroad by September 1905, but was held back by the Peking authorities. By December 1906, when it was clear that adequate capital could not be raised in Chang's provinces, Bland judged the time opportune for an approach to the viceroy.

His hopes rested on the pledge that Chang had given Fraser in 1905. The position, however, had been complicated by the success of the French in obtaining for themselves in the Anglo-French negotiations a standing in the Hankow–Canton business. In view of Chang's known antipathy to the French-opposition to French involvement in it had been one reason for Chinese determination to buy out the ACDC's contract for the railway—and the suspicion with which the Chinese authorities viewed foreign company methods, especially any appearance of combination between foreign interests, it was necessary to proceed with caution. Jordan warned Bland that open intervention by the French representative at this stage might give Chang an opportunity of evading British claims and turning to the Japanese. In the opinion of Jordan, and of Fraser in Hankow, action at this stage was premature, but if Bland did proceed he alone should interview the viceroy. Bland was determined to see Chang. He understood the possible consequences of overt association with the French, but felt that its realities had to be accepted. If Casenave insisted on a joint interview with Chang, Bland would have to go with him.

In the event, Bland alone saw Chang on 12 December, but damage was done by Casenave's request through the French consul for an interview with the viceroy as representative of the Banque de l'Indo-Chine. Moreover his card described him as *Ministre de France*. Bland's meeting with the viceroy went badly. Chang, holding himself pledged to deal only with British financiers, refused to admit French participation. His attitude may have been influenced by fear that if he gave way the road could be opened to a new battle of concessions, but it was influenced too by his particular objection to the French. He had been consistently opposed to them since the Tongking War of 1885–6, when he had been viceroy of Yunnan, but he may well have been affected additionally by knowledge of relations between French agents and the revolutionary groups associated with Sun Yat-sen that had brought protests to France from Peking in October 1906.[14]

The December fiasco necessarily resulted in a reconsideration of tactics. Bland, evidently holding that the activity of the French consul had been the essential error, proposed to the board of the British and Chinese Corporation that all intervention by French officials should be eliminated from business in which the British executive control was recognized. If there were to be diplomatic intervention it should come from British and not from French representatives, but he felt that 'the less official intervention—whether British or French brought to bear on our business with the Chinese, the better our prospects of success'. In making this point, Bland later maintained, he was guided by advice from Jordan and Fraser that diplomatic intervention should be kept out of the affairs of the corporation. His view did not find support from the board, which was clearly desirous of maintaining

[14] FO 371/214, Jordan to Grey, 23 Dec. 1906; papers communicated by BCC to FO, 18 Mar. 1907; Bland Papers, vol. 30 (reel 22) Diary 11, 12 Dec. 1906.

close relations with the Foreign Office and passed copies of the correspondence to the Far Eastern Department. Bland was instructed that
in the opinion of the Board,

the concurrence of the British minister or the British Consul as the case may
be should as a rule be sought on all occasions when you are, so to speak,
breaking new ground in the course of your negotiations. The Board is assured
that the sympathy and support of His Majesty's officers may always be
counted upon and while their 'intervention' in the sense of taking a direct and
active part in the negotiations may not be possible or desirable they should
always in the opinion of the Board be fully informed as to all important steps
you may think fit to take in your dealings with Chinese officials. Such confidence cannot but greatly strengthen your hands while conversely, if there is
any objection on the part of His Majesty's representatives it is better to learn it
in time than to wait for it to be raised afterwards.[15]

Close co-operation between the group and British officials was
henceforth maintained, so much so that the negotiations could be
described as a combined operation in which the Foreign Office was
very closely involved. When in June 1907 a further approach was made
to Chang, Hillier, who represented the corporation while Bland was
on home leave, was accompanied by Consul-General Fraser.

In the meantime, the possibility of Japanese participation in the
Hankow railway projects had been assessed by the British and French
governments. A share in the construction work had already been
reserved for Japan by Chang in the undertaking to Fraser. Now the
question of a place for Japanese interests in the financing of the trunk
line was considered, the matter first being raised by Cambon with
Grey in November 1906. The suggestion had come not from the
Japanese but from the French government. Japan, having failed to
raise an additional loan in London in 1906 because the market was in
difficulties through excessive lending abroad, had turned to Paris.
Pichon, foreign minister in the new Clemenceau Cabinet, had immediately seen opportunities—to establish closer relations with Japan
and to further the efforts of the Anglo-French railway partnership in
China, as well as to assist Russia in her difficult negotiations with
Japan for settlement of matters left over from the Treaty of Portsmouth. When Pichon knew that his overture for a political and
economic agreement had been welcomed in Tokyo, he asked Cambon

---

[15] FO 371/214, papers communicated by BCC, 18 Mar. 1907; Bland Papers, vol. 23,
box 1 (reel 15), Bland to Addis, 25 Apr. 1907.

to gauge reactions in political and financial circles in London. Cambon in his conversation with Grey apparently confined himself to the economic aspects, making the point that if Japan joined the railway partnership this might help in overcoming Chinese hesitation about taking up a foreign loan. At the same time the French group informed their British colleagues of the Japanese approach for access to the Paris market.[16]

It was certainly true that the Japanese were active in the Yangtze Valley, and that they were favoured by Chang. They had every intention of involving themselves in railway operations in the area. A Japanese railway engineer, Dr Haraguchi, had been attached to Chang since 1905, and the French proposal was carefully considered in Tokyo. When he was made aware by Jordan of the routes included in the Chinese Central Railways agreement, Hayashi, Japanese minister in Peking, advised that, as the lines the Anglo-French group were planning would be important economically, Japan must join it for the future development of her trade with China. There was also some suggestion from Haraguchi that in order to put themselves in a favourable position for a share in construction rights of the whole undertaking, the Japanese should encourage Chang to begin construction by Japanese enterprise as soon as possible of 50 to 100 miles of the Hankow–Szechwan line where it would be profitable. This, he recalled, was the method Japan had used in her early railway building, constructing the remunerative links between Tokyo and Yokohama and Kobe and Osaka initially in order to acquire funds and to encourage local lenders. Haraguchi thought that if this model was followed in Hupeh and Hunan it could produce a similar result.[17]

Then in April 1907 came two developments. First, Cambon withdrew the proposal for Japanese participation—even though Grey had immediately welcomed it on political grounds and had found that it was equally welcome to the British group in London, and discussions had taken place between the British and French groups on the share to be given to the Japanese. Grey made this clear to Cambon, who claimed that the British group was opposed to Japanese participation.

[16] *DDF* 2nd series, 10, no. 283, Pichon to P. Cambon, 16 Nov. 1906; FO 405/168, Grey to Bertie, 23 Nov. 1906. Bland Papers, vol. 23, box 1 (reel 15), Addis to Bland, 27 Feb. 1907.

[17] *NGB* vol. 56, Kurino to Foreign Ministry, 10 Nov. 1906; Foreign Ministry to Hayashi, 20 Nov. 1906; vol. 59, Jordan to Hayashi, 6 Jan. 1907, Hayashi to Foreign Ministry, 24 and 26 Jan. 1907, with enclosure.

This, Grey said, was by no means so. 'They did not think that Japan would help the company much financially but perhaps their co-operation might politically be useful. The English group had made an offer to their French partners as to the manner in which the shares should be divided if the Japanese were admitted.[18] The second development was a proposal for a loan from the Yokohama Specie Bank to Chang for railway construction. This seems to have resulted from the efforts of the Japanese minister in Peking who pressed successfully for Odagiri, agent of the Specie Bank, to be sent to Hankow, following hints from Chang of a wish to borrow from Japan.

Chang could see an opportunity of playing off the Japanese against the British and so obtaining better terms from them. Whether he approached the Japanese or they him is uncertain, but Hayashi and Odagiri were ready to seize the chance of installing Japanese interests in a favourable position. Their weakness, however, was lack of investment capital. The proposed loan was too large for the Specie Bank to handle itself, and Odagiri intended to bring in the Hongkong Bank and others and to issue the loan in the London market. Negotiations in London, however, came to nothing because the British side was not prepared to allow the Japanese to draw on British capital to finance a loan that would substitute Japanese for British preponderance in major railway projects. It is clear, too, that the British side, who kept their French partners informed of the approaches from Japan—as the French had kept them informed of Japanese activity in Paris in 1906— had no intention of approving a separate Anglo-Japanese arrangement for a railway loan to China that could not have been reconciled with the Anglo-French agreements. They were, however, most ready to allow the Japanese to underwrite any part they might wish of an Anglo-French loan. The Japanese government, on Grey's instruction, was officially made aware of Chang's pledge as well as of the Anglo-French partnership, and thereupon the Yokohama Specie Bank was instructed to retire from the business. In fact Takahashi, the director of the bank, who had been in negotiation in London and Paris for Japan's own financial needs, had on his return to Japan recalled Odagiri from Hankow. It would in any case have been impossible for the Specie Bank to have proceeded without the support of the London market, for it would not have been able to place more than a small proportion of the loan bonds in Tokyo. The Japanese intention, as it

---

[18] FO 371/226, Grey to Bertie, 3 Apr. 1907.

was now presented to the British, had always been limited. They had sought not financial participation but a place for the Specie Bank in the issuing of a railway loan for Chang's province as a matter of 'face'. What they were most anxious to secure was a share in the construction work in which, while making use of the Chinese labour available, they hoped to find employment for Japanese foremen. They did not wish to encroach on the British construction rights through the Chang–Fraser agreement of September 1905 now formally revealed to them.[19]

In announcing to Grey the withdrawal of the French proposal for Japanese participation, Cambon had given as the principal reason the fact that the Chinese were very much opposed to Japanese enterprise, and he therefore doubted whether Japanese participation would further the aims of the Anglo-French syndicate. It was certainly the case that Chinese feeling towards Japan had moved to hostility, yet it is open to question whether their participation would have been a hindrance in view of Chang's persistent inclination towards them. Moreover France continued to improve direct relations with Japan. The Paris market organized the loan sought by Japan, and in July 1907 came the Franco-Japanese agreement placing their relations on a firm basis—though it was badly received in China, where its terms were held to detract from China's sovereign power.[20]

Whatever were French motives for withdrawing the proposal for Japanese participation in the railway loan, there was no doubt of British readiness both on the part of the Foreign Office and of the financiers in London to admit them, and this was made plain to the Japanese. There was a coincidence here between general policy—the maintenance of cordial relations with Japan, increasingly essential in view of the European situation—and the special issue of Chinese railways. All hope of a railway system in southern China and the Yangtze Valley financed and constructed virtually entirely by British enterprise had been abandoned by the end of 1905. The admission of the Japanese, in what in any case would be a minor role because of their lack of capital for investment, would not threaten British preponderance in the undertaking, would strengthen the Anglo-Japanese

[19] FO 371/228, Jordan to Grey, 7, 11, 16 May 1907; Grey to Jordan, 13 May 1907; Lowther to Grey, 31 May, 10 July 1907; *NGB* vol. 59, Jordan to Hayashi, 24 May 1907, Midzuno (Yokohama Bank) to Hayashi, 11 May 1907; to Hillier (Hong Kong Bank) 1, 4, 6 July 1907; Hillier to Midzuno, 3 July 1907.

[20] See E. W. Edwards, 'The Far Eastern Agreements of 1907', *Journal of Modern History* 26 (1954), pp. 340–55.

alliance, and might have assisted in removing Chinese obstruction. At least that is how the situation seems to have been viewed in London. Grey had told Cambon that British financiers 'were very independent and it was not in the power of the government to influence them to any great extent'. This was a useful device for forestalling requests from foreign governments for pressure to be exerted on the City. The financiers engaged in Chinese business knew differently, as Addis continued to make clear to Bland. 'Our own governments are determined to support the Entente Cordiale and to use us for that purpose', he wrote in February 1907.[21] Grey was equally determined to preserve good relations with Japan, but he did not have to press the British group to admit the Japanese. He did not, however, attempt to modify the Hongkong Bank's refusal to allow the Yokohama Specie Bank to issue bonds in London for its projected loan to Chang Chih-tung, but this matter was so handled by the bank as not to offend Japanese susceptibilities.

The men on the spot were cool about the Japanese. In March 1906 Satow had warned Grey:

There seems to be an impression in England that because of the alliance we can count upon the Japanese to back us up in putting pressure upon the Chinese in relation to railway and mining concessions. I am inclined strongly to doubt this. Japan has entered into an alliance with us for certain definite objects,and we can rely with confidence upon the strict performance of her engagement, but outside of these undertakings she will not sacrifice her own interests or sympathies for our benefit. She proposes to secure as large a share of the trade in China as she can by all the contrivances she can think of. In regard to mines and railways Japan has never allowed the foreigner to get any footing at all . . . All this of set purpose to keep the control of the sources of wealth and means of communication in her own hands. She will not, I feel pretty sure, lend her aid even to an ally for the purpose of compelling the Chinese to accept the contrary system . . . While she cannot sympathise with the ownership of Chinese railways by foreign governments or companies she is nevertheless quite ready to obtain such privileges for herself as far as possible. In regard to China's territorial integrity and independence she values our alliance because it goes a long way in checking foreign aggression. It also secures her equality of opportunity in commercial matters and her proximity and other natural and acquired facilities will enable her to turn that opportunity to the best account. So we must not be under any illusion as to the alliance being of any economic advantage to us.

[21] Bland Papers, vol. 23, box 1 (reel 15), Addis to Bland, 20 Feb. 1907.

In July 1907 E. G. Hillier reported to the Hongkong Bank, following his visit to Hankow to attempt to open loan negotiations with Chang Chih-tung, on Japanese activity in the Yangtze Valley.

Of the forces which are working to shape the future of Hankow and of the upper Yangtze at the present moment none is more conspicuous or striking than the growing influence of the Japanese. There are said to be some 5000 Japanese in or about Wuchang. They are found at Changsha and at Ichang their flag is to be seen everywhere on the river and the Viceroy, strongly pro-Japanese in his sympathies, is surrounded by a ring of Japanese advisers whose influence is perceptible at every turn. Their distinct methods of business and their peculiar way of acquiring information separate them from other foreigners. That they have great ambitions in the Yangtze valley there can be no manner of doubt and their object seems to be to conquer as much by a process of absorption by numbers as by the ordinary competition of trade. They evidently have reason for attaching a great deal of importance to obtaining a share in the present railway scheme. They have no money to contribute but they have labour and they have materials and it is, therefore, obviously of the greatest importance to them to arrange if possible, that the loan with which the railways are to be built should carry with it no vexatious conditions likely to affect them in these fields of industry.

In 1905 Hillier's attitude towards Japanese participation had been favourable. The change in his views reflected a growing uneasiness among the British community in China as to Japan's ambitions. G. E. Morrison, up to 1905 strongly pro-Japanese, had by 1906 become as strongly hostile to them, and so had many of those who corresponded with him. Jordan, while thinking it tactically wise that Japan should be given some place in the railway loan, was clearly suspicious, and was gratified when the terms required by the British group led to the withdrawal of the Japanese proposals. These he had seen as an attempt at 'poaching in our preserves at Hankow', in which the Japanese aim was 'to get the construction of the railway into their own hands and only to make use of us as suppliers of the capital.'[22]

As the discussions with the Japanese were ending, the second direct approach to Chang Chih-tung, this time by Hillier, had failed. When Chang absolutely refused to agree to a joint Anglo-French loan the negotiations reached an impasse, for there was no question of the

[22] FO 800/44, Satow to Grey, 31 Mar. 1906; FO 371/228, Jordan to Grey, 25 July 1907, with enclosure, Hillier to Townsend (Hongkong Bank) 13 July 1907; FO 350/4, Jordan to Campbell, 30 May 1907; Lo, Hui-min (ed.) *The Correspondence of G. E. Morrison* (2 vols., Cambridge, 1976–8), I, pp. 356–436.

British divesting themselves of the French partnership, which on political and financial grounds was deemed indispensable. There emerged, however, the possibility of a way out, for in Kwangtung the viceroy seemed to be more amenable. The Canton–Kowloon agreement had been concluded in March 1907 on terms satisfactory to the British, and now the viceroy was ready to deal with the French and had applied to Casenave for a loan for the construction of the southern section of the Hankow–Canton railway, which would run through his territories. Casenave proposed that if the French took responsibility for this section, the northern section through Chang's provinces could be financed by British capital, and thus the deadlock would be broken. An alternative suggestion was made by the Hongkong Bank to the Banque de l'Indo-Chine: that the negotiations at Hankow be conducted solely by the British, the French participating '*en sous-main*'.

It would become evident that both proposals would meet strong opposition. The second, though apparently acceptable to the French group, was rapidly rejected by the French government. A secondary role for France, Grey was told, was not acceptable. That was not the form in which what would be the first operation of the Anglo-French railway entente had been envisaged in France. It was inadmissible, the French note added, that a high Chinese functionary should be ready to accept British capital and refuse French, especially when the loan was of an official nature and supported by the imperial guarantee.

The French government would insist upon the maintenance of the principle of equal participation, as promised in the London agreements. For France, clearly, it was a matter of national prestige as well as of economic advantage. But economic advantage was not neglected, for France looked to more than a financial participation in the two projected trunk lines, the Hankow–Szechwan and the Hankow–Canton. Cambon made it clear that France intended to share in the construction and supply of materials and in the management and operation of the lines.[23]

As for the first proposal, to which the French memorandum made no reference, it was strongly contested by the Colonial Office, where the inclusion of the French in the Hankow–Canton project on any basis had always been disliked and Chang's opposition to them foreseen. The new suggestion, that the southern section should be built by

[23] FO 371/228, Jordan to Grey, 17 and 22 June 1907; Cambon to Grey, 26 June 1907.

French capital was 'especially objectionable ... the Hong Kong government could not view with equanimity the prospect of the line from Canton northwards being controlled even partially by French engineers', so much so that though the line was expected to benefit the trade of Hong Kong significantly, the Colonial Office felt delay in its construction to be a price worth paying to prevent French control.

In face of this situation, with French insistence on the full bond and the Colonial Office's opposition, Grey was in no doubt as to the course to be adopted. At a time when he was apprehensive of the cordiality manifested in Franco-German relations, he judged it essential to do nothing to irritate the French. The Colonial Office was informed that 'there can be no question of repudiating their claim for equal participation', though it was accepted that building of the southern section by them would be objectionable. It was also accepted that the French claim to extend participation to the operation of the railway could not be admitted, and Cambon was informed that in the British view any further attempt to force Chang to take a joint Anglo-French loan would not succeed. Since it was felt that there was no likelihood that Chang would obtain a loan from other European sources on the loosely defined terms on which he was insisting, the best course was to leave the matter in abeyance. This was accepted by the French and relations between the two sides remained cordial, the French expressing gratitude at the loyalty shown by their British partners in keeping them informed of the approaches made by the Japanese for an Anglo-Japanese loan to Chang.[24]

Attention was now concentrated in securing final loan contracts for two other lines, the Tientsin–Pukow and the Soochow–Ningpo, for which preliminary agreements had been signed in 1899. The first of these was an international concern. Initially it had been a joint venture between the Deutsch-Asiatische Bank and the British and Chinese Corporation in which the British share was the portion of the line from the Shantung border to Pukow, about one-third of the whole. With the formation of Chinese Central Railways the corporation's interest had passed to the new company, and the subsequent Anglo-French agreement had brought in the French. British policy had been to mark time on the Tientsin–Pukow line and to concentrate on the Soochow–Ningpo scheme, a solely British project of importance in

[24] FO 371/214, Colonial Office to FO, 10 July 1907; FO to Colonial Office, 25 July 1907; FO to Geoffray (French Embassy), 17 Sept. 1907.

Yangtze Valley communications, which was meeting determined provincial opposition.

Now, after some pressure from Chinese Central Railways, the Foreign Office agreed to push both lines. Negotiations for the Tientsin–Pukow contract were in the summer of 1907 largely in the hands of Cordes, the Deutsch-Asiatische Bank's agent. This was the consequence of Bland's return on leave to Britain. The Foreign Office had been consulted by the British group as to the advisability of Bland's leave, an indication of the very close official oversight of railway negotiation. Jordan approved Bland's departure only with misgivings. He feared, despite the entire confidence that Chinese Central Railways placed in Cordes, that the Germans, who unlike the British had no more contracts to negotiate, would take the opportunity of Bland's absence to ingratiate themselves with the Chinese by accepting conditions for the loan that would leave the lenders less control than was desirable. This in fact was what occurred.[25] Though belatedly the already heavily burdened Hillier was deputed to replace Bland temporarily, Cordes concluded a draft agreement on terms much more accommodating to the Chinese than the British thought wise. This determined the shape of the final loan agreement signed on 13 January 1908.

The Tientsin–Pukow agreement marked an important advance by the Chinese, for it was much more responsive to their views on the vital question of lenders' control than agreements made hitherto—the most recent example being that concluded for the Canton–Kowloon line by Bland on behalf of the British and Chinese Corporation in March 1907. When the preliminary agreement for the Tientsin–Pukow line had been made in 1899, the loan had been secured by a mortgage on the railway and provision that the lenders were to work the line during the currency of the loan. The final agreement, in contrast, firmly established Chinese control. Security for the loan was now to be the *likin* and internal revenues of three provinces the railway traversed, not the line itself. The chief engineers were still to be British and German, but their appointment was to be in the hands of the Chinese government. The Canton–Kowloon agreement, on the

[25] FO 371/225, Jordan to Grey, 6 Aug. 1907; Chinese Central Railways to FO, 8 Aug. 1907; FO 350/4, Jordan to Campbell, 25 July 1907; Bland Papers, vol. 23, box 1 (reel 15) Addis to Bland, 27 Feb. 1907; Bland to Addis, 10 Aug. and 10 Sept. 1907. On the Soochow–Ningpo loan see E-tu Zen Sun, pp. 61–8 and M. Chi, 'Shanghai–Hang-chow–Ningno Railway Loan', *Modern Asian Studies* 7 (1973), pp. 85–106.

other hand, had conceded less to the new spirit in China. In particular the practice of securing the loan by a mortgage on the railway had been preserved.[26]

The contrast was plain. Cordes had acted shrewdly in German interests. The Tientsin–Pukow agreement was to be an important step in their efforts to improve their relations with China. For some years Germany had been looked upon with suspicion in Peking, the consequence of her policy in Shantung and during the Boxer Rising. But, as Jordan had noted, the very fact of Germany's political isolation as the other powers with interests in China were drawing together had gone some way to restore her position in the eyes of the Chinese. As the network of agreements linking Britain, France, Russia, and Japan expanded, Germany, outside the group, benefited in China, and Cordes had now added to her standing and opened the way for a further advance.

[26] MacMurray, 1, pp. 615–27; 684–92, cf. Lee En-Han, *China's Quest for Railway Autonomy, 1904–1911* (Singapore, 1977), pp. 160–8, 178–83. Lee claims that the terms of the Canton–Kowloon contract did give the Chinese authorities a significant role in management of the line but agrees that the Tientsin–Pukow settlement was much more favourable to them. He implies that the British group was content with the terms negotiated by Cordes for the Tientsin–Pukow contract. This was not so.

6

The Origins of the China Consortium

UNEASINESS on the British side as to the possibility of a German bid for the Hankow–Canton loan was perhaps one factor in the re-opening of discussions with the French, early in 1908, to find a solution to the problems caused by Chang's refusal to deal with an Anglo-French combination, and the insistence of the French government, but not the French banks, upon full equality for France in the negotiations. As early as July 1907, just after Cordes had negotiated the draft Tientsin–Pukow agreement, Chang had suggested to Hillier that German capital should be introduced into a Hankow–Canton railway loan. In February 1908, Bland reported that Chang had threatened to turn to the Germans. Bland and Casenave advocated negotiation by the British alone as the only way to overcome the obstacle presented by Chang's refusal to accept the French as parties in a transaction arising from an undertaking that he had given solely to the British. Jordan took a similar view of the chances of German competition and the tactics necessary to defeat it.[1]

The British group, well aware of the French incubus and of the danger that the Deutsch-Asiatische Bank might bid for the Hankow–Canton business, saw an opportunity of easing the situation when the matter of a redemption loan for the Peking–Hankow line became active. The Chinese authorities, for political and financial reasons, were anxious to have complete control of this important and profitable railway. The Peking–Hankow line was a going concern, but 20 per cent of its profits went to the Franco-Belgian Société d'étude de chemins de fer en Chine, which had constructed the line and had control over the appointment of staff and supply of materials. Under the original contract of 1898, redemption was allowed after 1 September 1907. A loan to China for this purpose was doubly attractive to British interests; as a business enterprise that would bring prestige

[1] FO 371/228, Jordan to Grey, 9 July 1907; FO 371/422, Jordan to Grey, 15 Feb. 1908; Addis to FO, 25 Feb. 1908.

and profit, and as a reversal of the bitterly resented triumph of the Société d'étude in gaining the contract in 1898. The Hongkong Bank from the first saw the securing of the loan as important in relation to its position as the leading foreign bank in China, and Hillier had been seeking the business for the bank on its own account since the summer of 1907. The Société d'étude was also seeking the loan. The situation promised rivalry to the advantage of the Chinese, but to the disadvantage of Chinese Central Railways and particularly of the Banque de l'Indo-Chine, which was not a partner in the French element in the Société d'étude.

The French government had for long been dissatisfied at the limited role in the Société d'étude to which the dominant Belgian group had confined their French partners, and by early 1908 had decided to support participation of Chinese Central Railways in the redemption loan and to work against the Société d'étude.[2] Its aim was to secure a contract ensuring that the rights of supplying materials and appointing personnel to the railway staff should be entirely in the hands of the French group within Chinese Central Railways. A proposal on these lines, which admitted as a *quid pro quo* a similar position for the British in the Hankow–Canton line, was put to Addis on behalf of the French group in February 1908. This came just at the time when Chang Chih-tung threatened to turn to the Germans unless the British made definite proposals for the Hankow–Canton line that would exclude direct French interests and contain no stipulation as to the provision of materials.

Addis reported these developments to the Foreign Office, where it was agreed that the French proposal entirely disregarded present conditions in China in railway business. Continuing control over supply of materials was an understandable aim of the French, whose prices were well above the level of competitors and who knew that in a free market they would be seriously damaged, but it was now an unrealistic demand. Addis discussed the matter in Paris with Simon, and on 24 February reached an agreement that was approved by Caillaux as minister of finance. This provided that Bland was to negotiate by himself the conditions of the Hankow–Canton loan, and to sign the agreement on behalf of the corporation alone. There would be, however, a supplementary clause to which it was understood that the Chinese government would agree, stating that the French group

[2] Kurgan-van Hentenryk, *Leopold II*, pp. 737–48.

should be admitted to a half share. As to the Peking–Hankow redemption loan, it was proposed that the groups should combine to negotiate either together or separately, and that the French group should occupy the same position in this agreement as should be occupied by the British in the Hankow–Canton agreement. This provision related to indirect advantages accruing from loan contracts—appointment of personnel and orders for material. While China would have freedom to choose personnel and to place orders, the British group would not contest a special place for France; and the French would observe a similar detachment in the Hankow–Canton business. It seems that Caillaux was not prepared to accept this part of the agreement unreservedly because it was decided after some discussion to leave it for settlement by the British and French governments.

In fact neither government raised objection. Indeed in the Foreign Office satisfaction was registered, and with reason, at Addis's success. In the ensuing months, while the Hankow–Canton business remained dormant, negotiations for the Peking–Hankow loan proceeded but not as smoothly as the partners had envisaged. It was to cause serious problems for Addis but his handling of the difficulties considerably enhanced his standing at the Foreign Office, which he kept well informed of the negotiations. Following his return from Paris in February he had a long interview with Grey, and by September 1908 when the Peking–Hankow business was moving to its climax he noted, 'I am at the F.O. almost daily'.[3]

The root of the matter was the question of supply and operating rights. The Chinese were determined that the railway should pass entirely into their hands. They would not accept a tied loan that would leave some share in control to the lenders. Failing to secure the assent of the Société d'étude to such terms—for supply of materials that would bring orders to their industry was the main reason for Belgian involvement in railway enterprise in China—they turned to the Hongkong Bank, which had indicated its interest in the business. The situation opened the likelihood of a purely financial loan free from any ties. The bank, though reluctantly, was prepared, on grounds of prestige, to take the loan on this basis. The Foreign Office was similarly unhappy at the prospect of a financial loan, but Campbell was cautious towards Addis's suggestion that there should be official

---

[3] FO 371/422, Addis to FO, 20 and 25 Feb. 1908; Grey to Bertie, 4 Apr. 1908; Addis Papers, Diary, 25, 26 Feb., 17 Sept. 1908.

insistence in Peking that if the bank dropped the loan it should not be placed elsewhere. Addis, however, following further discussion, did decide to press the Chinese for a statement linking the loan to the Peking–Hankow railway. This, if it could be secured, would still be no more than a face-saving concession in what would remain a financial loan, free from all the supplementary benefits to the lenders that in the past had been attached to railway loans but which, as the Tientsin–Pukow settlement had demonstrated, were less and less likely to be conceded by the Chinese. Jordan had seen the signs clearly. The days of the British and Chinese Corporation, he told Campbell, were numbered.

The choice lies between adapting our methods to Chinese requirements or abandoning railway construction to our rivals. Cordes has shown them what the Germans are prepared to do. So long as the terms offered are such as to satisfy the financial world at home I do not think we should be justified in retarding railway construction by demanding more in the interests of any individual corporation. At any rate public opinion out here demands railways to promote trade.[4]

The lines along which the Peking–Hankow negotiation was likely to proceed were not pleasing to either of the associates of the bank— the British and Chinese Corporation and Chinese Central Railways— who saw the loss of profits to be drawn from operating rights and commission on supply. Additionally for the French there was the sacrifice without return of the benefits they had looked for from the Addis–Simon agreement, for without a stipulation in the loan contract the Chinese would buy railway supplies in cheaper markets than France. Moreover there would be the loss of French presence in an important railway.

Acrimony soon developed within the British group, with Addis, as the bank's representative, finding himself assailed by some of his co-directors; and in China between Hillier and Bland. The central issue was the assertion of the bank against its partners that it was in no way bound to limit its freedom in negotiating a financial loan with the Chinese government for any purpose whatever, provided that it did not include the financing or construction of public works accompanied by conditions of supervision and supply of material. Its agreement with the British and Chinese Corporation, it maintained,

[4] FO 371/422, memorandum by Campbell, 8 Sept. 1908; Addis to FO, 22 Sept. 1908; FO 350/5, Jordan to Campbell, 6 Aug. 1908.

was specifically for this class of business. In respect of it the bank considered itself bound to assist and further the interests of the corporation so long as the Chinese were prepared to accept those conditions. The opposing view argued that if the policy of financial loans were adopted and the Chinese were able to borrow money for railway construction (though that purpose would not be avowed) without restriction as to the way in which the money would be employed and without supervision by independent agents of the lender, the further existence of the corporation would lose its justification. Moreover, purely financial loans meant loss of construction rights and therefore of control over purchase of supplies through nomination of the chief engineers, a matter of concern to British and French industrialists.

The issue came to a head in July 1908 and seriously worried Addis. As spokesman of the bank, which recognized the objections to financial loans, he maintained that circumstances in China sometimes made it imperative to offer loans free of ties. Failing this, the bank's position would be at risk. Opinion within the bank hierarchy was that if China wished to raise loans nominally for general purposes and could offer suitable security, she could easily get the money. The bank could not afford to remain 'out of the picture' because of the interests of the corporation and Chinese Central Railways. Bland, who was in London in the autumn of 1908, was strongly opposed to financial loans and saw himself as the defender of investors in the corporation. He made his views known in the Foreign Office to Campbell and to Tyrrell, Grey's private secretary, and also made two visits to Paris to win support. He found Caillaux of similar views to his own but Simon of the Banque de l'Indo-Chine took Addis's position, saying that his bank would not give any undertaking binding it not to do any business that the Chinese might offer.[5]

There certainly seems to have been reason for the Hongkong Bank to fear competitors for the loan. Addis and Hillier felt that they were fighting a battle of vital importance for their bank. To secure the redemption loan business would be a significant advance. To lose it to the Belgians, who were still in the field as serious contenders with backing from two British banks, Schroders and Martins, would be a heavy blow to its standing in the Far East. Neither the Hongkong

---

[5] Bland Papers, vol. 23, box 1 (reel 15), Bland to Addis, 7 June 1908; to Macrae 30 Oct. 1908; to Rutherford Harris, 24 Nov. 1908; vol. 24, box 11 (reel 16), Landale to Bland, 1 July 1908; BCC to Bland, 28 Aug. 1908; Jamieson to Bland, 23 Dec. 1908; vols. 32 (reel 24), Diary, 5, 9, 12, 17 Sept., 5 Oct. 1908.

Bank nor the Banque de l'Indo-Chine wished for an untied loan, but Addis was determined that come what may, the Hongkong Bank should not only not be excluded but should have the leading role. He envisaged an international loan and was ready to admit the Banque de l'Indo-Chine to share in the issue (though not in the negotiations), but would have gone ahead without it. Since the loan would clearly have to be 'financial', he was committed under the agreement of 1895 to offer participation to the Deutsch-Asiatische Bank. This prospect was an additional cause of anger to the French government but was fortunately disposed of quickly because the German bankers, their market short of investment capital, declined. 'This was just what we wanted', noted Addis, 'and it was a double coup to get over and without friction and indeed with gratitude for our consideration in making the offer.'

The Chinese exploited the situation, playing off the Anglo-French group against the Société d'étude. Hillier, instructed that the Hong-kong Bank could not afford to let the business go out of its hands, had to agree to a Chinese government loan of £5 million with no more safeguard for the application of its proceeds than a clause tying the bulk to railway redemption, and at a price very favourable to the Chinese. Security for the loan was to rest in specified provincial revenues, not in the Peking–Hankow line itself. Moreover, the banks had to undertake not to interfere in future with the affairs of the railway.[6] To secure money on such terms, with no element of control over the railway in the hands of the lenders, was an unprecedented success for the Chinese and a clear warning to the foreign banks of a China able in the presence of competing financial suitors to free herself from the detested shackles hitherto imposed on her freedom. For the banks, anxious for business but aware that in present conditions China might outrun its credit and endanger trade and interests, there were serious reasons for restoration of a situation in which precautions could be taken through controls to ensure that the money of foreign investors was not dissipated by Chinese authorities. Following upon the Tientsin–Pukow agreement, the Peking–Hankow loan must have impressed upon the Hongkong Bank and the Banque de l'Indo-Chine the damaging effect of competition for loan contracts;

[6] FO 371/422, Jordan to Grey, 25 Sept.; Addis to FO, 26 Sept. 1908; Addis Papers, Diary, 7 July 1908; Lee, En-han, pp. 217–23; E-tu Zen Sun, pp. 137–40; MacMurray, 1, pp. 747–51.

for in the present climate in China where officials were responding to the rights recovery movement, it was plain that every opportunity to secure financial loans would be exploited.

The Anglo-French combination had secured the Peking–Hankow business, and the Hongkong Bank had preserved its leading position in Chinese finance, but the affair had left bitterness behind it in Paris. The bankers, as Bland discovered, understood why Addis had agreed to a financial loan

When I appealed to the French group, Bankers and 'Industrialists' together, to support the policy of the B & C and to bring pressure to bear on the H & S Bank there was absolutely no hesitation on the part of Simon and the other financiers there present. They said they were entirely of Addis's opinion as far as giving any assurance to the industrialists on future loans to China that if the market would take a loan they could not afford to lose opportunities . . .

The French government, however, under pressure from industrialists for tied loans, which were particularly important to them because of the uncompetitive prices of French materials in a free market, was less understanding of the bankers' position. In September, Caillaux had been quite definite about not going into the loan on Addis's terms, and equally clear that if the Hongkong Bank went on its own way there would be serious political complications. He had had to accept the situation but had done so most reluctantly, for the French had counted on retaining at least residual advantages in the Peking–Hankow enterprise.[7]

The leading British railway contractors, Pauling and Co., who had been unsuccessfully seeking business in China for some time, were also disturbed by the Hongkong Bank policy in negotiating for financial loans, which they felt meant the abandonment of any attempt to direct construction contracts into British and French hands. They did have an 'effective if somewhat indefinite' understanding with the British and Chinese Corporation for mutual assistance when reasonably possible in their respective spheres of operation, and in September 1908 had sought to recast it in more precise terms. The corporation agreed in principle, but while entirely in favour of an arrangement whereby railway loans they arranged should provide for construction by contract through Pauling's, they refused to bind

---

[7] Bland Papers, vol. 23, box 1 (reel 15), Bland to Harris, 24 Nov. 1908; vols 32 and 33, (reel 24), Diary, 9 Sept. 1908.

themselves on the point—an indication of the victory Addis had won for the Hongkong Bank's freedom of action in the battle within the corporation.

Addis's policy had certainly aroused opposition from those who felt that he had been guided too much by narrow regard for the interest of the bank. In the Foreign Office, however, there was no criticism of him. He had kept in close touch throughout with the department, though the redemption loan was not a matter covered by the Anglo-French agreement of 1905. Clearly any question in which the French government was involved was regarded as politically sensitive, and Addis had secured official approval in advance of the line he proposed to take with the French. He was felt to have done well in difficult circumstances. The loan, even if untied, was judged to be a gain in the general interests of the British position in China as well as of the Hongkong Bank. It had taken an important railway out of the hands of the Franco-Belgian group that had built it; and as Jordan pointed out, though it was regrettable that the Chinese had successfully resisted controls, contracts for materials would now be open to the British market 'and that is a great gain'. In the Far Eastern Department, Addis's policy of primacy for the bank had done him no harm. He had successfully adjusted the British financial arm to meet a changing situation, and his standing was high. 'The correspondence enclosed', Alston minuted on a record of the negotiations, 'reflects great credit for lucidity and diplomacy on our friend Mr Addis', and Campbell added, 'He is a very good man.' Official satisfaction was more tangibly expressed by an invitation to Addis from the governor of the Bank of England at the suggestion of the government to accept appointment as British censor of the State Bank of Morocco. This meant little in material terms, but as Sir Thomas Jackson, the doyen of the Hong-kong Bank hierarchy, told Addis, it was 'a very great compliment not only to yourself but to the Bank'.[8]

The Peking–Hankow redemption loan agreement was signed on 8 October 1908. By this time there were indications that the Chinese authorities—perhaps encouraged by their success in the redemption loan—were ready to open negotiations for the Hankow–Canton loan. They had already begun construction financed by local funds. By May 1908, eighty miles of track were under construction in Kwangtung and

---

[8] FO 350/5, Jordan to Campbell, 1 Oct. 1908; FO 371/422, Jordan to Grey, 11 Oct. 1908, with minutes; Addis Papers, Diary, 16 and 18 Dec. 1908.

the first twenty-four miles were open to traffic. The work was directed by a Chinese chief engineer with a team of subordinates of various nationalities. 'The line' it was reported, 'is well-built ... The engineers working under Kwang all seem to consider him a thoroughly good man. They recognize however that he has enormous difficulties to contend with through having a Board of Directors over him utterly ignorant of railway construction but all wanting to interfere with him and all suspecting him of making money over contracts etc.' Here, no doubt, is one reason why the central government, anxious to see the railway completed, wished to take trunk lines out of provincial control. Chang Chih-tung had been appointed to Peking as administrator-general with control of the whole Hankow–Canton project in his hands in July 1908, and in October he indicated to Hillier that he was ready to borrow.[9]

Because of the need to place the redemption loan, it was not until the end of December that discussions opened. Then Chang, fulfilling the 1905 undertaking to make the first offer to British interests, indicated his proposals to Bland as representative of the British and Chinese Corporation for a loan of £3 million for construction of the Hupeh and Hunan sections of the railway. From these it was immediately evident that if the obstacle of the French 'presence' had been removed, another had now emerged. What Chang wanted was a loan on terms similar to those for the Peking–Hankow redemption and Tientsin–Pukow contracts, with no suggestion of financial supervision or administrative control by the bondholders, and with security resting in the *likin* revenues of Hupeh so that neither the railway nor its earnings were pledged for the service of the loan. Construction of the line was to be under engineers already engaged by the viceroy of Hukuang on the recommendation of Consul-General Fraser. Financial supervision, however desirable in the interests of the bondholders, was, Chang stressed, an impossible condition in face of the determined opposition of gentry and people. The successful flotation of the Peking–Hankow loan, he argued, proved the complete confidence of foreign investors in Chinese railway administration.

Bland made it plain that the corporation was not prepared to lend on Peking–Hankow terms, which had related to a line already in existence; for a new line it was essential that investors should be assured either of efficient construction by well-known contractors, or

[9] FO 371/432, Jordan to Grey, 13 May 1908; E-tu Zen Sun, pp. 98–100.

effective supervision of finances and construction by British employees of good standing. As this seemed unwelcome, he thought a construction contract was the only immediate solution. It was unreasonable, he added, to suggest that British and French funds would be forthcomning unconditionally and for the possible benefit of manufacturers of other nationalities without privilege or benefit of the country supplying the capital; under no circumstances could China obtain such terms in any quarter.

The interview ended with both parties undertaking to make rough drafts of their respective proposals, and with a meaningful stress by Chang on the presence in Peking of representatives of German, Japanese, and Belgian financial groups. 'There would appear to be little room for doubt', Bland noted, 'that these gentlemen have been invited to take an interest in the business with a view to stimulating competition.'[10]

Chang, in fact, lost no time in making contact with the German group. In mid-January 1909, the Deutsch-Asiatische Bank informed the Hongkong Bank that they had been approached for a loan of £3 million for railway purposes. Aware that the Hongkong Bank was already negotiating the matter and desirous of avoiding competition, they now asked for participation. When this was rejected on the grounds that under the 1898 agreement between the groups, the railway concerned (the Hankow–Canton) fell within the British sphere, the Germans—arguing that the loan requested, being for railway purposes and not for a railway concession proper, was in fact within the terms of the agreement of 1895 between the two banks—threatened to go their own way if the participation to which they claimed to be entitled was refused them. The threat was serious. Indications were that Germany was preparing a major advance in her economic interests in China. By the end of January the German group had denounced the loose 1898 agreement that had limited their railway sphere to the Hoangho Valley and Shantung—a sign, Addis informed the Foreign Office, of an apparent determination to gain a footing both in the Yangtze Valley and in southern China.

The Germans were well prepared. Jordan judged them more efficient than the British and Chinese Corporation for business with the Chinese; more of them spoke the language. He was to tell Campbell in June 1909:

[10] Addis Papers, memorandum by Bland of his interview with Chang Chih-tung, 24 Dec. 1908; E-tu Zen Sun, pp. 101–2.

To me, it seems strange how our big business establishments have continued to ignore the language. Even the Hongkong Bank has still only one man—Hillier—who is competent to transact business with a Chinese official. He is a host in himself but the neglect seems almost criminal . . . Our people will have to bestir themselves a bit if they mean to keep pace with the Germans in the industrial race in China . . .

Further, the Germans were now well provided with the sinews of financial war. In 1908 Germany had been compelled for financial reasons to decline participation in the Peking–Hankow loan. Now money for investment was abundant. Germany, Addis warned the French group, 'is now in a position to make an effective bid for the industrial advantages in China by which she sets such store.' How was the German challenge to be met? One method was competition, which would probably secure the loan and the construction rights for the Anglo-French group but on terms that for the banks would not make them worth the having. This was what Addis wished to avoid—a situation in which in order to preserve construction rights under Chang's pledge of September 1905, the British and French would have to sacrifice profits in order to outbid competition for the loan.[11]

From the first, the inclination in London was towards compromise. 'In my opinion', Campbell advised, 'the best thing will be for the British, French, and German groups to come to an agreement as to the terms to be offered and all stick to those terms and share the loan and not by competing with one another to allow the Chinese to obtain the loan on ruinous terms.' This view, no doubt formulated in discussions with Addis, was accepted by Grey. 'Our attitude', he told Bertie, the British ambassador in Paris, was correctly defined by Addis as 'one of reluctant acquiescence.'

We have a great interest in the Canton–Hangchow (sic) Railway loan for which we are bound to stand up, because the Hong Kong colony advanced the money to China to repurchase the Railway concession, in the expectation that we should secure a considerable share of the construction. I was informed that there was a great danger that, if the Germans were not allowed to participate the Anglo-French group might lose the loan altogether. I therefore agreed that, if necessary, rather than risk the loss of the whole loan, and any share in the construction of the railway, German participation should be admitted.[12]

---

[11] FO 371/622, Grey to Jordan, 13, 15, 19 Jan. 1909; memorandum from Addis, 30 Jan. 1909; FO 350/5, Jordan to Campbell, 7 June 1909.
[12] FO 371/622, minute by Campbell on Jordan to Grey, 21 Jan. 1909; FO 800/51, Grey to Bertie, 1 Feb. 1909.

The British attitude reflected the general trend of official thinking on major economic issues in China since 1895. A preference for
compromise rather than competition had been evident in the
Foreign Office in the discussions over the first indemnity loan, when
the official view had favoured an international agreement against
the Hongkong Bank's pressure for a purely British loan. The battle
for concessions had been forced on Salisbury, though once entered
upon it was vigorously pursued and of course was popular with
the British community in China. In the initial phase the bank
(despite its agreement of 1895 with the Deutsch-Asiatische group)
became competitive on national lines—certainly in railway matters,
as indicated by its part in the formation of the British and Chinese
Corporation, one motive for which was its desire to free itself
from railway aspects of the 1895 agreement. The distaste of the
London capital market for Chinese loans modified zeal for a purely
national policy. By 1905 the Foreign Office and the bank, as a
response to the lack of British investment capital and the situation in
China, as well as, in the case of the Foreign Office, to the needs of
general policy, moved to accept the French partnership in a realistic
settlement; but there was no enthusiasm for it on the part of Addis or
of Jordan.

The experience of the Peking–Hankow loan, however, changed
Addis's attitude. Hillier in 1907 had twice urged the Hongkong Bank
to combine with the Banque de l'Indo-Chine and the Deutsch-
Asiatische Bank to negotiate with the support of their governments a
major international loan to provide for the Peking–Hankow re-
demption and the building of the Hankow–Canton and Hankow–
Szechwan lines. Addis, like Jordan, had been unsympathetic, as was
Morrison when Addis discussed the proposals with him in
November 1907. Addis had then thought London already sufficiently
entangled with German agreements. He felt that the weight of
French and German influence had been declining while that of
Britain had been increasing. 'I am therefore on general grounds
opposed to further continental amalgamations, by which it seems to
me, we have much to lose and little to gain', he told Bland. The
French connection had been hampering Britain over the Hankow–
Canton business, and Addis seems to have felt that the Foreign
Office was using the British group for political ends. Jordan's view
was similar. Presented by Campbell with the importance of the
entente cordiale and the necessity of fostering its growth even at the

expense of railway advantages he confessed, 'It is not always easy for the man on the spot to "think imperially" '.[13]

There was another aspect of the Peking–Hankow negotiations, which now influenced Addis's mind towards combination—the danger that the Hongkong Bank would encounter competitors for Chinese business among British as well as foreign rivals. Schroders and Martins banks had been involved in discussion with the Société d'étude, and the signs were that there was now no shortage of capital in London for investment in China. The Hongkong Bank issued three loans in 1908—the Tientsin–Pukow, the Shanghai–Ningpo, and the Peking–Hankow—all of which were well subscribed. The success of the last of these was especially significant: not only did it allow the lender no control over the railway, but it was issued in October 1908 just as the Bosnian crisis opened. Despite Addis's fears that the market would be adversely affected by the European situation, the loan was fully covered. The prospects were disquieting for the type of business—the more or less tied loan—for which the British and Chinese Corporation and Chinese Central Railways were designed and to which, through commissions on purchasing and participation in railway operation during the duration of a loan, they looked for profits. The bank's view at the end of 1908 was explained to Bland, the vehement defender of the tied loan. Both the Hongkong Bank and the Banque de l'Indo-Chine, he was informed by George Jamieson of the board of Chinese Central Railways, would be prepared to tell China straight that railway loans were the business of the British and Chinese Corporation and the Central Railways if there were no other competitors in the field,

but the difficulty is with the British public—money is a drug in the market and is likely to be so for some time. The British public are grabbing at fresh issues and Chinese loans in particular, and what Addis is afraid of is that if they tell the Chinese plump down that they will do no more loans on the basis of the Anglo-French redemption loan, the Chinese may say very well we will go else-where, and he has reason to think—or says so at least—that there are in fact two or three London houses in the field. He believes they might in the present temper of the money market bring out a Chinese loan over the Bank's head and this is a possibility the Bank could not tolerate . . . I mention this as show-ing the Bank's difficulty. They honestly want us to get the business but they cannot afford to let it go by them.[14]

---

[13] Bland Papers, vol. 23, box 1 (reel 15), Addis to Bland, 2 Dec. 1907; FO 350/5, Jordan to Campbell, 20 Aug. 1908; Morrison Diary (reel 236), 23 Nov. 1907.

[14] Bland Papers, vol. 24, box 11 (reel 16), Jamieson to Bland, 23 Dec. 1908.

In 1907 Grey had accepted Jordan's unfavourable judgement on Hillier's proposals for a three-bank international combination. Now in the Foreign Office there was no disagreement as to the best way to meet the German threat. The Colonial Office, an interested party because of the importance to it of a Hankow–Canton line connected to Kowloon, was informed on 27 January 1909 that the association of the British, French, and German groups was the most effective means to preserve British rights under the Fraser–Chang agreement of September 1905 to the provision of engineers and material, which could fall to the ground if a foreign group were to secure the loan. Addis's plan was to negotiate a financial loan, with the Hongkong Bank replacing the corporation in order to preserve construction rights by separating the two aspects, construction and finance. Retention of these rights he saw as essential, and a solely financial transaction was not in his mind. But a separate financial loan could bring in the Deutsch-Asiatische Bank under the agreement of 1895. He obtained advance approval in principle from Simon of the Banque de l'Indo-Chine to the admission of the Germans, though what Simon had in mind was a *entente générale* for all railway loans, which would put the groups in a stronger position in relation to the Chinese, and then notified the Germans of his proposal to which they had agreed. This would involve a diminution of the Hongkong Bank's share of the loan in order to secure the construction rights for Britain.[15]

Before the scheme was put to the Colonial Office, Addis had already set off for Paris and Berlin, first to get the assent of the French and then to lay it before the German group. Its basis was stated in three clauses:

1. The loan agreement was to be negotiated by Hillier alone and to be signed on behalf of the Hongkong Bank alone.
2. The three banks should share the loan in equal proportions.
3. The French and German banks were to agree not to take any action to prejudice the preferential rights of the British group to the appointment of engineers and to the supply of materials in virtue of the Anglo–Chinese agreement of 1905.

Addis had clearly anticipated difficulty in securing German assent to an agreement that would give them no share in the coveted construction rights, though he had already been assured that the

[15] FO 371/622, FO to Colonial Office, 27 Jan. 1909; Addis to Townsend, 26 Jan. 1909; Addis Papers, memorandum from French group, 25 Jan. 1909.

German groups were ready to agree to a threefold division of the loan to include the French. In the event he found the major obstacle to be in Paris—not from the French group, which had accepted German participation in advance for an *entente générale*, but from the French government.

Clauses 1 and 3 of Addis's draft caused no trouble. The 'stone of stumbling', as he put it, was Clause 2. The French group was now ready to accept admission of the Germans *ad hoc* as Addis proposed; the French government refused to agree to an isolated German participation confined to the Hankow–Canton loan. But following a meeting of the French Cabinet, Addis was informed by Caillaux that 'if the scope of the British proposal were extended to embrace an English–French–German *entente générale* for the whole of China (and possibly elsewhere) he might reconsider his decision'.

It may well have been that the attitude of Caillaux, who had links with the French group, was motivated by a wish to ensure for French finance in China an entry into the association between the Hongkong and the Deutsch-Asiatische Banks. In view of the atmosphere in China it was increasingly likely that future railway transactions would be on the basis not of construction contracts but of loans 'for railway purposes' (i.e. financial loans), and would thus come under the 1895 agreement entitling the two banks to share in each other's contracts. By admitting the Germans into the Hankow–Canton loan, the British group would not be making a major sacrifice because they would be able to claim reciprocal treatment from the Germans in future. But the French, if the Hankow–Canton admission were to be *ad hoc*, would make a concession without any guarantee of recompense from the German group in future. A general entente, which was certainly desired by the French group as well as by the French government, promised to safeguard their position. The proposal, however, was beyond Addis's competence to discuss. He then went on to Berlin—not, as he had anticipated, to negotiate an agreement, 'but as an act of courtesy and evidence of goodwill that I should explain to our German friends in person the efforts we had made on their behalf and our regret that they had been rendered fruitless, not through any lack of zeal on our part, but solely by the action of the French'.[16]

Addis's frankness in Berlin provoked an outburst from Clemenceau, the French Prime Minister, already misinformed that Addis in Paris had claimed to be authorized to say that the British government

[16] FO 371/622, Hongkong Bank to FO, 30 Jan., 1 Feb. 1909.

desired German participation in the loan. 'There is a cleft in the entente', Clemenceau declared to *The Times* correspondent in Paris, 'and care must be taken that it does not widen.' The differences over the loan had come at a delicate moment for France, as negotiations for the Franco-German agreement on Morocco were moving to conclusion and the French government was clearly embarrassed and angered by Addis's words, even though he had referred to the possibility that France would accept a general financial entente. There was also friction between the British and French governments over Ottoman finance, which added to the irritation felt in Paris.

Addis returned to London disappointed with his mission to find, 'rather to my surprise', that Campbell was much pleased, and had told Grey that Addis had got much more than they expected or even hoped. Campbell's satisfaction was evidently with the 'frank recognition by the French of the British preferential rights to the appointment of engineers and the supply of materials', and the undertaking by the Germans that if they did compete for the Hankow–Canton line it would be fair competition. As to the French proposal for sharing all future loans, Campbell found it 'rather a large order', but saw it as almost unavoidable. To him it was more a question for the financiers than for the Foreign Office. Addis had seen difficulties in the division of industrial advantages though not in the sharing of loans, but Campbell thought these could be overcome. From a national point of view the chief interest was to get the railway built. A general agreement by the three governments not to sanction any loan to China for railway or other industrial purposes except on adequate security that the money would be devoted to the purposes for which it was borrowed seemed to Campbell the one way out of the present impasse and the one way to prevent similar difficulties in the future. The Hankow–Canton line was clearly regarded as a matter of high importance and a triple entente as the best solution in the circumstances. Campbell was well aware of the situation in China where, he pointed out to a critic of the British group, 'we are no longer in a position to insist in return for the loan on the Chinese building by contract or to make any detailed conditions in relation to construction'. Agreement between the groups would prevent competition to the advantage of the Chinese and ensure provisions that loan funds would be properly applied.[17]

[17] FO 371/622, minutes by Campbell on Bertie to Grey, 27 Jan. 1909, and Hongkong Bank to FO, 1 Feb. 1909; Campbell to d'Erlanger, 28 Jan. 1909; Addis Papers, Diary, 30 Jan. 1909; *BD*, 7, no. 148, Bertie to Grey, 1 Feb. 1909.

It was evident, however, that if the French financiers were disposed to fall in with Addis's proposals, the French government was not. A sharply phrased memorandum now rejected British preferential rights in respect of engineers and material for the Canton–Hankow railway; claimed equality for France, and threatened that if it were not granted, all agreements as to joint action were to be considered at an end. Addis was attacked for working for 'financial loans pure and simple', which would mean that orders for materials might go to countries where the price was low, to the prejudice of those who furnished money without conditions or guarantees. The French government, influenced by the direct pressure of French industrialists, was clearly in favour of tied loans. There was, too, the fact that France had got no industrial advantages from the Peking–Hankow loan, and they now wished to repudiate the Addis–Simon agreement of February 1908 by which they had relinquished industrial participation in the Hankow–Canton loan. There was also a hint of political pressure, for the memorandum argued that the two governments had a common interest in not allowing the Hongkong Bank to involve British finance in loans without guarantees, and in an Anglo-German understanding in opposition to French finance and contrary to the Anglo-French *rapprochement.*

This was a somewhat audacious attempt to exploit British political dependence on France, at a time when France herself was concluding negotiations kept secret from the British for agreement with Germany on Morocco. That agreement, signed and announced on 9 February, was not received with enthusiasm in London and may have influenced the Foreign Office to rebut the French charges more firmly than Addis had expected, and in turn to make critical observations on the French claim to equality in construction rights. But agreement with France on the railway issue was desired in the effort to avoid a return to competition.[18]

The rejoinder was quickly followed by a concrete British proposal for an English–French–German *entente generale* for railways in China, to be based upon the agreement of 1895 between the Hongkong Bank and the Deutsch-Asiatische Bank. The scheme, formulated by Addis, was put by him to a joint meeting of representatives of the Foreign Office and the Colonial Office on 25 February as a means of prevent-

[18] FO 371/622, memorandum communicated by Cambon, 2 Feb. 1909; Addis to Campbell, 9 Feb. 1909; memorandum to Cambon, 15 Feb. 1909; E. W. Edwards, 'The Franco-German Agreement on Morocco, 1909', *EHR* 78 (1963), pp. 483–513.

ing the Anglo-French group being forced into acceptance of Tientsin–Pukow terms for the Hankow–Canton loan, and of ending the prospect of continuing international competition to the advantage of the Chinese and the detriment of sound investment. The object was to bring the Germans to agree to Canton–Kowloon terms as a minimum for the loan, and the bait was a modification by the British of their preference under the Chang–Fraser agreement for the supply of materials for the line—an attractive offer, for the industrial gains were of obvious importance to the lenders. Addis was authorized to put the proposal to the French and German groups and both accepted it in principle, somewhat to his surprise. He had expected opposition from the Germans to retention by the British of the right to appoint a British chief engineer for the line, and from the French to the provision that the Chinese would be allowed to buy materials on a free-trade basis as between the markets of the lenders—clauses intended to preserve in effect advantages for the British, for orders for materials would tend to allow the nationality of the chief engineer.[19]

The course on which British policy was now set was not to the liking of Jordan—always a unilateralist, unhappy with the links with the French, and now opposed to the further extension of international co-operation upon which the government had embarked. He would have preferred to have conceded Tientsin–Pukow terms in order to get the loan without any arrangements with the Germans. In London, however, financiers and officials were at one that in view of the agreement with the French, adequate control over loan funds (on which the French insisted) must be maintained, and Bland on 4 March was instructed to refuse to negotiate on any other basis. This was a significant decision because the Chinese authorities, only too well aware of the dangers in the present state of Chinese opinion in accepting the greater degree of foreign control provided under Canton–Kowloon terms, refused to give way. The negotiations were broken off, but despite the agreement in principle between the three groups Cordes signed a preliminary agreement on Tientsin–Pukow terms on 8 March, thus securing a strong tactical position for the German group. The instruction to Bland, Addis maintained, 'was the order of our own government in concert with the French government'; but it appeared to him and to the Foreign Office to have been implemented

[19] Addis Papers, Diary, 25, 26 Feb. 1909; FO 371/622, memorandum by Addis, 26 Feb. 1909.

too hastily by Bland, who could have spun out the negotiations until the groups had met further. Bland for his part felt that he had been deceived by the Chinese, who had undertaken to submit any proposals from another quarter to Jordan before accepting them so as to give the British opportunity to reconsider their position but had broken their pledge.[20]

In the subsequent group negotiations, the Germans, while maintaining their desire for a triple entente to include all financial loans (but excluding Shantung), continued to drag out matters so as to allow Cordes to conclude a final agreement for the Hankow–Canton line on behalf of the German group. Apprehension grew on the British side. The Germans were manœuvring for position so as to get a larger stake in the eventual compromise and were now claiming a share in the Hankow–Szechwan line, to include the appointment of the chief engineer. Jordan telegraphed on 27 March, 'I consider the situation very grave and that our interests in the Yangtze valley are seriously threatened.' An acrimonious meeting of the bankers in Paris on 2 and 3 April brought a breakdown of the discussions, the Germans claiming that their government would not permit them to withdraw from their engagement with the Chinese and threatening that if there were no intergroup agreement, they would probably be able to obtain the financing of the entire Hankow–Canton line as well as the Hankow–Szechwan, together with the engineers, material, and prestige that would go with a project involving a sum of about £22 million.

This brought conflict within the British ranks. Grey, in view of the apparent weakening of the French group, who were now reported to be ready to accept German terms (i.e. Tientsin–Pukow conditions for the Chinese), inclined to a similar course and suggested that Jordan's opinion be sought. Addis was determined to hold out because if the British gave way now, the Germans would make very hard conditions in the future. He was summoned to the Foreign Office to be told of Grey's attitude. 'The Secy of State is ratting', he noted, 'I *will not* give in.' The outcome of his discussion with Campbell was that both agreed to stand firm. Grey, told that the French government was still opposed to Tientsin–Pukow terms, fell into line, agreeing to hold out when it appeared that the British protest in Peking against the conclu-

[20] FO 371/622, Jordan to Grey, 1 Mar., 22 Apr. 1909; Grey to Jordan, 4 Mar. 1909; papers communicated by Addis, 5 Mar. 1909; Bland Papers, vol. 24, box 11 (reel 16), Bland to Jordan, 6 and 11 Mar. 1909; E-tu Zen Sun, pp. 103–5. *GP* 32, no. 11603, Rex (Peking) to Bülow, 12 Mar. 1909.

sion of the German loan had brought modification in the attitude of the Chinese and of the Germans, who were now ready to come to arrangements with the Hongkong Bank and the Banque de l'Indo-Chine.[21]

By the end of April, however, hopes that the Chinese would relax their insistence on Tientsin–Pukow terms faded and the situation remained at deadlock. Addis, still determined not to give way, approached the Japanese ambassador in London—for Japan had also been promised rights under the Fraser–Chang agreement—suggesting Japanese intervention in Peking. Jordan was ready in the last resort to go in with the Germans rather than stand aside. New compromise proposals, emerged, however, for the Chinese were aware of the reality of British threats that their breach of faith would damage their credit in Britain. They now accepted a proposal that, while leaving Tientsin–Pukow terms intact, satisfied the British and French insistence upon control over the use of loan funds: the substitution of the certificate of an auditor, who was to be a European appointed and paid by the lenders, for that of the chief engineer.

There remained the thorny matter of division of shares in construction rights among the groups, for the loan to be negotiated was now the Hukuang loan to cover the extent of both lines radiating from Hankow through the provinces of Hupeh and Hunan. Tentative agreement between the groups preceded their meeting in Berlin in mid-May. Neither Grey nor Addis was very confident about what would emerge. The weakness of the British position was that the Fraser–Chang agreement left British interests open to competition. 'We are putting to sea in an unseaworthy vessel', Grey told Addis before he left for Berlin, 'you must save what you can.' The outcome, however, was much better than had been feared, for the agreement reached between the groups on the Hukuang loan on 14 May provided for a British chief engineer for the whole of the Hankow–Canton line; limitation of the German engineer to the Hankow–Ichang section of the Szechwan line, with a British engineer for the concluding section to Chengtu and a French engineer for the middle section; equal participation of the three groups for the supply of material throughout the two lines; and effective guarantees from the Chinese for the proper employment of railway loan funds. A general agreement for joint

[21] FO 371/623, Jordan to Grey, 18 Mar. 1909; Addis to Campbell, 5 Apr. 1909; minutes by Grey and Campbell on Bertie to Grey, 3 Apr. 1909; Addis Papers, Diary, 3, 8 Apr. 1909.

action by the three groups in respect of any future loan for railways in China was drafted for signature in the near future.[22]

Addis had done well to achieve a settlement, as he put it 'on terms so favourable to British interests', and his satisfaction was shared in the Foreign Office. He had proved himself a resourceful and determined negotiator, and his conduct of affairs had reinforced his already high standing in the Far Eastern Department. There was a community of interest: Addis's aim was to retain for the British group as much as possible of the rewards promised by the Fraser–Chang agreement; that of the Foreign Office to ensure that these rewards went as far as possible to a British concern—a matter of particular significance to Hong Kong, always apprehensive of the construction of a deep water port to rival Kowloon, and this could only be the British group as recognized under the Anglo–French agreement of 1905. Addis was the tactician, but the policy followed was agreed and not imposed by the Foreign Office or resisted by the group. Both parties accepted, as the situation developed, that co-operation with Germany as well as France was preferable to competition. Campbell, for whom the overriding aim was to get the major railways built in the overall interests of British trade, had indeed long favoured international co-operation as the most effective course.

For those who still held to the view that British predominance in the Yangtze Valley railways was not only desirable but possible, there was nothing in the situation to rejoice at. For them it marked one more stage in a retreat. If in 1905 France had been accepted into partnership, that at least had been tempered by the fact of the *entente cordiale*; but Germany was Britain's rival on the world stage and now she had achieved a major success. It was hard for Jordan 'to see the German legation who probably never gave it an hour's work romping in at the last moment and carrying off the spoils.' He did not conceal his chagrin or his criticism of the Hongkong Bank group, which, he charged, had not recognized that on political grounds it was necessary to incur risks and accept sacrifices.[23] Public criticism was to come through *The Times*, from Morrison

---

[22] FO 371/623, Addis to FO, 30 Apr. 1909; Jordan to Grey, 30 Apr. 1909; FO 371/624, Addis to FO, 17 May 1909; Addis Papers, Addis to Murray Stewart, 20 June 1909. The agreement assumed that the Szechwan line would eventually be prolonged beyond Hupeh province. The Japanese were pressing Chang to preserve their rights under the Fraser agreement; see Bland Papers, vol. 24, box 11 (reel 16), Bland to Jordan, 16 Feb. 1909; vol. 23, box 1, (reel 15), Bland to Harris, 31 Mar. 1909.

[23] FO 350/5, Jordan to Campbell, 20 Mar. and 17 Apr. 1909; *GP* 32, no. 11604, Bülow to Kaiser, 15 May 1909; no. 11605 Rex to Bülow, 21 May 1909.

and from Chirol, the foreign editor, who visited Japan and China in the spring and early summer of 1909. Chirol, Morrison, and Bland were strongly anti-German in their views on general policy. Before he left London in March, Chirol had on the basis of information from Bland endeavoured to influence Foreign Office opinion against Addis. Now in Peking, he completely accepted the position of the embittered Bland, who felt that he had been made the scapegoat for what he thought to be the devious and pro-German policy of the bank that through Addis had won over the Foreign Office.

The attack against the Hongkong Bank in *The Times* opened with a series of articles by Chirol in July and August on his Far Eastern tour. It was countered by the bank in what Chirol privately described as a regular campaign of intrigue and lies[24] but it was to continue over the next few years. For the moment, however, Grey's concern, as the prospect emerged of a general agreement between the three groups, was with another aspect that was already bringing difficulties: the commitment to exclusive support of the British group in respect of the Hankow–Canton and Hankow–Szechwan railways. This was a special situation that Grey was clear could not be extended. He informed Addis before the Berlin meeting that if a general agreement were reached the government would not be bound to his group beyond the existing commitment and would be free to support other British groups as it pleased. Addis was instructed to make this clear to the French and German groups. The invidious situation in which Grey was placed because of the existing pledge had been brought home when appeals for support from Marcus Samuel and Co. and Pauling and Co. in the Canton and Szechwan lines had had to be refused. He made it plain that he did not intend to find himself in a similar situation over future railways in China. He also indicated to Addis what he saw as a solution: the elimination of competition among British enterprises involved in the Far East and the amalgamation of the principal firms of financiers and contractors of good standing in the field, as was the case with the French and Germans. On the British side, he pointed out, Armstrongs and Vickers Maxim had combined for certain undertakings in Japan.[25]

---

[24] *The Times*, 29 July, 22, 26 Aug. 1909; Lo, Hui-min, pp. 505–8, 519–20; China Association Papers, Minute Book D, 1906–10, General Committee, 23 Sept. 1909; J. O. P. Bland, *Recent Events and Present Policies in China* (London, 1912), pp. 265–81.

[25] FO 371/624, memorandum by Grey on conversation with Addis, 11 May 1909; Grey to Jordan, 12 May 1909; FO 371/625, Jordan to Grey, 23 June 1909.

This was a revealing indication of the extent to which official thinking on economic diplomacy had moved from the detachment of the past in response to the changing scene. The problem now, as Grey saw it, was not the existence of the group headed by the Hongkong Bank but its restriction. What he looked for was not the restoration of free competition in which independent British enterprises struggled against each other as well as against foreign rivals, but the extension on the British side of combination so as to enable the Foreign Office to concentrate its efforts to advance British economic interests. His hint did not bear fruit. The Hongkong Bank did not intend its rivals to share in the rich prospects that the triple bank agreement brought. It was in a strong position to resist suggestions to widen its ranks because of its links with French and German banks, closely bound to their respective governments in agreements having the support of those governments; though the French group certainly would have liked to see other British banks brought in so as to reduce the risk of their appearing as competitors. Moreover the Hongkong Bank had now long-established ties with the Far Eastern Department, and the degree of rapport between Addis in particular and leading officials was close and was to remain so despite the attacks of *The Times*.

For the moment, the Berlin intergroup agreement seemed to open the way to the conclusion of the Hukuang loan. It was not to be, however, for two further complications developed. One, which was quickly resolved, arose from the resentment of Chang Chih-tung against the British and Chinese Corporation, and still more against its agent Bland. Bland and Chirol maintained that this was the result of intrigue against Bland by the Germans, who were determined to oust him from the British group because of his resolute anti-German views. At all events, Chang refused to allow the corporation to appear in the business. Jordan advised that failure to give way might mean the loan would fall through. Accordingly, though yielding was a blow to British pride, the Hongkong Bank was formally substituted for the corporation—which was, however, to act as its agent, a concession secured at the price of an explicit undertaking that Bland would cease to represent the corporation and would have nothing to do with the present business. Thereupon the loan agreement, which provided for the portions of the Hankow–Canton and Hankow–Szechwan lines running through Hunan and Hupeh to be divided between the three lending groups for construction purposes, was initialled on 6 June by the Chinese and representatives of the three bank groups.[26] Already, however, a much more formidable obstacle to its ratification was emerging, the assertion by the United States of an interest in the Hankow–Szechwan line.

[26] FO 371/624, memorandum by Campbell, 1 June 1909; Grey to Jordan and Jordan to Grey, 3 June 1909; FO 371/625, Jordan to Grey, 8 June 1909; MacMurray, 1, pp. 880–5. It was Hillier's view, shared to a large degree by Jordan, that much of the difficulty over the Hukuang loan arose from the Hongkong Bank's use of BCC as a 'stalking horse' to evade its obligations to the Germans under the 1895 agreement. Jordan also noted that Bland was not kept well informed by his board (FO 350/5, Jordan to Campbell, 20 Mar. and 3 Apr. 1909).

7

The American Intervention

AN indication of the revival of American interest in financial and industrial enterprise in China had come in December 1908 through Rockhill, the American minister in Peking, who had been instructed to compete with the other foreign legations to secure American financiers equality of opportunity, particularly in the Hankow–Canton loan. In the summer of 1909 the intention of the Taft administration to take an active role in the affairs of China was given vigorous expression. A note of 3 June 1909, recalling the pledge by China in 1904 that British and American capital would be given the first chance over other competitors to participate in the Hankow–Szechwan railway, informed Grey that notwithstanding disinterest shown in response to British enquiries in 1905, American capital would now be glad to co-operate with British interests in accordance with the understanding of 1904.[1]

Examination of the motives influencing the American action is outside the purpose of a study concerned with British policy. It was already clear from reaction to Rockhill's hint that American participation in the railway projects in negotiation would be unwelcome in the Foreign Office. Campbell had commented:

we have hitherto found the Americans quite useless and unreliable in the matter of providing capital for railways in China. The Hankow–Canton line is a case in point. It was originally an American concession, but the Americans did nothing . . . I should be very chary of recommending the Chinese to let them have another finger in that pie.[2]

Grey had not dissented. Now the American note, coming just when it seemed likely that China would sign a final agreement for the Hukuang loan, was felt to be a high-handed attempt to share in the

---

[1] FO 371/624, Reid to Grey, 3 June 1909. Addis said the Americans were relying on a pledge of Sept. 1903 (Hongkong Bank to FO, 15 June 1909, FO 371/624).

[2] FO 371/435, Jordan to Grey, 12 Dec. 1908, with minutes. Jordan received no hint of the American action in June 1909, which took him by surprise (FO 350/9 Jordan to Campbell, 22 June 1909).

fruits of three or four years of arduous negotiation. The first reaction was a refusal to interfere in the arrangements arrived at. It was soon recognized, however, that in international law the Americans stood on firm ground, and it was obvious that they could obstruct the sanction-ing of the loan by the Chinese government.[3]

The problem was not over American admission to financial partici-pation in future loans or even in the Hukuang loan, to which the British group would not object, but over construction rights. Addis was in no doubt that if the Americans abandoned all claims to the supply of material, there would be no support from France or Germany for excluding them from what would be a purely financial role in which, in view of the limited interest of the New York capital market in foreign loans, they would be dependent upon the European markets to float what share of Chinese loans they might be allocated. Since 'it will not do for us to be more anti-American than the French or Germans', it was made clear to Reid, the American ambassador, that the British government had no objection in principle to American participation in Chinese railway loans—even to equal participation in the Hukuang loan—so long as this did not disturb the agreement between the three European groups.[4]

As Addis anticipated the French took a similar view, but in Germany the banking group, though not the government, were opposed. They felt that though American inclusion would not be of significance financially, in the matter of the supply of railway material

the Americans must be regarded as a competitor which we should not under-rate. Their materials are cheaper than English and German products, but on the other hand the quality is considerably inferior, a fact which is to be regretted still escapes to the eyes of the Chinese at the time being . . .[5]

As yet there had been no consultation between the British, French, and German governments on the American demand, but information about attitudes in Paris and Berlin coming from the groups through Addis indicated that responses to the United States had been on similar lines. Then came a change of front by France, away from confining American interests to future participation to limiting them

[3] FO 371/624, minute by Alston on Reid to Grey, 12 June 1909.
[4] FO 371/624, memorandum by Campbell on conversation with Addis, 16 June; Grey to Reid, 23 June 1909.
[5] FO 371/624, Addis to FO, 17 June, enclosing Urbig (German group) to Addis, 14 June 1909.

to financial participation solely in the Hankow–Szechwan line. The cause was Russian pressure for participation, which though not based on any real claim, would be difficult for France to resist if it were accorded to Americans for the future. The point was appreciated in the Foreign Office, where similar pressure from Japan was anticipated, but in Campbell's view, 'it will not be practicable to keep the Americans out of future business unless the English–French–German consortium are prepared to face formidable competition'.[6] Nevertheless, the British fell into line with France, accepting American inclusion in the Hankow–Szechwan line.

Here the influence of Addis was significant. He had become alarmed at what he judged to be the attempt of the German government to ingratiate themselves in Washington 'by representing that they are charmed at the idea of American co-operation and that the difficulties are made by England.' He could also see some advantage in the future for security of loans from inclusion of the Americans.

> It would be difficult in case of default to enforce the shadowy loan guarantees which are all that are left to us of the early mortgages, etc. The pressure of American diplomacy, over and above that of England, France, and Germany would increase the security of China loans by 1 or 2 per cent.

On his suggestion, Bryce, the British ambassador in Washington, was instructed to inform the American government that Britain would cordially recognize American co-operation in the Hankow–Szechwan line if the Hukuang agreement were not endangered and the American protest against it withdrawn, and if satisfactory arrangements for the purpose were made between the American banks and the European groups.[7]

The immediate difficulty was the vagueness of the American claim. Was it confined to the Hankow–Szechwan line or did it extend to the Hankow–Canton line, which was the serious British concern? Addis argued that they had no earthly claim to share in the latter, but he had little confidence in Grey's determination to resist. 'Sir Edward Grey, after approving my memo to exclude Americans from Hankow–Canton and to confine their participation to the Hankow–Szechwan

---

[6] FO 371/624, Addis to FO, 18 June 1909, with minutes.
[7] FO 371/624, Bryce to Grey, 19 June 1909, with minutes; Grey to Bryce 21 June 1909. Addis to FO, 22 June 1909.

line is wobbling again. It is clear that he will yield eventually to the US demands rather than provoke a rupture.'[8]

Grey had to take a broader view than the banker. The maintenance of good Anglo-American relations was an object for which British governments had made sacrifices in the past, and however important Chinese railway business was to British interests in the Far East it was less significant in the overall needs of British policy than equable relations with Washington.

When the European groups met the Americans on 7 July, they had on the previous day signed their draft agreements providing for co-operation in railway business and in loans to the Chinese government and provinces so as to strengthen their position in advance. The meeting with the Americans brought deadlock; for the American group, while agreeing to accept only 25 per cent of the Szechwan loan instead of the 50 per cent to which they claimed to be entitled, demanded 25 per cent of the loan for the Hupeh section of the Hankow–Canton line as well. In face of the rejection of this demand by the Europeans, the American bankers were themselves ready to withdraw it, but the United States government instructed them not to give way and the meeting was adjourned *sine die*.

Now President Taft took an unprecedented step: telegraphing a protest direct to the prince regent of China, in defiance of all diplomatic usage. In Peking, though Chang Chih-tung was for resisting American pressure, it was soon evident that the Chinese would yield recognizing that only to the United States government could they look for support against the Japanese in Manchuria. Jordan therefore advised that the European groups give way, and Addis now took the same line. 'Then let it be so', Grey instructed. Addis had seen the danger of a contest in China between Europe and America that could block all progress in the railway programme, especially the Hankow–Canton line felt to be of major importance to British interests. He now advised the European groups to agree to the American demand to be put on a footing of equality in every respect with themselves in the whole Hukuang loan, otherwise American pretensions would increase and Russian and Japanese claims would be provoked. Admission of the Americans on these terms was agreed on.[9]

---

[8] Addis Papers, Diary, 5 July 1909.

[9] FO 371/625, Grey to Bryce, 12 July 1909; Jordan to Grey 22 July 1909, with minutes; Addis to FO, 23, 24 July and 9 Aug. 1909; MacMurray, 1, pp. 833–5 (for terms of agreement on loans for railway purposes between British, French, and German groups, 6 July

Russià had in fact already made known in London a wish to participate. Opinion in the Foreign Office at the first mention of Russian
interest had been unwelcoming, but when Benckendorff presented a
memorandum on 20 July, Hardinge (plainly viewing the question in
the broad perspective of British foreign policy) minuted, 'I think we
must be careful to say something friendly as regards Russian participation in the future'. Grey's reply accordingly made it clear that
Britain would not object to participation of the Russo-Chinese Bank in
the purely private interbank agreement or in future undertakings—but
this was a matter for arrangement between the banks. The Japanese
as yet made no request for participation, but information from Tokyo
early in September of an arrangement between a Japanese syndicate
and the British contracting firm, Pauling's, for a bid for a concession
for the Hankow–Canton line indicated their continuing interest in
that area.[10]

More immediate was the need to soothe ruffled feelings in
Washington over the resistance to American claims. Grey therefore
assured Reid of British goodwill, saying that if he had had any idea
that the Americans intended to abandon their attitude of indifference,

I should not only have agreed to their participation originally but I should
have welcomed it. Moreover had I known that the American group were going
to claim their rights with regard to the Hankow–Szechwan line and that they
were willing to act in partnership with the British group I should probably
have advised our own people to stand firm on their rights and work in partnership with the Americans. As it was, however, the complications in connection
with the Canton–Hankow railway had made it desirable that our people
should come to terms with their competitors in China and when the Americans intervened at the last moment it was impossible for me to throw over our
own people by ignoring the arrangements they had made. The American
action had placed us in a difficult position.[11]

Grey's remarks must be judged in the context of the Chirol–Bland
campaign against Addis. When Grey spoke to Reid, Chirol had
brought to notice approaches by the American International Banking
Company in April 1909, rebuffed by the Hongkong Bank, for co-

1909); for the agreement on administrative loans, FO 371/625, papers communicated by
Addis, 7 July 1909.

[10] FO 371/625, memorandum communicated by Benckendorff, with minute, 20 July
1909; Grey to Benckendorff, 27 July 1909; FO 405/198, Rumbold to Grey, 6 Sept. 1909.

[11] FO 371/625, Grey to Bryce, 27 July 1909.

operation in the Hukuang loan. When Addis was questioned, he explained that the approach was from a single bank and similar to approaches received from numerous other banks. There had been no question of an American syndicate—nationally speaking—and the United States government was not mentioned. He had not thought it worthwhile bringing the matter to the knowledge of the Foreign Office. He had replied to all such requests that the Hongkong Bank could not entertain them because they were pledged to the French and Germans.

The Far Eastern Department readily accepted Addis's explanation. Grey himself, for all the soothing language he now used to Reid, had fallen in with the department's cool attitude to American participation when Rockhill's hints had been considered. What had changed the situation for him was the intervention of the American government. Chirol linked the failure to disclose the overture from the International Banking Company to the scheming of the Hongkong Bank, which he maintained 'deliberately sold us to the Germans'. Earlier knowledge of American interest, he thought, would have made possible resistance to the German thrust. He made some impression on Tyrrell and put his views to Grey when he returned to London, as did Bland, in August 1909. It does not appear, however, that the campaign damaged Addis's standing in the Foreign Office, despite Chirol's claims. There is in fact no evidence in Addis's private papers or in those of Bland, or in Morrison's published correspondence and unpublished diary to support the charge that Addis or the Hongkong Bank worked to assist major German interests. The relations between the bank group and the Deutsch-Asiatische Bank had not been markedly cordial since 1898. There had been for years a good deal of friction over the Tientsin–Pukow railway partnership. Addis in 1905 had wished to end the 1895 agreement between the two banks, but had been restrained by the Foreign Office. Chirol had been won over completely by Bland, determined to cause trouble for the Hongkong Bank after his dismissal.[12]

---

[12] FO 800/106, Chirol to Tyrrell, 24 and 29 June and 18 Aug. 1909, with minutes; FO 800/43, Grey to Jordan, 13 Aug. 1909; FO 371/625, Hillier to Addis, 23 June 1909, communicated by Addis, 12 July 1909; Chirol to Grey, 6 Sept. 1909; FO 371/851, minute by Campbell on Jordan to Grey, 22 Dec. 1909; Peter Lowe, *Great Britain and Japan, 1911–1915* (London, 1969), pp. 143–5: Lo, Hui-min, I, pp. 513–15, 516–18. There were instances of loan facilities granted by the Hongkong Bank to German firms based in China but these were minor affairs in the normal way of business.

The success gained by the Americans was as much the result of the situation in China as of the reluctance of the European governments to disturb relations with the United States on an issue not of major significance. Certainly the British felt the construction of the Hankow–Canton line to be urgently desirable, and considered sacrifices to prevent further delay through American obstruction to be justifiable. Sacrifices there had to be on the part of the European groups, and of construction rights as well as financial, now that American interests were admitted to full participation. Each group was of course intent on retaining as much as possible, and the following months were taken up by wrangling over the redistribution of the shares. Grey, harassed by parliamentary questions, was determined to uphold British interests: 'I would rather upset the whole thing than give in and am prepared if need be to tell the other 3 parties that I will go to all lengths at Peking to block the business until the French and Germans agree to what is fair.'

By the end of September, Hillier, who was conducting the negotiations in Peking for the British group, was thoroughly disenchanted with the Americans.

It seems to me that the attitude of the Americans, marked as it has been by insufferable bounce and an entire want of generous consideration for the circumstances in which their action has placed us, offers no guarantee that we shall ever be able to work together with cordiality and accord.[13]

This irritation, also felt in the Foreign Office, was added to there as the political objects of another aspect of the forward policy of the Taft administration, the Chinchow-Aigun railway project, became clear.[14] The Americans were pushing into the sensitive area of Manchuria, deliberately mounting a challenge—with Chinese support—against the position there of Japan and Russia. The proposal for the neutralization of Manchurian railways added still further to the embarrassments that the China situation was now causing British policy.

The Chinchow–Aigun project was in essence a revival of an earlier scheme brought forward in 1907 for an extension of the Northern

---

[13] FO 371/625, minute by Grey on Jordan to Grey, 27 Aug. 1909; FO 371/676, Addis to FO, 12 Oct. 1909 enclosing Hiller to Addis, 22 Sept. 1909.

[14] See E. W. Edwards, 'Great Britain and the Manchurian Railways Question, 1909–1910', *EHR* 81 (Oct. 1966), pp. 740–69; M. H. Hunt, *Frontier Defense and the Open Door* (New Haven and London, 1973), pp. 200–17.

Railway in the form of a branch from Hsinmintun to Fakumen with a possible further extension to Tsitsihar. That scheme, in which Pauling's and the British and Chinese Corporation were involved, had been launched by the Chinese with support of unofficial American interests. Initially Grey had welcomed it as an economic venture in which British interests were engaged on account of the Chinese government. Jordan was instructed to support Pauling's in the matter, and was further told he could support a British firm in any endeavour to secure a contract from the Chinese government for this or any other railway in Manchuria. But when the Japanese refused consent because the line would compete with the South Manchuria Railway, Grey immediately retreated. 'We cannot press for this line to be built', he ruled, 'if the Japanese had valid ground of objection, but that is a matter to be settled between Chinese and Japanese.'[15]

The maintenance of good relations with Japan was a basic principle of Grey's policy. The Anglo-Japanese alliance gave Britain 'security with economy' in the Far East, and thus was a vital factor in making possible the concentration of British naval power in home waters against the German North Sea fleet. The realities seem to have been recognized by Addis, already well aware that political considerations counted for more than economic in shaping British policy. The British and Chinese Corporation stood to lose business if the Hsinmintun–Fakumen scheme fell through, for under the terms of the draft contract it was to issue the loan of £2½ million for the line that Pauling's were to construct. Yet, though he saw gains to be made in Manchuria, claimed that the project was 'a matter of the first importance to us', and warned the Japanese that their obstruction might affect adversely their credit in Britain and the United States, Addis did not press too hard upon the Foreign Office or upon Japan, with which the Hongkong Bank did an important and lucrative business in finance for the South Manchuria Railway.[16] Though mobilization of public opinion by Pauling's and the China Association caused Grey to face sharp criticism in Parliament and the press, the foreign secretary did not deviate from his position that unless Japan was prepared to

[15] FO 371/229, Grey to Jordan, 27 Nov. 1907; FO 371/410, minute by Grey on BCC to FO, 6 Dec. 1907.
[16] Nish, *The Anglo-Japanese Alliance*, p. 349; FO 371/410, Addis to FO, 2 Mar. 1908; Bland Papers, vol. 23, box I (reel 15), Addis to Bland, 31 Jan., 1 May 1908; Collis, p. 123.

consent to the Hsinmintun–Fakumen line, Britain could not press for its construction.

Despite the plain lessons of the Hsinmintun–Fakumen fiasco, American interests launched the Chinchow–Aigun project for which Pauling's were to be the contractors which was followed in November 1909 by the grandiose proposal for neutralization of the Manchurian railways. As Russia and Japan took action to defend valuable interests from attack, Grey was faced with an even more embarrassing situation because the United States government was now firmly and publicly involved, and made plain its naive expectation of British support. In the British view of international relations, the United States occupied a special position. It had become axiomatic that there must be no conflict with the United States, and it was well understood that she was potentially a very great power. It was equally well understood that however desirable an Anglo-American entente might be in world politics, it was virtually impossible to achieve because of the refusal of the United States to participate in maintaining a balance of power. Consequently Grey, now forced by American policy to choose between his ally Japan and his associate Russia—friendships judged essential in British political strategy—and the United States, had no option but to side with Tokyo and St Petersburg. This left bitterness in Washington, where the Anglo-Japanese alliance was already regarded with increasing suspicion.

No doubt the chagrin of the State Department contributed to the continued wrangling over the division of construction rights in the Hukuang scheme in which the Americans were frequently opposed to the British. On this issue there was also friction with France bringing at one stage talk from Pichon of a rupture of the *entente cordiale*, and later from the British side a suggestion that the Chinese Central Railways Company should be dissolved.[17] If matters had been left to the financiers, who were anxious for the business to go forward, there would have been less difficulty. It was the governments that imposed an additional rigidity, so that it was not until May 1910 that agreement on reapportionment of construction shares was reached—on a basis not unsatisfactory to the British, who had preserved their rights over the Canton–Hankow line and secured equality in the Szechwan line. 'We have come out of it fairly well and the policy of holding out is

[17] FO 371/626, Addis to FO, 21 Dec. 1909, with enclosures, FO 371/851, Addis to FO, 1 Mar. 1910, with enclosures.

justified', Campbell commented. What pleased him particularly was that a return to competition had been averted.[18]

Now the task was to obtain the assent of the Chinese authorities to the settlement, which had been arrived at on the assumption that the section of the Hankow–Szechwan line to be financed and constructed initially would be extended beyond Ichang (the point at which it was to end under the draft agreement between the European banks and the Chinese of 6 June 1909). It was soon evident that the American government, whose intervention had forced modification of the 1909 agreement and set matters back by a year, was not disposed to show similar zeal in securing the assent of the Chinese to the new arrangement. This was thought in the Foreign Office to reflect its chagrin at the complete failure of the Manchurian policy, of which the only result had been to draw Russia and Japan closer together in joint resistance to American aims. American blundering in a delicate situation had left only irritation behind it. As for the Hukuang loan, the American representative did indeed join with the agents of the European banks in presenting identical notes to the Chinese asking them to complete ratification of the loan, but these were without result. The Chinese, partly perhaps because of American lukewarmness, partly because of their fear of provincial reaction, raised successive objections.

By the end of the year little progress had been made. Jordan became increasingly anxious at the effect of the delay upon the major British interest, the construction of the Hankow–Canton line. When the Chinese raised yet another issue, demanding that half the loan funds be deposited in native Chinese banks during the construction of the railways (a proposal to which Addis not unreasonably objected), Jordan telegraphed urgently, 'Further delay is dangerous and the political and commercial advantages to us of through railway to Hong Kong far outweigh all minor objections'. Addis saw dangers in the deposit proposal. To accept it meant the sacrifice of almost the last trace of financial control, which it was the object of the international agreements to preserve. The Hongkong Bank and its allies, as Jordan was aware, stood to lose financially if the loan funds went to Chinese banks, but he pointed out that China would not accept control of her loan funds by foreign banks at rates of interest involving heavy sacrifice. Furthermore the French, German, and American ministers

---

[18] FO 371/851, minute by Campbell, 25 May 1910, on the terms of the group agreement signed 23 and 24 May 1910.

and the representatives in Peking of the four bank groups, shared his view that the Chinese demand should be conceded. Because of this and of indications that Grey would adopt Jordan's view the banks gave way partially, agreeing that one-quarter of the loan funds should be deposited in Chinese banks on condition that the amount be credited to a special construction account and applied to railway expenditure in China before any transfer of loan proceeds held in London be made for that purpose. The Hongkong Bank and its allies were thus made to yield against their financial interest in the cause of a wider objective: to get the railway built. But the bank looked for support in return:

In taking this step contrary to their own opinion, the groups feel they may rely upon their respective governments to supply, in case of need such diplomatic pressure as may be necessary to counteract the loss of control involved by this concession made in deference to the opinion of their ministers.[19]

The Hukuang loan was now at long last moving to completion. The central government braced itself to defy provincial opposition. An imperial edict of 9 May 1911 brought all trunk lines under the ownership of the state, including those for which provincial companies had been founded before the present year but on which construction had been delayed. Jordan was delighted. The decree, he wrote, 'is beyond doubt the boldest and most statesmanlike pronouncement that the Chinese government has made on any question of policy in recent years.'[20]

A few days later, on 20 May 1911, the Hukuang loan agreement was signed. Its terms, apart from the reallocations made necessary by the inclusion of the American group, showed no significant difference from those of the draft agreement of 1909. The amount of the loan was now £6 million in place of £5$\frac{1}{2}$ million, and the term was extended to 40 years. The issuing price to China remained at 95 per cent and the interest at 5 per cent. No change was made in the security, the salt and *likin* revenues of Hupeh and Hunan. Construction and control of the railways was to be entirely and exclusively vested in the Imperial Chinese Government which agreed to appoint engineers-in-chief for each of the sections (British, German, and American), and to inform the banks of the selection made. The engineers were to work under the orders of the director–general and the managing director of the

---

[19] FO 371/1080, Jordan to Grey, 13 Apr. 1911; Addis to FO and Grey to Jordan, 19 Apr. 1911; Jordan to Grey, 20 Apr.; Addis to FO, 24 Apr. 1911.

[20] FO 371/1080, Jordan to Grey, 10 May 1911, with minutes.

section. After construction and during the currency of the loan the Chinese government was to continue to appoint Europeans and Americans as engineers-in-chief, but these appointments would be made without reference to the banks. Provision for control over loan funds was as in the draft agreement. Requisitions from construction accounts were to be on the authority of the managing director or his duly authorized representative, preceded by a certificate to the auditor. There were to be two auditors, one for the Hankow–Canton line, the other for the Hankow–Szechwan, who were to be appointed and paid by the banks, and during the construction of the lines the accounts were to be open to their inspection.[21]

The terms of the loan demonstrate the extent to which China had strengthened her position in relation to the foreign banks. The Chinese had registered a considerable advance towards gaining control of their railways in 1907–8 in the Tientsin–Pukow and Peking–Hankow negotiations. They had maintained this in 1909 despite the drawing together of the European banks. The virtually complete control conceded by the Europeans approximated to the advice of Satow in 1906, but it was more than the British group and the Foreign Office had wanted, and certainly much more than the French had desired. The Germans, willing to accept the Chinese demands, had given ground that could not be recovered. The Europeans in 1909 and the four-power consortium in 1911 were not able to force their terms on China. A financial blockade was not possible because the London market could not be closed. The Hongkong Bank, unlike its European associates, did not control its market, and its rivals would move in to lend to a China that seemed to have achieved political stability and to be intent on modernization. The consortium groups were eager for business and had to give way on control. The British government was above all concerned with the building of the railways, which were expected still further to increase the volume of trade with China now more significant as a market for British goods.

---

[21] MacMurray, 1, pp. 866–77. The loan was still limited to the construction of the sections of the Hankow–Canton and Hankow–Szechwan lines within Hupeh and Hunan. The price arrangements meant that China would receive £95 for every £100 bond sold by the banks at whatever price they could obtain from investors; if above £95 the banks gained, if below they lost (E-tu Zen Sun, p. 47). The price of 95 agreed for the Hukuang loan was another indication of China's improved negotiating position. The Northern Railway loan in 1898 and the Shanghai–Nanking in 1903 were both priced at 90; the Canton–Kowloon (1907) and the Peking–Hankow Redemption (1908) at 94.

But the question of the supply of materials was important to the governments and the groups, as the wrangling over the allocation of construction sections in the two railways had indicated. In this area the groups were able to secure pledges relating to the nationality of the engineers-in-chief of the sections. Clearly they expected the engineers to have considerable influence in the allocation of construction work and in the purchase of materials, which from the first had been a matter of concern to them. Their general agreement of July 1909 on railway loans had stipulated as one condition for loans to China that orders for materials should be equally divided among lenders. While the Hukuang contract provided for an overall preference for Chinese materials at equal prices and qualities over materials from the countries of the lenders, lenders' manufactures were to have preference on a similar basis over other foreign materials. The role of the engineers-in-chief could be crucial in these matters. On past experience the groups could expect that the bulk of orders for each section would go to the country of origin of the engineer.

By this time the American group had been brought fully within the banking consortium. In July 1909 when the European groups had made their agreements on railway and administrative loans they had offered participation to the Americans on equal terms, for they were fully aware that the pressure brought by the United States on China over the Hukuang loan could be repeated in future business. If the Americans were part of the consortium, that danger would be averted. The American bankers, however, looked for more than equality. Well aware of the limited capacity of their own market for Chinese loans, they wanted as a condition of entering the July agreement an undertaking that the European groups would obtain official quotation on their respective bourses for American bonds issued in connection with future loan business. This would mean that the European money markets would bolster a status for the United States in China loans that could not be sustained on investment from American sources alone. The French government had refused its consent to the undertaking required, so the American group remained outside the consortium.

The resulting situation promised and produced friction. In September 1910 there was trouble over a loan to the governor of Manchuria, which the European groups were negotiating and to which the Americans advanced a prior claim. In the Foreign Office, Campbell (who had from the first recognized the power of the Americans to obstruct Chinese business) was once more for compromise. Unless the Americans were given participation, he observed, 'there will always be trouble'.[22] The problem for the European groups was that the Americans had little to offer in financial resources. Admission would be a one-sided bargain—and there was the further factor that if they were brought in, Russia, with still less to contribute, would press for entry.

For Addis, however, there was a countervailing element: the growing possibility of serious competition for Chinese loans from London rivals of the Hongkong Bank. Jealously of the British and Chinese Corporation and annoyance at being excluded from official support, it was noted, 'is leading British firms of good standing to offer money right and left', and to do so for loans that were not guaranteed by Imperial Edict and thus lacked adequate security. In September 1910, in fact, the London City and Midland Bank was involved in the issue of such a loan for £450,00. In the end the Stock Exchange Committee, apparently without any Foreign Office intervention but perhaps in response to promptings from Hongkong Bank interests, held up application for quotation of the loan. Clearly, however, the situation was disturbing for the bank, for there was a danger that if the Americans independently negotiated a Chinese loan they might issue it in London with the aid of other British financial houses. As Addis knew, the London market was so large that in present circumstances with ample funds available they would have no great difficulty in so doing.[23]

What brought the matter to a head was the currency reform loan. Reform of the chaotic Chinese currency was a long-standing objective of all the commercial powers. The obligation to carry it out was first imposed on the Chinese government by Britain in the Mackay Treaty of 1902. Now, in 1910, the Americans took the lead while negotiations with China over the Hukuang loan were still in progress. Following a hint from the State Department, the Chinese government approached the American group for a loan of $50 million for currency reform.

First news of what was afoot came to the Foreign Office through the Hongkong Bank, and a few days later Whitelaw Reid announced that a preliminary loan agreement had been signed on 27 October with the American group. The European banks, it seems, were involved from

---

[22] FO 371/871, Addis to FO, 8 Sept., 1910, with minutes; FO 371/873, Addis to Alston, 28 Oct. 1910. In Sir E. Cassel's view no loan could succeed in the city against FO disapproval (70 371/1322, Gowe to Grey, 13 July 1912).

[23] FO 371/873, Max Muller to Grey, 22 Sept. 1910, with minute.

the first but Addis, having been sworn to secrecy, had not kept the Foreign Office informed—an unusual omission. 'We may have to take the matter up with the H & S Bank ', Alston observed, 'though it is very unlike them to act behind our back.'[24]

Whatever the initial understanding between the groups, however, friction developed immediately on the conclusion of the preliminary agreement. The Americans needed European assistance to float the loan. Since they were not bound by the 1909 group agreements, they were not obliged to require signature of the final agreement by the European groups as well as themselves. If the American group alone signed, with the Europeans as subsidiary participants, then to the United States would accrue all the credit and political advantages attaching to the agreement—even though the loan would be financed largely by the European markets. The provision in the preliminary agreement for the appointment of an American financial adviser to oversee the application of the reform seemed an early indication of an intention to use the loan to strengthen the position of the United States in Peking.

A meeting of the four groups was rapidly arranged for early November in London. Before it took place the situation was assessed in the Foreign Office, which hitherto had assumed that the American group, when it adhered to the group agreement on the Hukuang loan in July 1909, had at the same time been admitted to the general agreements between the banks for future railway and administrative loan business. The situation was delicate because outright British opposition to the Americans would sour still further relations already troubled by the Manchurian railways question. The British, like the French and Germans, wanted joint signatures, but Addis was advised not to take the initiative in opposing the Americans. He said that he might have to choose between them and the French and Germans. If he supported the Europeans, the Americans might proceed in their own way, using the London market—a serious threat to the Hongkong Bank. Moreover the Hongkong Bank itself in previous loan negotiations had secured liberty for one group alone to sign. Yet he felt he could not desert the French and Germans. Campbell agreed, but before the groups met there was a further conference between Grey, Campbell, Jordan (who was on leave in London), and Addis. It was

---

[24] FO 371/873, Grey to Max Muller, 21 and 28 Oct. 1910; memorandum by Campbell, 2 Nov. 1910; minute on Max Muller to Grey, 25 Oct. 1910; *FRUS*, 1912, pp. 89–92.

decided that Addis should strive for signature of a general agreement between all four groups as a priority, for that would stipulate that all parties should use their utmost endeavours to secure joint signature of loan agreements. If the general agreement was signed, the Americans could give participation in the currency loan only to the present British group; and if they declined, in the event of the Americans not obtaining joint signatures of that agreement, the Americans would have to issue the loan on their own market and the British and continental markets would be closed to them. If necessary Addis was to tell the Americans that, while the British desired nothing more than to co-operate with them in China, if French and German opposition prevented general agreement, the Hongkong Bank could not separate themselves entirely from the French and Germans with whom they had worked so long.[25]

The outcome was that general agreements covering railway and administrative loans were signed by all four groups on 10 November 1910. The Americans undertook to use their best endeavours, with the co-operation of the State Department, to get joint signature of the currency loan agreement. If they failed, they would offer the European groups the proper shares in the loan; and if the groups declined to participate, the four-bank intergroup agreement would be cancelled and the European groups would revert to the position they held under the agreements of 1909. The Americans would then have to issue the loan in Europe only through their own channels.

This was as satisfactory a settlement as could be expected. If the British had to choose, financial considerations added to the political need to keep in line with the French were to prevail over the desirability of smoothing American umbrage. Grey himself found much to criticize in American policy. Not only had their 'ill-timed proposals' for internationalization of the Manchurian railways made increasingly difficult the task of keeping the door open in Manchuria, they had reversed their policy of resistance to Russian taxation of foreign residents in Harbin without consultation with the British legation in Peking, which had in the past been co-operating with them. This showed 'an absence of purpose coupled with a disregard of us'. Moreover, they had shown 'an inconsiderate determination' to convene an opium conference at The Hague without consultation with Britain.

[25] FO 371/873, Addis to Alston, 4 Nov. 1910, with minute by Jordan; memoranda by Campbell, 4 and 7 Nov. 1910; W. V. and M. V. Scholes, *The Foreign Policy of the Taft Administration* (Columbia, 1970), pp. 197–200.

But despite his irritation, Grey fully accepted 'the extreme desirability of working with the Americans and not imperilling our good
relations with them in other parts of the world by adhering too literally
to a policy of strict reciprocity in the Far East'. Bryce had been
instructed to

lose no opportunity of assuring the United States Government of our desire to
work with them in all matters in the Far East so far as circumstances permit
and [to] lay stress on our anxiety to maintain the *status quo* in Manchuria
where any change of the kind feared by the United States could not fail to
affect our interests quite as much as theirs in a most detrimental manner.[26]

Grey was therefore somewhat disconcerted to find that at the meeting of the groups, Addis had placed upon him the responsibility for
the possible breach with the Americans over the currency loan. Addis
said he had been forced in open conference to say that if the British
group were offered only participation in the currency loan and not
joint signature they would refuse, and had indicated that this was
Grey's wish. Grey, however, had understood that in this situation the
decisive factor for Addis was not his wishes but the impossibility of
abandoning the French and German groups.[27]

The agreement reached on 10 November did not end the problems
that the currency loan posed for Grey. The proposal for an American
financial adviser was obviously one more blatant attempt to push the
United States, with a minor proportion of China's trade, into a position of influence in Peking. Yet to appear again as a leader in opposition to American policy was something Grey wished to avoid if at all
possible, all the more so since it was reported that Taft himself had
suggested the American financial adviser. When, however, as the
British had hoped, France objected to the American adviser, Grey's
position was eased. While the issue remained unresolved, the British
kept in the background. 'We must continue to keep out of this opposition to the adviser', Grey instructed. When the Americans made a
formal request for support, the British attitude was presented in mild
terms: the adviser proposal was judged impracticable because of the
opposition of other powers, but the Americans were assured of Grey's
wish to do anything possible to advance American co-operation in
China. He was, however, prepared to support an adviser from one of

---

[26] FO 371/873, Addis to Grey, 11 Nov. 1910; FO 371/920, Grey to Bryce, 22 Sept.
1910; MacMurray, vol. 1, pp. 828–32.
[27] FO 371/873, memorandum by Campbell, 11 Nov. 1910, with minute by Grey.

the non-interested powers. This in fact was the solution accepted by Taft. It opened the way for the final agreement signed on 15 April 1911 by the four groups and the Chinese government.[28]

American action had made the currency loan an affair of governments, with the bankers filling a subsidiary role; and it remained such when, with the agreement signed, a more thorny issue than the adviser question came to the front—the place of Russia and Japan. Both powers had made it plain as American policy on Manchuria developed that they claimed a special place there; and this was given emphasis by their agreement of 4 July 1910. The inclusion of the United States within the consortium added to fears in St Petersburg and Tokyo of movement by international finance into Manchuria. The currency loan agreement gave some justification, for it specified that a proportion of the loan funds was to be devoted to the promotion and extension of industrial enterprises in Manchuria. Furthermore, Article 16 of the agreement provided that if China were to decide to invite foreign capitalists to join with Chinese interests in Manchurian business contemplated under this loan, the consortium banks should be given the first option. It seems clear that all the consortium groups (and not the Americans alone) wanted to obtain a stake in what was plainly an expanding market. Certainly British interests were alive to the prospects in an area that the Foreign Office was told was now of first-class importance to many British firms and even to various manufacturing interests.[29]

Russia's intention to protect its Manchurian stake was made known before the final agreement was signed. The withdrawal of the proposal for an American adviser against which Russia and Japan had objected in Peking diminished fears of American influence over the central government, but the threat to Manchuria remained. The Russian reaction was to disclaim interest in railway business in favour of the consortium in the eighteen provinces of China proper, but to reserve freedom of action in this field in Manchuria and Mongolia, and throughout the Chinese empire in respect of 'political loans', which by the consortium groups was taken to mean financial loans as distinguished from railway loans. For these purposes, the consortium were informed, Russia was forming an international

[28] FO 371/1068, minute by Grey on Jordan to Grey, 27 Jan. 1911; memorandum by Campbell, 27 Feb.; Grey to Phillips (American Embassy), 2 Mar. 1911; MacMurray, I, pp. 841–9.
[29] FO 371/843, China Association to FO, 5 July 1910.

banking group consisting of the Russo-Asiatic Bank, the Belgian Banque d'Outre-mer, the London City and Midland Bank, Lloyd's Bank, the Bank of Scotland, and the Eastern Bank. Moreover pressure was brought on the French government to argue that advances under the currency loan should not be assented to until there was satisfaction that expenditure proposed in Manchuria should not be on projects that Russia could fairly claim were detrimental to her interest.

Grey accepted this as a principle, but on Addis's advice he demurred to a further stipulation advanced by France; that Russia should agree to the earmarking of the various Manchurian revenues enumerated in the loan contract as security for the loan. He did, however, assure the Russian ambassador that he would not give diplomatic support for the construction of railways in Manchuria; and when the United States agreed to insist that the small part of the loan allotted to Manchuria for industrial enterprises should be used strictly for those named, this seemed to Grey to offer a satisfactory safeguard. When the French baulked at admitting Chinese loans to be issued by the Russo-Asiatic Bank to quotation on the Paris Bourse, and when the London City and Midland Bank dissociated itself from membership of the Russian group, the Russian attitude became more conciliatory and they threw out hints of co-operation to the representatives in Peking of the consortium banks.[30]

Japanese reaction to American entry into the consortium and to the proposed currency reform loan was more restrained than the hostile attitude taken initially by Russia. That Japanese banks wished to join the consortium was soon made plain by Takahashi to the Hongkong Bank and to Jacob Schiff of the American group. The financial position of Japan now, he explained, was quite different from what it had been in 1906–7 when she had been invited to participate in railway business by Britain and France. Money was now easy, and some Japanese bankers wished to enter the consortium.

Discussions with Addis in London revealed that the British group would not oppose the entry of Japan for future business.[31] The terms

[30] FO 371/1068, Addis to Campbell, 17 Feb. 1911; Addis to FO, 17 May 1911; Grey to Cambon, 20 May 1911.

[31] *NGB*, vol. 66, Takahashi to Townsend, 14 Nov. 1910; Ono to Takahashi, 28 Nov. 1910; vol. 68, Takahashi to Schiff, 29 Nov. 1910; FO 371/873, Addis to FO, 16 Nov. 1910. Addis, in fact, did not wish to see the Japanese brought in. He said that the price of inclusion would be that Japan must bring something into the consortium as the other groups had.

of entry he indicated were acceptable to the financiers but not to the Japanese Foreign Office, where it was felt that Japan would have to renounce already-acquired participation rights to the syndicate and offer it rights she would secure in the future. Furthermore Japan did not admit the claim of the four groups to all the rights they now possessed. Hence it was decided in Tokyo that application to enter the consortium should be postponed. In the ensuing months there were frequent discussions with Russia over the currency loan, but Japan did not associate herself with the Russian scheme for a rival banking group.[32]

Manchuria apart, where the railway schemes sponsored by the Americans as well as the currency loan provisions met Russian and Japanese opposition, the position in China with the Hukuang and currency loans signed seemed to have developed satisfactorily for the consortium. Certainly Jordan. as he admitted to Campbell, had been surprised by the outcome.

You have the satisfaction of feeling that the principle of international co-operation which you consistently advocated and which I reluctantly accepted has proved a triumphant success in the end. The spectacle of the four Powers working together in perfect harmony certainly made a great impression upon the Chinese and was one of the factors which moved them to action.

A month later his optimism was unmitigated: 'Railway matters are progressing splendidly and I feel in a very triumphant mood', he wrote on 24 June 1911.[33] Jordan's mood was soon to be changed. By mid-October much of China was in revolution.

---

[32] *NGB*, vol. 66, political director of Ministry of Foreign Affairs to Takahashi, 30 Nov. 1910.

[33] FO 350/7, Jordan to Campbell, 24 May and 24 June 1911.

8

The Consortium and the Revolution

THE revolutionary movement spread rapidly in the south and centre of China but got little response in the north. When Yuan Shih-k'ai, dismissed from the imperial service in 1909 although he was its strongest personality and most capable administrator, responded (after some tactical hesitation), to the regent's appeal for him to return to take charge of affairs, the danger became obvious of civil war between the north, generally loyal to the Manchus, and the south. If serious conflict developed, the threat to foreign interests would be considerable. Commerce would be at best disrupted, and the lives and property of foreign nationals put at risk. On all counts the British, with the major commercial stake and the largest proportion of foreign nationals, stood to suffer most.

As the division in China became clear, British policy was defined. There was no disposition to favour the imperial regime. It was not well regarded in the Foreign Office, where Campbell judged it as 'corrupt and rotten'. What was desired was, as Grey put it, 'a strong and stable government which would ensure conditions favourable to trade'.[1] The nature of the regime—monarchical or republican—was immaterial. Grey saw his course to be neutrality between the government and the rebels, accompanied by efforts to bring them to agreement. Neutrality was held to be essential, both because of lack of confidence in the imperial authorities and because of the wide dispersal of British interests and nationals—some in government-controlled areas in the north, the bulk in the south and centre where the rebels dominated. A speedy agreement between the two sides was urgent for a further reason: civil war might bring military intervention from outside. The experience of the Boxer crisis was a sufficient indication of the danger such a development could contain for British interests.

The means to secure the desired stability were plain to Grey and his

---

[1] FO 371/1095, Grey to Jordan, 14 and 17 Nov. 1911; FO 350/1, Campbell to Jordan, 15 Nov. 1911.

advisers: diplomacy backed by financial pressure. For these to be effective, however, unity in policy among all the major powers involved in China was essential. The degree of co-operation already established between the four governments whose banks formed the consortium indicated a basic unanimity on China policy. Much would depend on the continuation of this, and much on the attitude of Russia and Japan—outside the consortium because they lacked financial resources, but rapidly able to bring military power to bear. In fact neither Russia nor Japan was in a position to undertake a major military move, for the strains of the 1904–5 war were still being felt in Tokyo as well as, more obviously, in St Petersburg, where defeat had brought not only exhaustion but a shift in policy towards Europe. Yet the Far East, though now in the background of Russian interests, was still an area of concern. In Japan, where the affairs of China were a central issue, there was division over the policy to be followed. Support for the rebels was widespread in some quarters, among them the army, but the conservative-minded government looked uneasily at the rise of republicanism in China—so much so that a suggestion of joint action to maintain the imperial dynasty was put to the British government, but was quickly turned aside by Grey.[2]

The attitude of the consortium was rapidly put to the test as both the Manchu authorities and the rebels, who had established a government at Nanking, requested loans. Approach to the Peking agents of the banks by the imperial government led Grey to call for caution on the part of the consortium powers and to emphasize the need for a common policy. He was in no doubt as to the course to be followed: financial stringency would force the opposing sides into agreement. He found general acceptance among the powers that there should be no loan until a responsible administration emerged in China. This was registered in the decision of the consortium banks on 8 November 1911 to follow a policy of strict neutrality. When Sun Yat-sen arrived in London, *en route* for China from America, he was given no encouragement. He was assured of an unimpeded passage through Singapore and Hong Kong, but that was all. Sun's efforts to secure a loan were unsuccessful. At his request he met Addis 'in utmost secrecy' at Addis's private house, presumably because he did not wish it to be known that he was in contact with the Hongkong Bank. Though Addis was rather impressed by Sun, in contrast with opinion

[2] P. Lowe, *Great Britain and Japan* (London, 1969), pp. 62–3, 70–3.

in the Foreign Office where Campbell judged him to be no more than 'an armchair politician and windbag' with little influence over the rebels, he made it clear to Sun that the bank would not make a loan to the rebels.[3]

The financial blockade imposed by the powers contributed to the agreement reached between the two sides in China in February 1912 with the abdication of the infant Manchu emperor and the proclamation of a republic with Yuan Shih-k'ai as its provisional president. The presence of Yuan at the head of affairs was a reassurance to the powers, and was particularly welcome to Britain where Jordan's long-standing admiration for Yuan had convinced the Foreign Office that, whatever its nature, monarchy or republic, a regime headed by Yuan offered the best hope of putting China on a stable foundation. 'Neutrality with a pro-Yuan bias', as Peter Lowe puts it, was the policy adopted.[4] It was immediately obvious that much depended on a solution for the acute financial problems of the Chinese government. It had already become apparent in the period of uncertainty up to February that the restraint decreed by the consortium governments would bring attempts to offset it from banks outside the consortium that saw the opportunity of profitable business. The Peking agents of the consortium banks, anxious for the standing of their institutions and apprehensive of rivals establishing themselves with the Chinese authorities, had been inclined to take up business before their governments imposed the blockade. Outside groups grasped the opportunity—particularly the Belgians, whose role in China had been much weakened by the Anglo-French entente and still more by the four-group consortium.[5] They had been quick to act. At the end of October 1911 it had emerged that a group of Belgian, British, and French banks was organizing a loan for the Peking government. This came to nothing in face of opposition from the British government, who refused to give it official support, and from the French, who blocked it in Paris, but there was also evidence that banks within the consortium were tempted to lend. Special interests were in conflict with political decisions.

In December 1911 the offer of a loan, apparently approved by the French government, from the French group to the director of Postal

---

[3] FO 350/1, Campbell to Jordan, 11 and 15 Nov. 1911; Addis Papers, Diary, 11 and 13 Nov. 1911.

[4] Lowe, p. 70.

[5] Kurgan-van Hentenryk, *Leopold II*, chap. 11.

Administration (a French subject), was reported to the Foreign Office. This French loan, the first example of unilateral action by a consortium bank, seems to have been withdrawn in face of British criticism,[6] and the French government reiterated its support for unity of action among the powers. In January, however, more alarming news had come from the south: loans to the rebels were alleged to have been made not only by the Japanese (who, though not within the consortium, had proclaimed adherence to the policy of neutrality, as had Russia), but by the Hongkong Bank itself.

Investigations revealed that both loans had been made to commercial concerns, though a proportion of the funds in each case was suspected to have passed to the rebel authorities. The Shanghai branch of the Hongkong Bank (which had made the British loan), and the Japanese Okura Bank both argued that it was imperative, for the safeguarding of future business, to assist their customers, but the transactions aroused suspicion. Within the consortium the French were very critical of the Hongkong Bank's loan to the China Merchants' Company, while on the British side there was concern that the Japanese were exploiting the situation to gain predominance in shipping and industrial enterprises in the Yangtze valley. The Foreign Office, alarmed by the policy of the Japanese, which seemed to point to a return of competition, was embarrassed by the action of the Hongkong Bank. The bank could be brought into line, all the more so since its loan had been a local arrangement made without knowledge of the London office where it was deplored.[7] Japan, outside the consortium, was a different matter. Protests in Tokyo blocked the Okura loan, but firmer links with Japan on financial policymaking were obviously desirable. This had been recognized in the Foreign Office. 'We must consult the Japanese about future loan proposals', Grey had instructed, following a report of resentment in Tokyo in December that Japan had been ignored when a temporary loan to the Peking government had been under discussion. Russia, too, it was agreed, would have to be brought into financial plans, which were bound to have political implications for China, an area of interest and of concern to both powers. For Grey, Russia and Japan had to be kept

---

[6] FO 371/1097, Addis to FO, 8 Dec. 1911; Jordan to Grey, 13 Dec. 1911; Grey to Bertie, 16 Dec. 1911.

[7] FO 371/1311, MacDonald to Grey, 26 Jan. 1912; FO 371/1312, MacDonald to Grey, 8 Feb. 1912; Grey to Bryce, 7 Feb. 1912; Jordan to Grey, 9 Feb. 1912; minute by Langley on telegrams communicated by Addis, 30 Jan. 1912.

sweet in the interests of Britain's general policy as well as in the particular matter of China. In Paris, too, similar considerations were
uppermost, particularly in regard to Russia. The fact that neither
Russia nor Japan, borrowers not lenders in international finance,
could bring any assets to the consortium was secondary to the political
necessity of keeping them in line in a common policy. 'The groups
won't like it,' one official observed, 'but that can't be helped.'[8]

With the February settlement, finance became the central issue in
relations between China and the powers. There were two aspects.
First, meeting the immediate needs of the provisional government and
the liabilities that the rebel government at Nanking had contracted. In
both these cases payment of troops was the urgent matter. Second,
long-term financial provision to give stability to China's financial and
economic structure. Both issues were politically charged and control
of policy in each was firmly maintained by the consortium governments, which were in general agreement on the necessity for the
continuation of collective action.

Only the German bankers showed reluctance to admit Russian and
Japanese banking groups as members of the consortium for all future
business, though they did not oppose their admission for the major
loan now under discussion that was intended to put China's finances
on a sound basis. The ground of their objections, shared if not voiced
by the other bank groups in the consortium, was that neither would
bring in any substantial financial weight.[9] Yet Russia and Japan acting
independently could make some funds available to China, as the
Japanese loans to the rebels had demonstrated. Grey was well aware of
the probable result of independent financial action: a return to unprofitable competition that would threaten the united front of the
powers. A similar view was held to Paris. Though the French did not
conceal their anger at the loan made by the Hongkong Bank to the
China Merchants Company, more important issues kept them close to
Britain. Agreement between the two major governments in the
consortium that Russia and Japan must be brought into financial as

    [8] FO 371/1310, minutes on MacDonald to Grey, 14 and 16 Dec. 1911.
    [9] FO 371/1314, Addis to FO, 29 Feb. 1912, with enclosures. The stated German view
was that the interests of Russia and Japan were political while those of the four-bank
group were financial and economic. This was justified, but the Germans were also
uncertain of the impact of the general policy ties that linked Russia and Japan to France
and Britain. The other major question occupying the powers was that of the recognition
of the republic.

well as political decisions was sufficient to bring the banks into line. Consent was then given by the consortium governments to small loans to meet immediate needs before Russia and Japan were admitted. Addis had stressed that financial disaster with serious effects on British trade and interests lay ahead if these loans were not made. If they were, he pointed out, the Hongkong Bank would be risking resources in an unstable situation. He was informed that the bank could look to the British government in the event of any difficulties over repayment, an acknowledgement that the bank was acting as the agent of the government in a political operation.[10] Yet it was also the case that the bank in its own long-term interests could not risk being supplanted by rivals outside the consortium winning the favour of the new regime by offering funds.

The decision of the four powers to admit Japan and Russia to the consortium did not end difficulties. Japan responded quickly, agreeing on 18 March to enter on the assurance that loans made by the consortium banks would not infringe her special interests in southern Manchuria. Russia proved more awkward. Sazonov, the Russian foreign minister, was alarmed by the projected size of the major reorganization loan (£60 million) that the consortium proposed to make to China. He was as much concerned as the Japanese to safeguard interests in Manchuria, but was even more concerned by the prospect of a regenerated China, united and militarily strong, which might result from the reorganization loan. Russia mounted a two-pronged campaign. Isvolsky, now ambassador in Paris, brought together with the aid of the Russo-Asiatic Bank a multinational group of banks outside the consortium groups. This was intended by the Russians to challenge the consortium, though the British and Belgian banks that provided the financial substance of the Russian group had a different aim: to secure membership of the consortium, not to break it. The Russian object was to draw France away from the consortium into association with a rival French–Russian–Belgian–Japanese financial formation. Sazonov, as a safeguard against failure of the attempt to destroy the consortium, brought pressure in London for assurances that membership of the consortium would not commit Russia in respect of any loans that might be used to infringe her position in Manchuria. Russia's place in the triple entente was used in a note of 26 March 1912 as it had been during the Manchurian railway

---

[10] FO 371/1314, Addis to FO, 5 Mar. 1912; FO to Hongkong Bank, 6 Mar. 1912.

disputes in 1909–10–to influence Grey. Russia, he was informed, did not refuse in principle to join the consortium but could do so only in conditions that allowed her not to distract her attention from her interests in Europe and the Balkans in order to concentrate on the defence of her situation in the Far East. This Russia thought to be a common interest of the powers of the triple alliance.[11]

Pressure was also brought in Paris, but Grey and Poincaré were determined to maintain the consortium and resisted an attempt to break its financial blockade. Plainly the consortium banks, placed in a monopoly position in respect of a major loan, would benefit as an indirect consequence; but the purpose of the blockade was political. It was intended to force China, by depriving her of alternative sources of funds, to accept terms for the reorganization loan that would put her finances in the good order necessary to bring the stability essential to healthy commerce. Hence when the Russian-sponsored group reached agreement with China in March 1912 for a loan of £1 million, this was immediately met by firm countermeasures by the consortium governments. Consequently, on 6 April Sazonov agreed to join; but because of Russia's determination to secure safeguards for her position in Manchuria, coupled with resistance from the existing consortium banks to manœuvres arising from the demands of the multinational group that was to represent Russia within it, it was not until June 1912 that the terms of Russian participation were finally agreed. Neither the Foreign Office nor the British group welcomed Russia's entry. As Jordan was told, 'We have throughout been very seriously pressed by Russia backed up by France and for political reasons it was absolutely necessary that an agreement should be arrived at.'[12]

France, indeed, had at one stage gone so far as to threaten withdrawal from the consortium if Russia were not ready to accept the compromise eventually reached by the consortium groups on the most difficult issue—the claim by Russia and Japan for a right of veto over the expenditure of loan funds for projects in their areas of special interest in Manchuria, Mongolia, and western China. Grey was not prepared to urge Poincaré not to support Russia on this issue, but when Sazonov accepted a provision that should any business contrary

[11] FO 371/1315, note from Russian embassy, 26 Mar. 1912; *DDF* 3rd series, 2, no. 334, note by Berthelot, 12 Apr. 1912; Kurgan-van Hentenryk, *Leopold II*, pp. 774–81.

[12] FO 371/1314, Grey to Bertie, 19 June 1912; FO 350/1, Langley to Jordan, 21 June 1912; MacMurray, 2, pp. 1021–5. Germany and the United States had held out for limitation of Russian and Japanese special interests to those deriving from treaty rights.

to the interests of Russia and Japan be concluded the Russian and Japanese groups were to be free to withdraw from the agreement, the consortium was saved. This was certainly a relief to Grey; his object all through had been to prevent a breakdown, which would have added political difficulties between the powers to the confusion in China. With Russia and Japan brought into the financial entente all the major powers were linked, and there was now what there had not been for many years: the prospect of a common attitude on China issues, and therefore of restraint—the aim throughout of British policy.

There was however another aspect, with domestic political implications given additional emphasis by the manœuvres of Russia, which was to cause Grey some embarrassment. This was the special relationship between the government and the Hongkong Bank, which with its affiliates was the sole British institution within the consortium. A greater readiness in the City to take up Chinese loans had shown itself some years earlier, and so had resentment at the dominant position of the Hongkong Bank. With the large and lucrative reorganization loan in prospect, in conditions of apparently greater stability in China, pressure for participation from the financial world became stronger. In January 1912 the Foreign Office had been informed by the Eastern Bank that it, together with J. H. Schroder and Co. and E. D. Sassoon and Co. was a member of an international syndicate formed to finance loans for the Chinese government. This was in fact the group brought together by Russia. The Eastern Bank requested official support for participation in any international loan that might be arranged. At the end of February it notified the Foreign Office of the imminent conclusion of its £1 million loan to China, and suggested the loan should be divided between the syndicate and the consortium groups. This at once brought up the question of the obligation of the government to the Hongkong Bank, the target of growing criticism in City financial circles as constituting a monopoly.

Addis feared that the Foreign Office was wavering, and vigorously argued for a continuation of the support the bank had been receiving: 'Had rather a scene at F.O. with Langley and Max-Muller over Bank's claim to exclusive govt. support. I went for them straight', he recorded on 5 March, and next day put his case in writing. He pointed out that the British group (in effect the Hongkong Bank) had with the other consortium groups entered into negotiation with the approval of the government to supply Yuan Shih-k'ai's immediate financial requirements against the issue of unsecured Chinese Treasury notes, repayment of which was to be provided out of the reorganization loan. What he sought was protection against China accepting offers from groups outside the consortium until the reorganization loan had been issued.[13]

Following an interview with Grey on 9 March, Addis got the assurances he sought. Grey, while disclaiming any intention of giving the Hongkong Bank a monopoly of government support, would not support negotiations for a loan that might interfere with the temporary arrangements made for financing the Chinese government, or conflict with the terms, or weaken support for the reorganization loan. This decision was certainly influenced by the fact that the financial arrangements by the consortium had been made with the approval of the member governments. To refuse support to the Hongkong Bank might have disrupted the consortium and the political entente behind it. But Grey's pledge was, as in 1909, limited to a special situation. The Hongkong Bank had served British interests well. Official confidence in it and particularly in Addis were important factors. But once more, as in 1909, Grey emphasized the desirability—in order to obviate difficulties likely to arise out of competition from other British firms and because of the impossibility of exclusive government support for one British bank alone—of forming a British group on the lines of the continental groups. Further, Addis was told that Grey expected the Hongkong Bank would arrange for the participation of competing British banks in the issue of the reorganization loan, provided such participation would really fall to British capital. The Eastern Bank was advised to approach the Hongkong Bank, and informed that the government deprecated a return to competition for Chinese loans.[14]

When in mid-March 1912 the international syndicate through its Belgian element, concluded its loan of £1 million with the Chinese government, the consortium banks protested strongly and suspended their payments to China. They were supported by their governments, which in their different ways placed obstacles to the financing of the loan in their markets. This action together with protests in Peking forced the Chinese government to cancel what had become known, because of the principal members of the international syndicate, as the Anglo-Belgian loan. The Chinese, with no option left to them, were

---

[13] FO 371/1315, Addis to FO, 6 Mar. 1912; Addis Papers, Diary, 5 Mar. 1912.
[14] FO 371/1315, FO to Addis, 14 Mar. 1912.

now forced to return to the consortium, and the way was seemingly clear for negotiation of the reorganization loan. As for the international syndicate they were bereft of any leverage when Sazonov, as he moved to enter the consortium, responded to French pressure to withdraw support in respect of the Anglo-Belgian loan from the Russo-Asiatic Bank.

The check to the manœuvres of the international syndicate brought renewed pressure on the Hongkong Bank from its competitors for a place in the financing of the British portion of the reorganization loan. The Chartered Bank, the oldest-established European bank doing business in China, was warned off a projected loan to a Chinese provincial government and advised to approach the Hongkong Bank for a share in the reorganization loan. This Addis was prepared to admit, but was supported by the Foreign Office in his insistence that the Hongkong Bank should be the sole issuing bank in London, just as the Deutsch-Asiatische was in Berlin and the Banque de l'Indo-Chine in Paris. The Chartered Bank protested, aggrieved both at a blow to its prestige and at the prospect that as China might be on the eve of commercial and industrial expansion, the Hongkong Bank would obtain a monopoly of the issuing of future loans. The matter was delicate, but Grey stood by his undertaking to Addis. While making it clear that exclusive support of the Hongkong Bank was only assured to it pending final issue of the reorganization loan, he was quite firm that it had a claim to be regarded as the sole issuing bank in Britain for the loan. It had acquired a special position by being first in the field with that loan, the Chartered Bank was informed, and it was to a large extent instrumental in bringing about the international combine 'which it is hoped will render effective the aim of His Majesty's Government to prevent any return to the former unprofitable policy of international competition in Chinese loans'.[15] The moral capital that the bank, and especially Addis, had built up in the Foreign Office was paying high dividends.

The Eastern Bank and its London associates also got no support in their efforts to share in the issue of the loan in London, or for official pressure on the Hongkong Bank to come to 'a fair understanding on China finance'. Russia pressed for the Schroder bank, as a member of the Russian group in the consortium, to be allowed to associate with the Hongkong Bank for the purpose of the issue of the Russian part of

[15] FO 371/1317, FO to Chartered Bank, 13 May 1912.

the loan only. This too, despite French support, was turned aside by Grey, who explained that it would be difficult, after one or two British banks had been refused participation, to allow the inclusion of some other bank. Regard for the interests of the Hongkong Bank was not the only factor influencing the Foreign Office. There was also the intention to prevent foreign intrusion into the London market. Within the consortium Addis got the support of his German, American, and Japanese banking partners for keeping Schroder's from issuing rights; but it, the Eastern Bank, and four Belgian institutions that had responded to Russian overtures to make the failed Anglo-Belgian loan did gain entry as the Russian group to the consortium, which had from the first been their main aim.[16] But in securing agreement from his consortium partners that the business organization of the loan should be centred on the Hongkong Bank in London, Addis made an important addition to the prestige of his bank that emphasized still more its predominance in China business.

It had already been agreed by the consortium governments that control of negotiations for the reorganization loan should rest firmly in their hands and not in those of the bank agents in Peking. Political interests were to prevail, not profit. The governments, determined to ensure strict control over Chinese financial administration, understood the danger that, given a free hand, the bank agents, eager for business, might relax demands for control. The agents were to conduct negotiations with the Chinese authorities, but every issue of significance was to be referred to their respective governments.

While Grey accepted that the terms of the loan should be decided by the governments not the bankers, he was ready to be more flexible than Poincaré on the security to be required from China and on the nature of the supervision to be exercised by the lenders over the employment of the funds to be made available. He was not opposed to strict supervision. This, indeed, had already been imposed by the groups on the disbursement of the temporary advances made to the Chinese government. Now Grey was ready to press for foreign advisers in government departments and extended employment of foreign specialists in railways and other industrial enterprises of the Chinese government, with a view to controlling revenue and increas-

---

[16] FO 371/1319, Grey to Bertie, 5 June 1912; Bertie to Grey, 7 June 1912; FO 350/1, Langley to Jordan, 5 July 1912; Kurgan-van Hentenryk, *Leopold II*, pp. 784–6. In Dec. 1912 Schroder's left the Russian group to join the expanded British group.

ing earnings. Where, however, Poincaré had in view direct foreign control, Grey—aware of the strong opposition this would rouse in China—preferred that foreign advisers should be appointed as officials of the Chinese government, though with adequate powers guaranteed under agreement with the consortium governments and groups so that funds could be cut off if China refused to follow the requirements of the advisers.[17]

The belief that the Chinese government would resist any major degree of foreign control was soundly based. Grey had been advised that the reviving of sovereign rights would be as prominent a feature in the programme of the new regime as it was in that of the old, with the difference that the new men would bring far more knowledge and experience of Western methods to the prosecution of the movement. T'ang Shao-yi, now Yuan's prime minister, successfully encouraged anti-loan agitation in order to force a relaxation of conditions, and at the end of June the Chinese formally rejected the supervisory conditions attached to the reorganization loan. In its place they asked for smaller monthly advances, to be covered by a loan of £10 million on easier terms. A relaxation of conditions was rejected by the consortium governments for any loan, and as an indication of their determination that loan funds should not be squandered they agreed that advances to China should be suspended.

There now reappeared the difference in view between the consortium governments and their banks. The banks feared that competitors would, with the approval of their governments, offer China easier terms, and were ready to accommodate the Chinese request for a loan of £10 million. Addis could see the danger that if the consortium insisted on conditions impossible for the Chinese government to accept, an impetus might be given to action by the richer provinces to contract loans. This, because of its likely consequences for the unity and stability of the country, the British were anxious to prevent. His argument, that in view of the reduction in the amount of the loan it would be inequitable and unwise to require the same security, the entire salt gabelle, was at first rejected by his partners, but by mid-July 1912 all with the exception of the American group had to some extent come round to his position. Addis certainly, and the French and Germans to a lesser extent, saw the matter as men of business with

---

[17] FO 371/1317, memorandum from French Embassy, 7 May 1912; memorandum to French Embassy, 29 May 1912.

great interests in China. The Americans, with less at stake, were perhaps looking for a way out of the whole affair. This, at least, was Addis's opinion.[18] The consortium governments, however, maintained their insistence on strict controls for even a reduced loan and refused to permit China to borrow outside the consortium until she had made provision for the repayment of advances already made by the consortium banks.

The Chinese government, desperate for money, sought to breach the blockade in its weakest point—the London money market, where resentment against the monopoly of official support in Chinese loans enjoyed by the Hongkong Bank continued to run high. Addis, determined to maintain the primacy of his institution in Chinese business, had admitted other houses to no more than subsidiary status. The fact that he could call on official support only strengthened feeling. *The Times* fuelled the flames, and Grey was under frequent attack. Moreover the Hongkong Bank was isolated. It did not control the London market as the French and German groups, each including major institutions, controlled Paris and Berlin. In these circumstances China could look for aid in London, and found it. C. Birch Crisp, a City financier, obtained through an American syndicate a contract to negotiate a loan for China. Armed with this he secured a promise of support from leading banks including Lloyd's, London and Westminster, and Capital and Counties. Highly optimistic statements on the situation in China and the economic prospects there were made to the press by G. E. Morrison, now political adviser to the Chinese government. Morrison had come to London partly for private reasons, but equally in order to work up support in the City for a loan that would allow China to breach the blockade.[19]

The prospect of the Crisp loan acutely embarrassed the Foreign Office and led to a reconsideration of policy. The gist of a memorandum by J. D. Gregory of the Far Eastern Department was telegraphed to Jordan on 30 August for his comments. Jordan was told that if China rejected the fresh scheme that the consortium groups were preparing, the exclusive support that had been given for a political objective—to secure through the reorganization loan 'the establishment and consolidation of a stable and efficient form of government in China, the

    [18] FO 350/1, Langley to Jordan, 9 Aug. 1912.
    [19] Lowe, *Great Britain and Japan*, p. 131; *The Times*, 26 Sept., 1 Oct. 1912; FO 350/1, Alston to Jordan, 4 Oct. 1912.

existence of which constitutes an important British interest'—could hardly be maintained. As it was, the Foreign Office was under increasing pressure from firms outside the consortium not to oppose their transactions. If the consortium failed to reach agreement with China, the reorganization scheme, even in modified form, was at an end. Then China would be free to borrow outside the consortium, and the British government would be able to consider on its merits any application from a sound British group for support in carrying through any financial operations in China. Provision for security, control of expenditure and repayment of advances to the consortium banks would be a condition of support. But there would be no exclusive suport for any group, and nothing more than the customary support given to British firms in dealings with the Chinese government.[20]

The embarrassments resulting from public and parliamentary criticism of exclusive support of the Hongkong Bank were clear. In terms of British domestic policy, the consortium had become a liability open to the charge of monopoly and, from the radicals, of exploiting the financial needs of China to keep her in tutelage. Jordan, however, while far from enthusiastic about the consortium, saw it as the lesser of two evils. He felt that if it would ease its terms, it offered the best means of success; if it broke up, the way would be open for competition and financial confusion. His advice was taken, and Crisp was told that the British government would put all possible pressure on China to drop the loan.[21]

No formal action was taken to block the loan in the London market. No secret was made of official disapproval, but contact with the market was avoided because to have acted formally would have impaired a useful instrument of policy. The position was explained to Jordan. The Stock Exchange Committee only gave the Crisp loan a quotation by six votes to five.

We were told that if we would write a letter to say that as a matter of policy we would be glad to have the quotation refused it would have been but Sir E. Grey quite rightly objected to do anything of the kind. We have always taken the line when talking to foreign governments that we cannot interfere in such matters as we have no control, and to intervene once, perhaps successfully,

---

[20] FO 371/1321, memorandum by Gregory, 26 Aug. 1912; Grey to Jordan, 30 Aug. 1912.
[21] FO 371/1322, Jordan to Grey, 3 Sept. 1912; Grey to Jordan, 10 Sept. 1912.

would have created a most undesirable precedent if at any time they desired us to intervene in a case where it could be inconvenient or undesirable.[22]

On another front Addis, who was understandably anxious to preserve the consortium, was supported by the Foreign Office in his efforts to get agreement among the groups to some relaxation in conditions. Grey let the governments know that the failure of negotiations would mean the relaxing of exclusive support. China could not be forbidden to obtain financial assistance on any terms from outside. Grey and Addis were well aware that the London market could be breached. The Crisp loan had been a warning: if most of the stock had been left with underwriters, a not inconsiderable portion had been taken up by investors.[23] The British arguments seem to have had some effect within the consortium, for none wished to see it break up. By early October Addis had been able to persuade his partners to accept some relaxation in the terms.

Negotiations with China were resumed by the consortium banks at the beginning of November 1912. A few weeks later the domestic embarrassment for Grey of the monopoly position of the Hongkong Bank was somewhat eased when Addis announced the widening of the British group to include Baring Brothers, the London County and Westminster Bank, Parr's Bank, and J. H. Schroder and Co. This was of course a response to pressure from various quarters—the Foreign Office, the bank's partners in the consortium and the Hongkong Bank representatives in China—but no doubt also to the Crisp loan affair, which had made it plain that there was support in the City for an attempt to breach the Hongkong Bank's privileged place. The bank, however, intended to retain its controlling position, and was supported by the Foreign Office. The Chartered Bank once more complained against Addis's refusal to allow it no more than a subordinate place in the extended group. This it would not accept, and remained outside.[24]

The negotiations in Peking did not long remain tranquil, for disagreements re-emerged within the consortium. There were purely financial questions at issue, but the main dispute was over the

---

[22] FO 350/1, Langley to Jordan, 9 Nov. 1912. The opposition of the Consortium powers forced China to cancel the Crisp loan in December 1912.

[23] FO 371/1322, Grey to British ambassadors to consortium governments, 27 Sept. 1912.

[24] FO 405/209, Addis to FO, 16 Dec. 1912; FO to Hongkong Bank, 21 Dec. 1912.

appointment of foreign advisers to oversee the administration of the salt tax. The Chinese were prepared to accept advisers from countries outside the consortium, but France, supported by Russia, insisted upon consortium nationals. Initially Grey was ready to agree on this, but he resisted French claims to nominate to posts giving control over key areas. In face of determined opposition by the Chinese to the appointment of consortium nationals, the British, supported by Germany, pressed for a more flexible attitude within the consortium, for the deadlock that now existed threatened the interests of the banking groups of both countries. Their stake in China, especially for the British, was considerable, and they could see danger to their prospects if China again sought financial assistance outside the consortium.

In January 1913 Grey responded rapidly to an appeal from Addis for action to end the deadlock. The French were warned that if they persisted in their demands a complete break of the consortium would result. Britain and Germany drew together. Addis was told that the Foreign Office would not interfere with his discretion in instructing his agent in Peking to sign independently the preliminary agreement for the reorganization loan with immediate advance of funds to China. Similar instructions were given to the German group. This certainly showed a care for the interests of the Hongkong Bank on the part of the Foreign Office, but wider considerations were also in view: if China turned elsewhere, she might obtain funds without the conditions judged necessary to secure the financial stability so desirable in the interests of British trade.

Breakdown was averted because, although the terms of the reorganization loan were still in dispute within the consortium as well as with the Chinese government, the consortium did agree towards the end of January 1913 to make an advance of £2 million. But the adviser question continued to cause acrimony within the consortium because the British suspected that the aim of France, backed by Russia, was to establish control over China's finances through the advisers, as had been done in Egypt. Grey was once more ready to face the breakdown if there were no compromise. Addis was instructed that if the groups could not agree, he was free to proceed with those who agreed to the most satisfactory terms possible. It thus seems that Grey was prepared to contemplate an Anglo-German entente in place of the consortium. More likely he expected that a British move would alarm the French and bring them to modify their position so that some degree of harmony would be restored. If so he judged correctly for the French gave way, reducing their demands for foreign advisers from six to four, including one for the revived currency loan.

The Chinese still baulked at the prospect of consortium nationals as advisers. Grey seems not to have been opposed in principle to neutrals, but since Britain had obtained the most important nomination (to the chief inspectorship of the salt gabelle), and the powers were now in agreement, he was not inclined to go out of line. Addis remained apprehensive that breakdown would come and the Chinese would look outside the consortium but now, with agreement reached with the powers, Grey was not prepared to allow the bank to act independently. Addis was clear that even if it meant loss of business, the bank, in its real and permanent interests, must not break with the British government.[25] Negotiations with the Chinese, however, remained at a standstill, for Chinese nationalists were strongly opposed to advisers from the consortium powers. The withdrawal of the American group from the consortium by the Wilson administration strengthened their resistance. Wilson's action, and the terms in which it was justified, was therefore in Addis's words 'a body blow',[26] though not to the financial capacity of the consortium to float the loan if agreement were reached.

What did bring negotiations to conclusion was the internal situation in China. Hostility between Yuan Shih-k'ai and the Kuomintang led by Sun Yat-sen was moving to climax. Yuan needed funds to be sure of his ability to deal by force with any rebellion against his authority. Sun Yat-sen, well aware of this, warned the Hongkong Bank that if the loan were concluded without the sanction of the National Assembly, it would be repudiated by all the provinces south of the Yangtze as well as Shansi and Shensi. Although the Hongkong Bank's officials in China were alarmed, the threat was brushed aside by the consortium powers under the leadership of Britain determined to do all possible to keep Yuan in power. Jordan warned that Yuan would certainly resign if the powers yielded to Sun Yat-sen's threats, and the consequence would be political and commercial chaos in China. The loan

---

[25] FO 371/1590, Grey to Bertie, 23 Jan. 1913; Grey to Jordan 24 Jan. 1913; FO 405/211, Jordan to Grey, 20 Jan. 1913; Grey to Jordan, 1 Feb. 1913; papers communicated by Addis, 8 Feb. 1913. Jordan was very critical of the co-operation between the agents of the Hongkong Bank and the German group in what he saw as a policy designed to break the consortium in order to open the way for a loan to China. This would be to the advantage of the two banks since it would ensure the repayment of earlier loans made by them to Chinese provinces (FO 800/31, Jordan to Langley, 10 Feb. 1913).

[26] FO 371/1592, Hongkong Bank to FO, with enclosure, 26 Mar. 1913.

agreement was signed on 26 April and its first portion issued in the financial markets on 21 May.[27] The issue was very successful, not least because the prospectus included a statement that the consortium governments recognized that the repayments of the loan were a binding obligation on the Chinese government. With the conclusion of the loan, the way was open for Yuan to deal with the Kuomintang and clear the way for a strong central government.

The consortium had kept together, despite friction, to bring out the reorganization loan, a matter of much satisfaction for Britain. By the summer of 1913 it was experiencing severe strains in respect of industrial loans, the business that had first brought the banking groups together.

---

[27] FO 405/211, Hongkong Bank to FO, 26 Apr. 1913; Jordan to Grey, 27 and 28 Apr. 1913; FO 371/1594, Addis to FO, 21 May 1913.

9

The Revival of Competition[1]

DURING the autumn of 1912 there were clear signs that the Chinese
government intended to accelerate the modernization of the country
and to welcome foreign participation. This promised a profitable field
of investment for financial and industrial concerns. The policy of the
consortium powers, however, presented an obstacle. As matters stood,
Britain, in common with her partners, was bound not to approve loans
to China from sources outside the consortium groups for administrative or industrial purposes during the negotiation of the reorganization loan and for six months after the final instalment under it had
been paid to China; and was equally bound to exclusive support of the
British group within the consortium. The group itself, under the interbank agreements of 1909, 1910, and 1912, was bound to share industrial
as well as financial loans with its French, German, American, Russian,
and Japanese partners.

Grey had never liked the pledge of exclusive support, which under
the pressure of circumstances during the Chinese revolution and its
aftermath had been significantly widened in scope. It could not be
reconciled with the *laissez-faire* traditions of British commercial
practice. There had already been ample evidence of City hostility to
the links between the government and the Hongkong Bank. Although
the bank had under pressure admitted other institutions to participation, the group was still small. Now, as China seemed to be opening
up, resentment was strengthened against the quasi-monopoly position
enjoyed by the group with government support. This was a serious
political embarrassment for Grey, and certainly contributed to his
wish to see industrial loans thrown open so that all substantial British
concerns could look to official support for business in China.

Side by side with this, another consideration influenced the desire
to free industrial loans from restriction: the threat of business lost to

[1] This chapter is largely drawn from my article 'British Policy in China 1913–1914:
Rivalry with France in the Yangtze Valley', *Journal of Oriental Studies* 15 (1977),
pp. 20–36.

British enterprise. Countries outside the consortium were not bound by its agreements and could undertake business. In itself this was not a serious matter because for any significant industrial loan, recourse would have to be made to the major capital markets. In Paris and Berlin such transactions could be vetoed by the French and German governments. In the London market, however, the British authorities lacked such powers. They could not prevent money being lent from London to China through an intermediary. 'British financial houses may contact us when they want our support but are not likely to do so when they are financing some foreign enterprise.'[2] This situation caused some unease in Paris, where it was argued that valuable industrial contracts blocked by the consortium governments as part of their coercive policy might pass to rival groups. In the Foreign Office, while there was certainly no wish to see British capital supporting foreign enterprise in China, the most disturbing element at the end of 1912 was evidence that while the British government scrupulously observed its obligations, certain of its partners were circumventing consortium agreements in order to secure a share in industrial contracts.

What had aroused concern on strategic as well as on economic grounds was a loan projected by Belgian financiers for the extension of the existing Pienlo railway to Lanchow in Kansu to the west, and to Haichow on the Yellow Sea to the east. This would complete the proposed north-western grand trunk system from the coast to the interior of China. The extension scheme, it soon emerged, was backed by French and Russian interests. Though the French group in the consortium disclaimed any connection with it, and Poincaré agreed to make representations in St Petersburg against participation in the loan by a banking house that belonged to the Russian consortium group, Jordan saw it as evidence of political aims.

This line, it is morally certain will be ultimately Russian or French, and will be one of great strategic importance which may ultimately affect integrity of China. With Mongolia and possibly Chinese Turkestan in Russian hands a line from the frontier of Mongolia to a port on the Yellow Sea raises grave political considerations.[3]

---

[2] FO 371/1942, minute by Langley on Jordan to Grey, 23 Mar. 1914. For French comment on the London market see *Asie Française*, Sept. 1912, Oct. 1912.

[3] FO 405/209, Jordan to Grey, 25 Dec. 1912; Kurgan-van Hentenryk, *Leopold II*, pp. 787–9.

Officially the French attitude over the Pienlo loan was correctly disapproving, but in April 1913 it was reported that French banks, with the acquiescence of the Ministry of Finance, had provided £3 million out of the £4 million total of the loan.[4] To the Foreign Office, as to Jordan, this loan bore a resemblance to the old pattern at the end of the nineteenth century, when the French, working through Belgian companies, built up a significant stage in Chinese railways.

By this time a more ominous development had added to the unease created by the Pienlo loan: the formation, as a joint venture between the Chinese government and French interests, of the Banque Industrielle de Chine to finance public works in China, including ports, railways, and mines. Jordan appears to have been unaware of the negotiations in Peking that had preceded the formation of the Banque Industrielle. The first news that the Foreign office had of it was through a private member's question in the House of Commons at the end of March. Enquiries in Paris revealed that the Chinese government had approved the statutes of the Banque on 11 January 1913, and was to subscribe one-third of its capital. The government assumed the moral obligation of facilitating for the Banque all the operations it might initiate in accordance with its objects. One of the directors of the Banque was André Berthelot, a former deputy, son of Marcellin Berthelot the distinguished chemist and leading republican notable who had been foreign minister in 1894–95, and brother of Philippe Berthelot, formerly head of the Asiatic Department at the French Foreign Ministry and recently appointed *chef de cabinet* to Pichon who had again become foreign minister. The Banque Industrielle, Bertie reported, was backed by the Foreign Ministry, which had solicited support for it from French financial houses; but not by the Ministry of Finance, where there was opposition to Philippe Berthelot's pleas that French banks be recommended to interest themselves in the venture. Bertie also reported that there were critical voices raised against the Banque in the press. According to Addis, the French consortium group did not favour the new institution.[5]

Although the suggestion was refuted by Pichon, the driving force behind the Banque Industrielle appears to have been Philippe Berthelot, who intended it to be the spearhead of the French economic

[4] FO 371/1623, Bertie to Grey, 12 Apr. 1913.

[5] FO 371/1592, Colonel Yate MP to Grey, 21 Mar. 1913, giving notice of the question; FO 371/1623, Bertie to Grey, 29 Mar., 7, 12 Apr. 1913; Grey to Jordan, 7 Apr. 1913; Addis to FO, 28 Mar. 1913.

penetration of China of which he had long dreamed. With the departure of Poincaré from the Foreign Ministry in January 1913, Berthelot acquired a preponderating influence on China policy and promoted a markedly nationalistic line. The strength of France, in a situation in which China seemed about to embark again upon a policy of industrial expansion, lay in the abundant capital available for investment. Berthelot, it seems, now judged the moment ripe to use this arm, counting on the support of French financial institutions. Industrial organizations in France, hitherto somewhat indifferent to opportunities in China, were by 1912–13 showing interest in railway schemes there and petitioning their Foreign Ministry to obtain a fair share of orders for them. Indications of a more independent line on the part of France were also apparent in the determined effort to impose rigid controls on China as a condition of the reorganization loan, and in the assertive attitude of Conty, the French minister in Peking.[6]

Since the Banque Industrielle had not undertaken operations there was no ground for British protest, but the developing industrial scene brought a reconsideration of policy. In January 1913, in response to pressure from British firms, Grey proposed to his consortium partners that industrial loans be separated from financial so that nationals of the consortium powers would be free to undertake business involving loans subject to conditions, and this was agreed to. In May, however, recognizing that conditional freedom would put consortium nationals at a disadvantage with competitors. Britain proposed unconditional freeing of industrial loans, to include the dissolution of the interbank agreements of 1909 and 1910 as well as of 1912. The date of dissolution was to be some months ahead. This again was accepted, but in September, Britain, the one consortium power pressing for freedom for industrial loans, accelerated the dismantling process. The stimulus came with reports in the summer of negotiations for a loan for industrial purposes from a German firm to the provincial authorities of Yunnan, followed by news of a second Belgian railway loan, again clearly, with French backing. These developments, together with Japanese activity in the Yangtze Valley, brought a decision for which Jordan (who was home on leave) and Gregory of the Far Eastern

[6] A. Bréal, *Philippe Berthelot* (Paris, 1937), pp. 58, 61, 202; G. Kurgan-van Hentenryk, 'Philippe Berthelot et les entreprises ferroviaires franco-belges en Chine (1912–1914)', *Revue d'histoire moderne et contemporaine* 22 (1975), pp. 284–92; FO 371/1629, Jordan to Langley, 31 Oct. 1913.

Department were largely responsible: to proceed immediately to the final stage in the restoration of competition in industrial loans.[7]

On 3 September 1913 the Hongkong Bank was informed, with particular reference as justification to the Belgian loans and the creation of the Banque Industrielle, that 'in the higher interests of the British commercial and industrial position in China as a whole', freedom of competition was to be immediate. The bank was told that it was clear that

the expected scramble for railway and similar enterprises in China has begun in earnest and that under present conditions, which preclude His Majesty's Government from supporting British industrial undertakings which may commend themselves, Chinese business is in imminent danger of being irrevocably lost to all British firms and groups including of course the individual members in the Five Power consortium.

The government recognized that in practice it was impossible for other powers to exercise any effective control over their nationals. In consequence the effect of the British government's continuing observance of its undertakings was merely to prevent British firms participating in competition for Chinese business while others in effect were free—an untenable position. Therefore the six-power agreement of June 1912, in so far as it reserved industrial loans from institutions within the member states to the banking groups forming the consortium, must be considered as inoperative and virtually lapsed. The Hongkong Bank was now requested to propose to its partners the immediate termination of the interbank agreements of 1909 and 1910, which had provided for the sharing of business between the groups then included in the consortium.[8] This was done, and by the end of September the consortium as an organization for industrial loan business had ended. It remained intact, less of course the United States, for the making of financial loans for administrative purposes. So, too, did the Anglo-French association represented by Chinese Central Railways with its existing rights. But the British decision ended exclusive support, and permitted any British enterprise to compete for and to claim official support in any industrial loans. It

---

[7] FO 371/1594, Alston to Grey, 19 Aug. 1913, with minute by Gregory; memorandum by Gregory, 19 Aug. 1913; Jordan to Gregory, 26 Aug. 1913. The German loan to Yunnan, on the Indo-China frontier, disturbed the French government, which protested to Germany (Poidevin, pp. 722–3).

[8] FO 371/1594, FO to Hongkong Bank, 3 Sept. 1913.

also promised to end, except for the financial consortium, the long special association between the Foreign Office and the Hongkong Bank. The 'cordial and loyal co-operation' of the bank over the years was appreciated and publicly recognized in the knighthood conferred on Addis in October 1913.

The new situation had been brought about as much to meet criticism of Grey from British opponents of exclusive support as by the wish to mount a counter-offensive against rivals on the part of the Foreign Office, where mingled with optimism there was clear awareness of the risk to individualist British enterprise confronted with the concentrated strength of foreign groups and deprived now even of the limited protection afforded by the consortium agreements.[9] Jordan, though taking the view that in the last resort the building of railways was more important for British commerce in general than the question of who built them and equally aware of the dangers of competition, had in January 1913 been confident of the ability of British firms to look after themselves.[10] Developments in the weeks following the ending of the international agreements governing industrial enterprise, however, bore out forebodings as to the risks to which British interests were exposed in conditions of determined competition.

In October 1913, to add to mounting evidence of increasing Japanese economic penetration in southern China, came disturbing news of French activity. Conty, it was reported, was working to undermine British predominance in the Chinese maritime customs administration. More alarming was the announcement that the Chinese government had negotiated a loan of £6 million with the Banque Industrielle for harbour works at Pukow and a bridge at Hankow—positions at the centre of British commercial interests in the Yangtze Valley—and had done so in disregard of repeated warnings that Britain claimed a prior right.[11] Though this development was taken with significant calm by the Hongkong Bank group, which had been negotiating for the contract through the British and Chinese Corporation, Jordan, now back in Peking, reacted sharply. In face of this concrete

---

[9] FO 371/1594, Addis (to Langley, 24 June 1913) pointed to the dangers. His was no doubt an interested argument, but Gregory was also aware that the restoration of free competition would carry risks for British enterprise (FO 371/1617, minute by Gregory on Jordan to Grey, 1 June 1913).

[10] FO 371/1590, Jordan to Grey, 6 Jan. 1913.

[11] FO 371/1629, Jordan to Langley, 31 Oct. 1913; FO 371/1623, Alston to Grey, 7 Nov. 1913; Addis to FO, 10 and 11 Nov. 1913; Jordan to Grey, 5 Dec. 1913.

instance of advance by foreign interests he took the strongly national attitude that usually marked his views on economic policy: 'I cannot view without grave misgiving the attitude adopted by French financial interests during the last few months', he wrote in December 1913, referring not only to the Pukow loan but also to the Belgian railway loan in July against which the French government had refused to protest, and to a reported loan by a French bank to Szechwan Province that might be used to finance a Chinese expedition into Tibet to the embarrassment of the government of India. This latter might not materialize but the Pukow loan seemed definite and called for action.

> To prevent future incidents of this kind I venture to suggest that we should impose certain obligations upon the British and Chinese Corporation and other companies as a condition of their obtaining our support for future railway undertakings. The British and Chinese Corporation do not, in my opinion, show sufficient regard for British interests in general as distinguished from the mere financial interests of the Corporation in carrying out large undertakings like the Tientsin–Pukow railway. It was their bounden duty, I think, to see that the port which forms the terminus of the two and the connecting link among the three lines which they had constructed was retained in British hands, and one cannot conceive of a German company showing such neglect of German interests. In the present instance while the Germans made an effort to compete with the French, the British and Chinese Corporation stood entirely aloof, with the result that British shipping will probably be subjected to port dues and other charges.

The obligation he proposed was that before Foreign Office support was accorded to their applications, British companies seeking railway concessions should undertake to ensure that British interests arising directly out of their concessions, as distinct from their own immediate interests, should be effectively safeguarded against outside interference.[12]

Jordan had frequently criticized the Hongkong Bank group, but up to the summer of 1913 the Far Eastern Department of the Foreign

---

[12] FO 371/1629, Jordan to Grey, 8 Dec. 1913. Jordan's argument, in effect that foreign investment should serve the national interest, raised a controversial issue of principle widely discussed at the time, particularly in France and Britain where international finance was attacked for placing profit before patriotism. For comment on the issue in France see Poidevin, pp. 543–9, 725–6, and R. Girault, 'Pour un portrait nouveau de l'homme d'affaires français vers 1914', *Revue d'histoire moderne et contemporaine* 16 (1969), pp. 329–49. In Britain, Bland attacked the Hongkong Bank and its affiliates for neglecting British interests. The general question is discussed by E. Staley, *War and the Private Investor* (New York, 1935), pp. 72–3.

Office had generally shown understanding for the views and policies of the bank and its affiliates and had accepted, indeed to some extent welcomed, the trend to co-operation between the financial and industrial groups of the major powers in China. This attitude, apart from brief exceptions, had never been shared by Jordan or his predecessor, Satow. But signs of change had appeared, precipitated by the Pukow–Sinyang railway contract negotiations, which had been successfully concluded in June 1913 with the signing of a preliminary agreement between the Chinese authorities and Chinese Central Railways. In the negotiations in 1904–5 for association between the British and French financial groups, it had been clearly accepted by the British, who had held a preliminary loan agreement for it since 1899, that the Pukow–Sinyang concession was among those conveyed to the joint association represented by Chinese Central Railways. When, however, Jordan renegotiated the preliminary agreement on behalf of Chinese Central Railways, he claimed that he had not known of the existence of the French interest, which was not revealed by the British group until the agreement was on the point of conclusion. Jordan, who had assumed he was supporting a purely British enterprise, was highly critical of the situation then established. Initially the British group argued in favour of the admission of the French to full participation, but took advantage of evidence that the Chinese would use this to terminate the agreement to limit the French group to financial participation. The neglect of French interests in this matter was resented in Paris, and was recognized in the Foreign Office as a contributory factor in the growing conflict between British and French policy in the Yangtze Valley.[13]

Among officials in the Far Eastern Department, as in the Peking Legation, the affair provoked irritation at the fetters that the existence of Chinese Central Railways as an international company appeared to impose on British enterprise, and a marked disinclination to enter into further agreements of this nature with any power. Langley, the head of the department, like his predecessor Francis Campbell, maintained the attitude of approval of international co-operation for industrial enterprise in China. Langley had been involved in the formation of the Anglo-French partnership in 1903–6. He now argued that it had

[13] FO 371/1619, Alston to Grey, 16 June 1913; FO 350/12, Jordan to Langley, 26 Jan. 1914; FO 405/216, memorandum by Gregory on railway construction in China, 1 Mar. 1914.

been brought into being largely by the Foreign Office and clearly wished that it should continue. For a time he also favoured some co-operation with the Japanese in railways in the Yangtze Valley, claiming that other powers would never recognize the vast area as a British sphere.[14] Other officials reacted differently. Alston, who had been posted to Peking to take over the legation while Jordan was on leave, had initially been ready to accept some co-operation with the Japanese, but soon turned against both this and the arrangements with the French. By November he was claiming that to secure equal participation for the French in the Pukow–Sinyang railway would be 'in the highest degree injurious to British railway interests in general', and was asserting that in view of the change in industrial loans policy, purely British interests such as this railway should not be sacrificed to obsolete international financial arrangements.[15] By 1914 the feeling against international concerns had become even stronger. A report of criticism aroused in China by disclosures of the links between British and French interests led Gregory to comment:

I can only express the malicious hope that the British and Chinese Corporation and the Chinese Central Railways will be irrevocably prejudiced in the eyes of the Chinese government and that future concessions will go instead to firms that are purely British, purely straightforward and purely patriotic.

He recognized that loans would in part be placed abroad in the prevailing conditions of finance, which was bound to become more and more international, but joint undertakings involving a degree of control by foreign nationals were to be condemned. 'It is dead against our interests to support joint undertakings under the new conditions prevailing in China and I would suggest that we should ruthlessly decline to support them in future.' Grey agreed, remarking in January 1914, 'We should certainly reserve our efforts for really British and desirable undertakings.'[16]

Jordan's proposal that pledges should be obtained from British companies was, however, not thought to be workable in practice, though a general remonstrance was sent to the British and Chinese

---

[14] FO 371/1621, minute by Langley on Jordan to Grey, 11 Apr. 1913; FO 371/1625, minute by Langley on Alston to Grey, 26 Sept. 1913. Campbell had died in Dec. 1911.

[15] FO 371/1619, Alston to Grey, 15 Nov. 1913. Alston's change of attitude resulted from alarm at Japanese activity during the rebellion in the south in the summer of 1913.

[16] FO 371/1935, minute by Gregory on Jordan to Grey, 26 Dec. 1913; FO 371/1937, minute by Gregory on papers communicated by BCC, 14 Jan. 1914. FO 371/1941, minute by Grey on memorandum by Gregory, 16 Jan. 1914.

Corporation. His suggestion that France and Japan be asked to restrict the activities of their financiers in enterprises materially affecting British undertakings in China accorded with thinking in the Foreign Office, and had indeed already been decided upon in relation to Japan as well as France.

The problem was to devise appropriate means to meet the situation. The Japanese were seeking to share with British capital the financing of an important railway project, the Nanking–Hsiangt'an line in the Yangtze Valley, and were reported to be anxious to lend to the Canton Provincial Railway Company. This would give them control of the southern portion of the Canton–Hankow railway, which would be injurious to Hong Kong. The first method adopted, after indications of British disinclination for co-operation had failed to dissuade the Japanese, was to propose in October 1913 that in return for Britain agreeing to benefits and privileges for Japan in the Yangtze region, Japan should accord British enterprise similar privileges in southern Manchuria. As expected this was not conceded by Japan, who showed no disposition to withdraw the demand for financial participation in the Nanking–Hsiangt'an railway, which would place a section of it under Japanese control.[17]

The weakness of the British position in the now-urgent matter of devising a strategy to fend off French and Japanese encroachment in the Yangtze Valley, the main centre of British interests, was that because of the termination, under British pressure, of the restrictions on industrial loans, there was now no formal ground on which protest could be made. What was decided, on the suggestion of Gregory, was to make a definite assertion of principle on future concession policy in an effort to reach a permanent solution. With China entering a new phase, probably a period of violent development, a policy was required to meet it. If discussion were merely confined to specific points there would be a succession of similar questions; it was necessary to go to the root of the matter.

The definition of 'spheres of influence' is not to be thought of but there are ways of declaring an equivalent position as we have already done to the

---

[17] FO 371/1621, note to Japanese ambassador, 11 Oct. 1913; memorandum from Japanese ambassador, 26 Nov. 1913. On the background see P. Lowe, *Great Britain and Japan*, pp. 149–57. The prospect of Anglo-Japanese partnership in railways in the region had developed from discussion in Jan. 1913, unauthorized by the FO, between Mayers, agent of the BCC and Odagiri of the Yokohama Specie Bank.

Japanese and there seems no reason why we should not definitely claim 'traditional and acknowledged fields' for our own industrial enterprise and concede the same to the French—or any other power that may come into the field. For present purposes we may not get much out of a communication of this kind but it may lead to some kind of reciprocal, if tacit, arrangements in the future . . .

Gregory did not think it wise to define exactly what the British meant by the Yangtze Valley or how much of it they intended to be their special preserve.

It would be absurd to claim the whole, but it is equally undesirable to earmark any particular district and exclude the rest allowing no room for expansion or development as time goes on. Our claim must therefore be to a vague and undefined region but it may clearly be to a wide area embracing all the present concessions now in dispute which would incontestably infringe on a sphere where British enterprise is firmly established and has a prescriptive right to develop.

That conflict existed with France as well as with Japan was not without advantages, for approach to the two powers would prevent the Japanese feeling that they were singled out. Langley was uneasy, but Grey was impressed by Jordan's strong opposition to French and Japanese penetration of the British preserve.[18] Accordingly, approaches were made to Japan on 31 December, and to France in broadly similar terms on the following day. To Japan the British reiterated the claim to reciprocity between the Yangtze Valley and southern Manchuria. The French were reminded that the dissolution of the intergroup arrangements had come about because circumstances in China had made the pre-revolution policy of joint enterprise on a permanent basis impracticable. This, though necessary, had at once created a completely new situation that the British government thought must forthwith be taken into account by the powers, for 'Unless the latter are prepared to regulate the activities of their nationals, the new competition will spread indiscriminately over the whole industrial area of China with manifest risk to the good relations existing between them'. Hence the British wished to suggest measures to meet this contingency. They were, as always, in favour of the open door and equal opportunities for all, but were convinced that 'friction must arise even among the most friendly powers unless this policy is

---

[18] FO 371/1621, minutes by Gregory and Grey on Jordan to Grey, 13 Dec. 1913.

by tacit agreement interpreted in a spirit of accommodation to the known aspiration of the individual powers to certain particular fields of industrial activity'.

Both France and Japan were told that while the British government did not wish to lend itself to the dangerous policy of defining spheres of influence, it was clear that harmony between the powers could only be maintained 'by each power discouraging its nationals from embarking on enterprises in areas where another power had by long association acquired special interests'. The Japanese were informed that, nevertheless, Britain was prepared to agree to participation by Japan in the Nanking–Hsiangt'an railway if Britain were granted an absolute *quid pro quo* in southern Manchuria. To France the point was made in broader terms. Britain was, in general, prepared, if the other powers would reciprocate, to pursue a policy of scrupulous non-interference in districts where the nationals of other powers could obviously claim some sort of prescriptive right to an exclusive promotion of their own industrial enterprises. But specific reference was made to the activities of the Banque Industrielle, notably on the matter of the Pukow Harbour loan contract acquired by the Banque 'in the heart of a district which lies in the traditional and acknowledged field of British industrial activity'. In the British view this was essentially a question where the principle of policy they proposed should be applied, and they now asked the French government to meet them in this matter and press the Banque Industrielle to direct its activities elsewhere.[19]

The communications to France and Japan marked a reversal of policy. Britain was now not merely accepting but advocating a recognition of spheres of economic preponderance. If this was presented as 'a purely informal arrangement', it was nonetheless an abandonment of the policy followed, voluntarily in respect of the association with France, since 1905. The British, having secured the removal of restrictions in order to obtain conditions of fair competition, had rapidly been forced to retreat to a defensive policy, albeit confined to industrial interests of a political complexion such as railways, docks, and mines. There was no intention of imposing or accepting restrictions on the freedom of commerce anywhere in China, or of excluding co-operation outside areas of special interest. But the Chinese authorities, as well as the French and Japanese governments, were left in no

[19] FO 371/1621 memorandum to Japanese Embassy, 31 Dec. 1913; to French Embassy, 1 Jan. 1914.

doubt as to British determination. Yuan Shih-k'ai was warned by Jordan that he would lose British friendship if he encouraged any more such pretensions as the Pukow contract and the proposed prolongation of the Lanchow–Haichow railway to a port on the Yangtze. The British, he was told, would not tolerate any attempt to encroach upon their position in the Yangtze Valley.[20]

Neither France nor Japan was prepared to accept the British argument. The Japanese maintained that their position in southern Manchuria, founded on political and strategic interests resting on treaty rights, was essentially different from the British claims in the Yangtze Valley, which had no foundation in a right by treaty. While they were ready to withdraw their claim to participation in the Nanking–Hsiangt'an line, they now looked to British support for a railway from Foochow to Hankow. It was recognized on the British side that Japan did have existing (if limited) interests in Fukien and the Hanyehping mines, but she could not be allowed to control the whole of the line to Hankow. The Japanese were accordingly offered British support for a concession for a section of the proposed line, but it was made plain once more that efforts to extend Japanese interests in the Yangtze area would be resisted. Strategic as well as economic considerations were involved because control of a line from Foochow to Hankow could give Japan, if she should ever gain possession of Foochow, military control of south-eastern China. The railway question remained unresolved by August 1914, but British determination to maintain pre-eminence in the area and to reject Japanese attempts to exploit the Anglo-Japanese alliance to extend her interests were matched by clear indications of Japan's intention to persist in her thrusting policy. The future course of Anglo-Japanese relations did not seem promising.[21]

With France by the summer of 1914 there was improvement. The French reply to the British memorandum of 1 January indicated that while the general principles put forward in it were acceptable, the Pukow agreement could not be cancelled but the French were prepared for co-operation with British interests in the enterprise. Yet though the Anglo-French agreement of 1905 had admitted French

---

[20] FO 371/1941 Jordan to Grey, 24 Feb. 1914. Yuan was ready to co-operate in order to keep out the Japanese but he expected the British to be accommodating over a new loan, (minute by Gregory on conversation with Barton, 5 Mar. 1914).

[21] See P. Lowe, *Great Britain and Japan*, chap. 5, for a close examination of the Yangtze question in Anglo-Japanese relations, 1913–14.

interests to the Pukow area and given them participation in railway projects radiating from Pukow, and though, as the French were to point out, the area had become one where international enterprise was well established, the advocates of a national policy in the Foreign Office were not prepared to compromise on the harbour contract. The French were now told, in a stiffly worded memorandum, that while there were areas where international interests were inextricably mixed and where joint enterprise was appropriate, there were others—and Pukow was one of them—where one set of national interests was predominant, and which were therefore indisputably earmarked for the individual enterprise of the nationals of particular powers. It was recognized that France was entitled to compensation in the Pukow–Sinyang dispute, but the British government, though ready for co-operation in appropriate areas, would not agree to joint enterprise at Pukow. In this they were not discriminating against France but asserting 'in rather pronounced fashion the predominant position of British interests in the Yangtze region under discussion against all powers having interests in China'. They would only be too glad to see the French do likewise in the area that tradition earmarked as their exclusive sphere. The French rejoinder of 6 April maintained their position, but by July the situation was much improved. A British memorandum of 6 July noted that in the matter of the Pukow–Sinyang railway there was now no difference in principle between the point of view of the two governments, while the Pukow Harbour contract seemed to be moving towards settlement by an arrangement between the British and French groups.[22]

The new situation marked a recognition of realities on the part of both governments. It was they, not the British and French bank groups (which had co-operated for nearly ten years in China), who had taken up opposing positions in support of national rather than joint enterprise. On the British side this had responded to a public mood at home and among the British community in China, anti-pathetic towards the Hongkong Bank, as well as to particular criticism of its privileged position from leading British companies apparently eager to undertake what would be purely British enterprises in China. Grey, always uneasy about the obligation to exclusive support and

<hr>

[22] FO 371/1941, memorandum from French Embassy, 5 Mar. 1914; memorandum to French Embassy, 17 Mar. 1914; FO 371/1942, memorandum from French Embassy, 6 Apr. 1914; FO 371/1932, memorandum to French Embassy, 6 July 1914.

recognizing by the end of 1912 that, as he put it, other governments were not finding it posisble to control the activities of their nationals in industrial ventures in China, had come to accept the ending of international agreements and the reduction of the consortium to a shell as necessary in order to maintain the British position. Yet the British and French banking groups, still linked by their agreement of 1905, continued to co-operate, and Chinese Central Railways remained in existence.

The remarkably accommodating attitude of the French group over the Pukow–Sinyang railway was matched by the mildness of the British group's reaction to the award of the Pukow Harbour contract to the Banque Industrielle. This certainly did not indicate acceptance of the Banque by the British group, nor it seems by the major French groups. Possibly because of its failure to reach agreement with the Banque de l'Indo-Chine and its associates, the Banque Industrielle met renewed opposition in France. In London the Hongkong Bank succeeded in blocking attempts by the Banque Industrielle to raise money on the London market through the Pekin Syndicate in which French interests had over the years secured a majority shareholding and dominated the directorate, which by 1912 included André Berthelot. The Hongkong Bank's operations were unknown to the Foreign Office until revealed plaintively by the Banque Industrielle, and were then warmly welcomed as a patriotic action.[23] By July 1914 the Banque Industrielle seems to have been checked in London and in Paris, where French banks resisted pressure from the government to come to its assistance. Consequently, in face of opposition by the Banque de l'Indo-Chine group and the Hongkong Bank to its efforts to raise capital it was unable to finance its Pukow concession, which French banks judged not to be a sound business venture. It then made overtures through the British Embassy in Paris for an understanding for co-operation in its concessions, including the Pukow Harbour project.[24] The outbreak of war in August left the situation eased though unresolved, but clearly one in which the efforts of the two governments in China, the French to advance a national policy and

---

[23] *Annales de la chambre des deputés, débats parlementaires*, session of 30 Mar. 1914, pp. 2384–92; FO 371/1937, Bertie to Grey, 31 Mar. 1914; FO 371/1941, minutes by Gregory and Langley on note communicated by Pekin Syndicate, 30 Mar. 1914; F. Farjenel, 'La vie politique et parlementaire à l'étranger: Chine', *Revue politique et parlementaire* 79–80 (Jan.–June 1914), pp. 587–96.

[24] FO 371/1931, Bertie to Langley, 8 July 1914.

the British to counter by a national policy of their own, as in 1898–1904, had run up against economic realities.

Jordan and his supporters in the Foreign Office had misjudged the situation. There had been some signs of recognition in the engineering industry of the desirability of grouping for business in the China market. The British Engineers' Association, which brought together many of the major firms, was incorporated in 1912 for the express purpose of watching and promoting British engineering interests there.[25] Yet, as Jordan pointed out in June 1913, its structure was far too loose to be effective. What was wanted was 'not the dissemination of further information about industrial affairs in China but the organization of British manufacturing and financial interests into one or two powerful syndicates equipped in such a way as to enable them to compete with the Associations which are being formed by our rivals.' The success of the Belgian railway syndicate, he remarked, was undoubtedly due to many years of careful organization. The British had no similar group prepared to make a large advance of money at a moment's notice and to seize any opportunity that offered. The Banque Industrielle, he added, showed similar carefulness and ingenuity in its design. British firms trusted to their individual efforts rather than to organized co-operation, but this was unsuited to the present requirements of China. He noted the formation of a new Japan–China Corporation and felt that it was high time for British engineering manufacturers to see that they were adequately equipped for the competition that was coming. 'The only way to meet competition of this kind is organization on a similar basis.'

The wisdom of Jordan's arguments was well appreciated in the Foreign Office, as was the difficulty of persuading firms to group. Gregory suggested that Jordan when home on leave should meet representatives of the Association but this, though welcomed by Jordan, came to nothing. The danger of inaction was well understood, as the pressures that were to lead Grey to break up the consortium for industrial loans had mounted. Gregory felt that the situation in China was completely new. Competition was much greater than in the pre-revolutionary period.

Consequently new conditions are required to meet it and if the consortium is to break up, there must be something to put in its place, or the risk to our industrial undertakings will be very serious.

---

[25] FO 371/1617, British Engineers Association to FO, 10 Apr. 1913.

If we could utilize what existing machinery there is, such as the British financial group, as a basis for a financial combine, and could endeavour to create a nucleus anyhow in the various industrial spheres we could afford safely to revise our present policy. Its continuance for the remainder of this year, which is now contemplated, may create an agitation that may have the effect of bringing all these considerations to a head and enable us to force combines into existence as the price of a reversal of the consortium policy.[26]

The problem when Gregory made his comment in June 1913 had appeared to be one of organization in which combination would replace individualism in British commercial strategy in China. Jordan and his supporters had assumed that British industry and finance were eager to expand in the China market, and that the restoration of free competition for industrial loans would bring a rush of activity. In fact British firms showed no eagerness, and the rivals of the Hongkong Bank did not attempt to finance rivals to the British and Chinese Corporation. 'Sir J. Jordan's main complaint at present is that there is such a dearth of British applicants for concessions', Gregory noted in February 1914, and in March Alston was lamenting that British traders did not compete as they should with their German and Japanese rivals: 'the British trader is proverbially indolent unless he sees the prospect of big profits'.[27] Jordan himself was despondent at the failure to create effective machinery to enable British enterprise to compete with its rivals and at its want of energy.

The representatives of British industry are nearly all retired military men who have no knowledge of business and are, in some cases, not capable to drawing up a contract ... what we really seem to want is a combination which will appeal to the Chinese as the Banque Industrielle does now and as the Sino-Japanese one now being organised is intended to. The Chinese are given an interest in these concerns. The Americans followed the same principle in their oil concessions and we cannot expect success on the old lines of exclusively British concessions ... Our people are slow to adopt new methods. As it is the auction of China is going on and all the best lots will soon have been sold.[28]

[26] FO 371/1617, Jordan to Grey, 1 June 1913, with minute by Gregory.
[27] FO 371/1931, Jordan to Grey, 24 Feb. 1914 with minute by Gregory; FO 371/1942, minute by Alston on Jordan to Grey, 30 Mar. 1914. Complaints by officials of the want of energy on the part of the British business community in China were nothing new; see, for example, FO 17/1403, Bredon to Bertie, 22 July 1899.
[28] FO 350/12, Jordan to Langley, 8 Mar. 1914.

By the spring of 1914 the realities were becoming plain. Gregory commented: 'It is extremely difficult to collect British firms to undertake business in China, especially mining. We are not really in touch with those sort of people and no one at present seems very eager to put money into China. We get very few applications for support in these days.' Gregory was prepared to follow Jordan's suggestion that a conference be held at the Foreign Office of all the financiers, banks, and business houses interested in China with a view to having some co-operative movement, but Langley opposed. In his view, 'the Foreign Office should only be so far concerned as to put the idea into some industrial or financial head. There are considerable difficulties in the way, connected with monopoly, which would probably become clear in any discussion with one of our financiers.' He agreed on approaches to the Board of Trade, the British Engineers' Association, and the China Association. The two associations could be told the position as to opportunities in China: 'We can hardly go further than that or take the responsibility of encouraging investments in China'.[29] His suggestion that Addis and Revelstoke of Baring's be sounded was adopted. Addis had already made clear over the matter of the Nanking–Hsiangt'an railway his reluctance to allow political considerations to override economic. When pressed to finance a loan for the line, which Jordan regarded as a highly important position in the Yangtze Valley, he refused to approach his partners in the British group. He could not, he said, appeal to Revelstoke and the joint-stock banks associated with him to put up money for political purposes as they would certainly refuse to put such a proposition before their directors. He could only apply to them on the ground that this was a sound business proposition, and in the state that China was in he could not say it was. If the board of the bank in Hong Kong would authorize the advance, he would not object. If not, Jordan could transfer his support elsewhere, but he warned that neither of the contracting firms (S. Pearson and Co. and Pauling's), would be eager to take the concession.[30]

[29] FO 371/1933, minutes by Gregory and Langley on Jordan to Grey, 15 and 19 Mar. 1914.

[30] FO 371/1941, minute by Langley on Hongkong Bank to FO, 19 Mar. 1914. The situation was a consequence of the BCC's lack of capital. It could not issue a loan in the present state of the market and could not carry any more advances to China on the uncertain security of Chinese Treasury bills. Addis's refusal to make funds available may have been a form of pressure on Grey to raise his veto on a new loan to the Chinese government and to agree to terms acceptable to the banks being negotiated with China.

In fact the Hongkong board did agree to make the loan on the terms offered by the Chinese, but Addis's attitude was significant. In the past he had been ready to fall in with official wishes; in 1911, when Jordan had urged that for political reasons the British group should, with the French and American groups, join with the German group in a loan to the Shantung provincial government, Addis, though disinclined to participate on business grounds, had said that his objections 'were subject to the opinion of the Secretary of State; if in his opinion it is considered desirable for political reasons to accept the German offer the bank will do so at once'.[31] But that was in the days of the special relationship between the bank and the Foreign Office. Now he and Revelstoke made it clear that their decisions would be governed by business considerations. They said there was plenty of money available for any sound Chinese concession on reasonable conditions, and advances could be made in cases where the expenditure of the money upon the object for which it had been found was guaranteed. But the conditions being offered at present were not reasonable, and they were not prepared to make advances for any undertaking on note of hand of the Chinese government as this course could lead only to bankruptcy. No financial organization, however large, could alter this.[32]

On the eve of war in 1914 the British position in the Yangtze Valley was still strong, and the railway concessions Jordan had secured in the new scramble had ensured British control of communications in key areas.[33] But could funds be raised to develop these concessions? Clearly the Hongkong Bank and its associates were likely to be less acquiescent to requests from the government than had been the case when they had received exclusive support. British industrialists for their part showed no inclination to abandon individualism and group for business in China on continental lines. Moreover, the bulk of engineering firms, with order books full, saw no reason for concerning themselves over much with a market where credit conditions were not attractive.[34] The prospect of the

Addis had urged the raising of customs duties as security which Grey, on Jordan's advice, had refused, FO 371/1933, Addis to FO, 20 and 24 Jan. 1914 with minutes; FO to Hongkong Bank, 17 Feb. 1914.

[31] FO 371/1069, Addis to Campbell, 5 Sept. 1911.
[32] FO 371/1933, Grey to Jordan, 30 Mar. 1914.
[33] FO 350/12, Jordan to Langley, 6 Apr. 1914.
[34] *The Times*, 8 Dec. 1913.

emergence of purely British enterprise in China as sought by the Foreign Office did not appear promising. As it was, the outbreak of war put an end to possibilities of economic expansion in China. All that was open to British diplomacy from 1914 to 1918 was to attempt to hold what had been gained.

10

Conclusion

BRITISH economic diplomacy in China between 1895 and 1914 revealed several changes of direction. The aim of policy—to safeguard commercial interests—remained constant, but methods altered in response to changing circumstances. Under Salisbury, though the emergence of determined competition from rivals operating through state-organized financial institutions came to be recognized as serious, there was reluctance on the part of ministers to move into closer relations with British finance in order to meet it. In a situation in which loans to China for administrative purposes and still more for industrial construction, particularly railways, were the means used to secure political influence as well as profit, this was a restrictive factor. Officials were more responsive, recognizing that a financial arm was a necessary weapon if counter-action was to be effective, and that the Hongkong Bank—the one British institution operating in China that showed eagerness to assert British interests and to co-operate with official policy—was the obvious, indeed the only possible, partner. By the end of Salisbury's period at the Foreign Office, links with the bank were well established and the government was involving itself in assisting the flotation of loans of political significance. The relationship was informal. For railway construction, the official function was to support applications for concessions by the subsidiary set up by the bank and Jardine, Matheson (the British and Chinese Corporation), that of the bank to finance them through loans raised in the London market. The relationship was not exclusive, but in fact there was no other serious British competitor for railway business. In mining the Pekin Syndicate, another substantial concern, received official support.

Salisbury, and still more Hicks Beach as chancellor of the exchequer, only uneasily accepted official links with a financial institution. Lansdowne was less inhibited and more ready to adapt British methods to the new conditions in economic diplomacy.[1] By the time

---

[1] This was so also in respect of Persia; see Mclean, *Britain and her Buffer State*, p. 143.

he left office at the end of 1905, the Foreign Office had become more and more involved with British finance in China. The old traditions of detachment and aloofness had given way to an active, indeed a directing role. But there were still limits to government action. Lansdowne could not follow advice to create a state-directed organization embracing finance and industry on the lines of continental rivals. In the British economy there were few links between banks and industry and, in an essentially competitive environment, few between major industrial concerns. The *laissez-faire* principle effectively prevented government action to bring together a continental-style group. It was necessary to work with the means available—the Hongkong Bank, the British and Chinese Corporation, and the Pekin Syndicate. Under Lansdowne the relationship between them and the government was cemented and extended, initially in continuation of the policy of competing against rivals. In 1904–5 came the important change from competition to co-operation with France, hitherto one of the major rivals. The Anglo-French railway agreement came partly because of the reluctance of British investors to finance loans for railway concessions in China, more because it accorded with the direction of general foreign policy. It also involved the British government in a formal relationship with the Hongkong Bank and its associates through the pledge of exclusive support for the specified objectives of the agreement between the British and French financial groups.

This was the situation inherited by Grey. It was to embarrass him considerably when City interest in China loans awakened, because not only was the pledge to exclusive support in conflict with established principles but it was confined in effect to one institution only. What he wished to see was not a return to detachment but, to meet domestic criticism, a wider-based group. He was quite content with the policy of international co-operation in major economic projects in China that from 1905 to 1912 was strongly supported by his advisers in the Foreign Office. Conditions in China, where the influence of the rights recovery movement was very evident in negotiations for railway loan contracts, strengthened the case for co-operation between the foreign banks. The Germans forced their way in to the Anglo-French association in 1909, and the Americans in 1909–10. In neither case was there enthusiasm on the British side for this extension, but a general agreement among the banks for co-operation in China business was accepted as necessary in the circumstances. Each stage in the movement for co-operation marked an erosion in the British position, for

each involved ceding to others shares in concessions that had originally been gained for British finance and industry. It had, however,
come to be accepted in the Foreign Office that it was more to the
advantage of British trade in China to get railways built, irrespective of
who built them, than to maintain a hold on concessions that could not
be exploited by British resources and merely blocked the way to
construction. In the formation of the consortium, Addis was the financial diplomat, the executant of policies devised in the closest cooperation with Grey and his advisers.[2] His reputation stood very high
among officials, and criticism of him and of the bank made no impression.

In the summer of 1911 the economic situation in China seemed set
fair and the policy of international co-operation to have justified itself.
A balance acceptable to the foreign banks and to the Chinese authorities had been struck in railway loans. The formation of the consortium had not halted the steady movement in favour of China in the
terms of loans. This had been evident from 1905 and continued after
the elimination of competition among the major lenders through the
formation of the consortium. The banks wanted business and had to
accept terms less to their advantage than those of earlier contracts.
China wanted loans and had to compromise, but was able to ensure
that control over railways now to be built would be firmly in Chinese
hands.

The revolution of 1911 and its aftermath reduced the consortium to
a shadow. Initially its existence as a six-bank group from 1912 made
possible a co-ordinated policy by the member governments in the vital
area of administrative loans to China. Strains in this area, however,
foreshadowed the break up of the agreements for co-operation in
industrial loans. Though Britain was responsible for the formal
dismantling, this was in part a reaction to self-seeking actions by
France and Japan in the key sector of railway concessions that
threatened further inroads to what the British regarded as their
preserves in the Yangtze Valley. It was also a reaction to widely
expressed resentment in Britain against exclusive official support of
the still narrowly based British group. What resulted was an attempt at

---

[2] For a view of Addis as negotiator, see O. Homberg, *Les Coulisses de l'histoire* (Paris,
1938), pp. 91–2. Grey did find an additional reason for urging the widening of the
British group: the City rumour that the Hongkong Bank was German-controlled (FO
371/1322, minute by Grey on Crowe to Grey, 13 July 1912). Foreign Office confidence in
Addis and the bank was, however, unshaken.

an independent national policy to defend the threatened positions. The situation in essentials recalled the battle of concessions of 1898 but was now symbolized by the termination, not the strengthening, of the special association with the Hongkong Bank in the area of industrial loans. This decision indicated the nature of the bank's relationship with the government. It was an instrument, valued as such, but to be dispensed with as new methods were adopted.[3]

The intention was to resist encroachments on the part of France and Japan, though one was the associate and the other the ally of Britain. Hitherto Grey had given precedence to the wider needs of foreign relations when clashes of interest had appeared in China. In the Manchurian railways controversy he had refused to support a British firm in the Hsinmintun–Fakumen contract, or American policy in schemes for the Chinchow–Aigun line and for internationalization of the Manchurian railways. The maintenance of good relations with Japan and Russia was given priority. Major British interests, however, were not felt to be at stake in the Manchurian issues. In the Yangtze Valley they were, and in 1913–14 there was determination that they should not be sacrificed.

The situation that developed is one of several illustrations in the years immediately before the outbreak of war in Europe of sharpening conflict between Grey's dominating political concern—the maintenance of political associations for reasons of the European balance—and the defence of British interests outside Europe against pressures from the very powers who were partners in these associations. This was most obviously so in Persia, which received the greatest public attention; but in China too, where since 1904 the preservation of wider political groupings had been judged to be of overriding importance and purely British interests had been subordinated to this in Manchuria and in the more important Yangtze area, reaction in 1913–14 was sharp. It was indicative of a changing attitude in the Foreign Office.[4] The maintenance of established political associations—the alliance with Japan, and the links with France and Russia—remained the basis of policy, but a less acquiescent response to pressures from those powers was evident. In the China question, international

---

[3] For business arising from the reorganization loan, the bank group as the British member of the consortium continued to receive official support.

[4] See Steiner, pp. 147–52; M. G. Ekstein in F. H. Hinsley (ed.), *British Foreign Policy under Sir Edward Grey* (Cambridge, 1977) pp. 342–8; Keith Robbins, *Sir Edward Grey* (London, 1971), p. 260.

co-operation was still the inclination of the financiers, but it was resistance to infiltration into what they held to be British preserves that was urged by officials who were now coming to the front in the Far Eastern Department, where the death of Sir Francis Campbell had removed a consistent advocate of compromise and co-operation. His successor as head of the department, Sir Walter Langley, was alone in resisting the call from Gregory, Alston, and Jordan for an independent policy in support of purely British enterprise. Relations with France and Japan, and Russia too (for there were areas of non-commercial friction outside the Yangtze), deteriorated sharply over China. The situation was ironic, for with Germany there were no conflicts. Jordan commented in July 1914:

Apart from the healthy commercial rivalry which always exists there is no antagonism of any kind between the two peoples. On the contrary there is a perhaps not unjustifiable jealousy on the part of some other powers that our relations with Germany are closer than political conditions in Europe would appear to justify.[5]

By then the differences with France had eased. Hopes of a strong independent British group emerging had been disappointed. Those officials who had urged a national policy could find no effective industrial and financial foundation for it. They had misread the situation. So had their counterparts in France. Moreover, Jordan was meeting difficulties in China. The Tibet question, he reported, was a severe handicap in obtaining concessions. 'This and the distracted state of home politics are telling against us just now in China and not since the dark days of the South African war has our task been more difficult in the Far East.'[6]

The signs pointed to a return to co-operation in industrial loans with the original members of the consortium, but not with Japan or Russia.[7] The framework for it remained in being. Ties between the British consortium group and its French partners had not been disrupted, and the Hukuang loan contract linked the British, French, German, and American groups. Co-operation had brought benefits to

---

[5] FO 405/215, Jordan to Grey, 21 July 1914. The Germans declined to accept the British claim to a privileged position in the Yangtze Valley but they did not cause problems for the British (FO 405/216, memorandum from the German Embassy, 11 June 1914; FO 371/1941, minute by Gregory on Jordan to Grey, 21 Jan. 1914.
[6] FO 350/12, Jordan to Langley, 27 July 1914.
[7] FO 371/1939, Buchanan to Grey, 26 Jan. 1914, with minutes.

British interests. The territorial integrity of China had been preserved despite the upheaval of the revolution. British investment had continued to expand and in 1914 still surpassed all competitors.[8] Railways built in co-operation could be, as the Tientsin–Pukow line had shown, of immense benefit to British trade.[9] Only those who had cherished unrealistic dreams of British predominance could be disappointed. Co-operation had proved the means of securing agreements with the Chinese on railways and finance that could provide the foundation for a healthy Chinese economy, a long-standing British aim, though financial stability had not come by 1914. China, seeking funds for administrative purposes, was once more attempting to break the consortium and was again in touch with Crisp, to the alarm of Grey.[10]

The outbreak of war, however, ended all negotiations. For the European powers the affairs of China sank into the background. When the consortium was resurrected it was in very different circumstances.

As for the Hongkong Bank it could look back upon twenty years of significant advance. The numerous loans issued by its London office and its association with European, American, and Japanese banks had raised its prestige and made it an important force in the world of international finance.[11]

[8] C. F. Remer, *Foreign Investments in China* (New York, 1933), pp. 229, 343.
[9] FO 371/1590, Jordan to Grey, 6 Jan. 1913.
[10] P. Lowe, *Great Britain and Japan*, pp. 139–41.
[11] *The Banker's Magazine*, Dec. 1913, pp. 139–41.

Bibliography

1. *Unpublished Material*

A. Official papers

Foreign Office Records in the Public Record Office, London:
General Correspondence Series China, 1895–1906 FO 17/
                                              1906–1914 FO 371/
                                 France 1904–1905 FO 27/
             Confidential Print China   FO 405
Cabinet Papers
Treasury Papers

B. Private Papers in the Public Record Office

FO 800/   Marquess of Lansdowne
           Sir E. Grey (Viscount Grey of Fallodon)
           Sir F. Bertie
           Sir Walter Langley
           Sir Beilby Alston
FO 350/   Sir John Jordan
PRO 30/33 Sir Ernest Satow

C. Other Private Papers consulted

Sir Charles Addis (now at School of Oriental and African Studies, London)
A. J. Balfour, (BL Add. MSS 49683–962)
Baring Brothers Archive (London)
Sir Edward Hamilton (BL Add. MSS 48599–699)
Sir Michael Hicks Beach (Gloucestershire County Record Office)
Sir Mathew Nathan (Rhodes House Library, Oxford)
Rothschild Archive (London)
3rd Marquess of Salisbury (Hatfield House)
China Association (School of Oriental and African Studies)
The Times Archive (London)

On microfilm:
J. O. P. Bland (Thomas Fisher Rare Book Library, University of Toronto)
G. E. Morrison, Diary (Mitchell Library, Sydney)

2. *Official Papers, Published*

British Documents on the Origins of the War 1898—1914 ed. G. P. Gooch and H. W. V. Temperley (London, 1926–38).
Documents diplomatiques français 1871—1914 (Paris, 1919–62)
Die grosse Politik der europaischen Kabinette 1871—1914, ed. J. Lepsius, A. Mendelssohn–Bartholdy and F. Thimme (Berlin, 1922–7).
Nihon gaikō bunsho (Japanese diplomatic documents) Ministry of Foreign Affairs, Tokyo (1936–).
Foreign Relations of the United States, Department of State, Washington.

3. *Other Printed Sources*

The Times
Asie Française
The Stock Exchange Year Book
The Bankers' Magazine

Books and Articles

Allen, G. C. and A. Donnithorne, *Western Enterprise in Far Eastern Economic Development: China and Japan* (London, 1954).
Andrew, C., *Theophile Delcassé and the Making of the Entente Cordiale* (London, 1968).
Baster, A. S. J., *The International Banks* (London, 1935).
Bastid, M., 'La Diplomatie française et la revolution chinoise de 1911', *Revue d'histoire moderne et contemporaine*, 16 (Apr.–June 1969), pp. 221–45.
Bays, D. H., *China Enters the Twentieth Century: Chang Chih—tung and the Issues of a New Age, 1895—1909* (Ann Arbor, 1975).
Bland, J. O. P., *Recent Events and Present Policies in China* (London, 1912).
Braisted, W. R., 'The United States and the American China Development Company', *Far Eastern Quarterly* 6 (1952), pp. 147–65.
Bréal, A., *Philippe Berthelot* (Paris, 1937).
Bruguière M., 'Le Chemin de fer du Yunnan', *Revue d'histoire diplomatique* 77 (1963), pp. 23–61, 129–62, 253–78.
Brunschwig, H., *Mythes et réalités de l'imperialisme colonial français 1871—1914* (Paris, 1960).
Cameron, M. E., *The Reform Movement in China* (Stanford, 1931).
Campbell, A. E., *Great Britain and the United States, 1895—1903* (London, 1960).
Campbell, C. S., *Special Business Interests and the Open Door Policy* (New Haven, 1951).
Chan, K. C., 'British Policy in the Reorganization Loan to China 1912–13', *Modern Asian Studies* 5 (1971), pp. 355–72.

Chandran, J. *The Contest for Siam, 1889–1902: A Study in Diplomatic Rivalry* (Kuala Lumpur, 1977).

Ch'en, J., *Yuan Shi-k'ai, 1859–1916* (London, 1961).

Chi, M., 'Shanghai–Hangchow–Ningpo Railway Loan: A Case Study of the Rights Recovery Movement', *Modern Asian Studies* 7 (1973), pp. 85–106.

Collis, M., *Wayfoong: The Hongkong and Shanghai Banking Corporation* (London, 1965).

Crisp, O., 'The Russo-Chinese Bank: An Episode in Franco-Russian Relations', *Slavonic and East European Review* 52 (1974), pp. 197–212.

Croly, H., *Willard Straight* (New York, 1924).

Dayer, R. A., *Bankers and Diplomats in China 1917–1925* (London, 1981).

Edwards, E. W., 'The Far Eastern Agreements of 1907', *Journal of Modern History* 26 (1954), pp. 340–55.

— 'Great Britain and the Manchurian Railways Question, 1909–10' *English Historical Review* 81 (1966), pp. 740–69.

— 'The Origins of British Financial Cooperation with France in China, 1903–6', *English Historical Review* 339 (1971), pp. 285–317.

— 'British Policy in China, 1913–1914: Rivalry with France in the Yangtze Valley'. *Journal of Oriental Studies* 15 (1977), pp. 20–36.

— 'Great Britain and China 1905–1911;, and 'China and Japan 1911–1914', in F. H. Hinsley (ed.) *British Foreign Policy under Sir Edward Grey* (Cambridge, 1977).

Esherick, J. W., *Reform and Revolution in China: The 1911 Revolution in Hunan and Hubei* (Berkeley, Calif., and London, 1976).

Fairbank, J. K., K. F. Bruner, and E. M. Matheson (eds), *The I. G. in Peking: Letters of Robert Hart, Chinese Maritime Customs, 1868–1907* (2 vols., Cambridge, Mass., 1975).

Fairbank, J. K., and Liu Kwang-Ching (eds), *The Cambridge History of China Vol. 11 Late Ch'ing, 1800–1911, Part 2* (Cambridge, 1980).

Farjenel, F., 'La vie politique et parlementaire à l'étranger: Chine', *Revue politique et parlementaire* 79–80 (Jan.–June 1914), pp. 587–96.

Feis, H., *Europe: The World's Banker, 1870–1914* (New Haven, 1930).

Field, F. V., *American Participation in the China Consortiums* (New York, 1931).

Fieldhouse, D. K., 'Imperialism. An Historiographical Revision', *Economic History Review* 2nd series, 14 (1961), pp. 187–209.

— *Economics and Empire* (London, 1973).

Gagnier, D., 'French Loans to China, 1895–1914: The Alliance of International Finance and Diplomacy', *The Australian Journal of Politics and History* 18, no. 2 (1972), pp. 229–49.

Gallagher, J. and R. Robinson, 'The Imperialism of Free Trade', *The Economic History Review* 2nd series, 6, (1963), pp. 1–15.

Gérard, A., *Ma mission en Chine, 1893–1897* (Paris, 1918).

Girault, R., 'Pour un portrait nouveau de l'homme d'affaires français vers 1914', *Revue d'histoire moderne et contemporaine* 16 (1969), pp. 329–49.

Grenville, J. A. S., *Lord Salisbury and Foreign Policy: The Close of the Nineteenth Century* (London, 1964).

Grey of Fallodon, *Twenty-Five Years: 1892—1916* (2 vols., London, 1925).

— *Speeches on Foreign Affairs, 1904—1914*, selected by Paul Knaplund (London, 1931).

Griswold, A. W., *The Far Eastern Policy of the United States* (2nd edn., New Haven, 1962).

Hargreaves, J. D., 'Entente manquée: Anglo-French Relations, 1895–1896', *Cambridge Historical Journal* 11 (1953) pp. 65–92.

Hinsley, F. H., (ed.), *British Foreign Policy under Sir Edward Grey* (Cambridge, 1977).

Homberg, O., *Les Coulisses de l'histoire* (Paris, 1938).

Hou Chi-ming, *Foreign Investment and Economic Development in China, 1840—1937* (Cambridge, Mass., 1965).

Hsu, M. C., *Railway Problems in China* (New York, 1911).

Hunt, M. H., *Frontier Defense and the Open Door: Manchuria in Chinese-American Relations, 1895—1911* (New Haven, Conn. and London, 1973).

Hyde, F. E., *Far Eastern Trade, 1880—1914* (London, 1973).

Inouye, Yuichi, *North China Railway Problems (1897—1901) and their consequence for the Anglo-Japanese Alliance* (London, 1981).

Ikei, M., 'Japan's Response to the Chinese Revolution of 1911', *Journal of Asian Studies* 25 (1962), pp. 213–27.

Jansen, M. B., *The Japanese and Sun Yat-Sen* (Cambridge, Mass., 1954).

Jeremy, D. J. (ed.), *Dictionary of Business Biography* (London, 1984–).

Joseph, P., *Foreign Diplomacy in China, 1894—1900* (London, 1928).

Kawai, K., 'Anglo-German Rivalry in the Yangtze Region, 1895–1902', *Pacific Historical Review* 8 (1939), pp. 413–33.

Kennedy, P., *The Realities behind Diplomacy: Background Influence on British External Policy, 1865—1980* (London, 1981).

Kent, P. H., *Railway Enterprise in China* (London, 1907).

Kiernan, V. G., *British Diplomacy in China, 1880—85* (Cambridge, 1939).

King, F. H. H., 'The Bank of China is Dead', *Journal of Oriental Studies* 7 (1969), 39–62.

— (ed.) *Eastern Banking: Essays in the History of the Hongkong and Shanghai Banking Corporation* (London, 1983).

Kurgan-van Hentenryk, G., *Jean Jadot: Artisan de l'expansion belge en Chine* (Brussels, 1965).

— *Leopold II et les groupes financiers belges en Chine* (Brussels, 1971).

— 'Philippe Berthelot et les enterprises ferroviaires franco-belges en Chine 1912-1914', *Revue d'histoire moderne et contemporaine* 22 (1975), pp. 269–92.

Lafargue, T. F., *China and the World War* (Stanford, 1937).

Langer, W. L., *The Diplomacy of Imperialism, 1890—1902* (2nd edn., New York, 1951).

Lau, K. 'Sir John Jordan and the Affairs of China, 1906–16', Ph.D. thesis, London, 1968.

Lee, En-han, *China's Quest for Railway Autonomy 1904—1911* (Singapore, 1977).

Levi, W., *Modern China's Foreign Policy* (Minneapolis, 1953).

Lo, Hui-min, *The Correspondence of G. E. Morrison* (2 vols., Cambridge, 1976, 1978).

Lowe, C. J., *The Reluctant Imperialists: British Foreign Policy 1878—1902* (2 vols., London, 1967).

— and M. Dockrill, *The Mirage of Power: British Foreign Policy 1902—1922* (3 vols., London, 1972).

Lowe, P., *Great Britain and Japan, 1911—1915* (London, 1969).

— *Britain in the Far East* (London, 1981).

Lung, Chang, *La Chine à l'aube du XXᵉ siècle: Les Relations diplomatiques de la Chine avec les puissances 1894—1904* (Paris, 1962).

Mackinnon, S. R., *Power and Poliltics in Late Imperial China: Yuan Shih-k'ai in Beijing and Tianjin, 1901—1908* (Berkeley, Calif., and London, 1981).

McLean, D., 'Commerce, Finance and British Diplomatic Support in China, 1885–86', *Economic History Review* 2d series, 26 (Aug. 1973), pp. 464–76.

— 'The Foreign Office and the First Chinese Indemnity Loan, 1895', *Historical Journal* 14 (1973), pp. 303–21.

— 'Chinese Railways and the Townley Agreement of 1903', *Modern Asian Studies* 7 (1973), pp. 145–164.

— 'British Banking and Government in China: the Foreign Office and the Hongkong and Shanghai Bank, 1895–1914', Ph.D. thesis, Cambridge, 1973.

— 'Finance and "Informal Empire" before the First World War', *Economic History Review* 2d series, 29 (1976), pp. 291–305.

— *Britain and her Buffer State: The Collapse of the Persian Empire, 1890—1914* (London, 1979).

MacMurray, J. V. A. (ed.), *Treaties and Agreements with and concerning China, 1894—1919* (2 vols. New York, 1921).

Malozemoff, A., *Russian Far Eastern Policy 1881—1904* (Berkeley, 1958).

Moulder, F. V., *Japan, China and the Modern World Economy* (Cambridge, 1977).

Monger, G. W., *The End of Isolation: British Foreign Policy 1900—7* (London, 1963).

Newton, Lord, *Lord Lansdowne* (London, 1929).

Nish, I. H., *The Anglo—Japanese Alliance: The Diplomacy of Two Island Empires 1894—1907* (London, 1966).

— *Alliance in Decline: A Study of Anglo—Japanese Relations 1908—23* (London, 1972).

— *Japanese Foreign Policy, 1869—1942* (London, 1977).

Overlach, T. W., *Foreign Financial Control in China* (New York, 1919).

Palmer, A. W., 'Lord Salisbury's Approach to Russia, 1898' *Oxford Slavonic Papers* 6 (1955), pp. 102–14.

Pearl, C., *Morrison of Peking* (London, 1967).

Pelcovits, N. A., *Old China Hands and the Foreign Office* (New York, 1948).

Platt, D. C. M., *Finance, Trade and Politics in British Foreign Policy, 1815–1914* (Oxford, 1968).

Poidevin, R., *Les Relations économiques et financières entre la France et l'Allemagne de 1898 à 1914* (Paris, 1969).

Quested, R. D., *The Russo-Chinese Bank: A multinational Financial Base of Tsarism in China* (Birmingham, 1977).

Reid, J. G., *The Manchu Abdication and the Powers* (Berkeley, 1935).

Remer, C. F., *Foreign Investments in China* (New York, 1933).

Renouvin, P., *La Question d'Extrême-Orient* (Paris, 1946).

— 'Finance et politique: A propos de l'entente cordiale franco-anglaise' in *Homage à Lucien Febvre* (Paris, 1953), pp. 357–63.

Robbins, K. *Sir Edward Grey* (London, 1971).

Robinson, R. and J. Gallagher, *Africa and the Victorians: The Official Mind of Imperialism* (London, 1961).

Romanov, B. A., *Russia in Manchuria, 1892–1906*, translated by S. W. Jones (Ann Arbor, 1952).

Rosenbaum, A., 'The Manchurian Bridgehead; Anglo-Russian Rivalry and the Imperial Railways of North China, 1897–1902', *Modern Asian Studies* 10 (1976), pp. 41–64.

Saul, S. B., *Studies in British Overseas Trade, 1870–1914* (Liverpool, 1960).

Scholes, W. V. and M. V., *The Foreign Policy of the Taft Administration* (Columbia, 1970).

Schrecker, J. E., *Imperialism and Chinese Nationalism: Germany in Shantung* (Cambridge, Mass., 1971).

Staley, E., *War and the Private Investor* (New York, 1935).

Steeds, D., and I. Nish, *China, Japan, and Nineteenth Century Britain* (Dublin, 1977).

Steiner, Z. S., *The Foreign Office and Foreign Policy, 1898–1914* (Cambridge, 1969).

Sun, E-tu Zen, *Chinese Railways and British Interests, 1898–1911* (New York, 1954).

Taylor, A. J. P., *The Struggle for Mastery in Europe, 1848–1918* (Oxford, 1954).

Tilley, Sir J., and S. Gaselee, *The Foreign Office* (London, 1933).

Vevier, C., *The United States and China, 1906–1913* (New Brunswick, 1955).

Viner, J., 'International Finance and Balance of Power Diplomacy 1880–1914', *South Western Political and Social Science Quarterly* 9 (1929) pp. 407–51.

Walsh, W. B., 'The Yunnan Myth', *Far Eastern Quarterly* 2 (1943), pp. 272–85.

Wilbur, C. M., *Sun Yat-sen* (New York, 1976).

Wright, M. C. (ed.), *China in Revolution: The First Phase, 1900—1913* (New Haven, 1968).
Wright, S. F., *Hart and the Chinese Customs* (Belfast, 1950).
Young, E. P., *The Presidency of Yuan Shih-k'ai* (Ann Arbor, 1977).
Young, L. K., *British Policy in China, 1895—1902* (Oxford, 1970).

Index